Six Weeks To
Professional
Excellence

CW00552912

Hodder & Stoughton

A MEMBER OF THE HODDER HEADLINE GROUP

Orders: please contact Bookpoint Ltd, 130 Milton Park, Abingdon, Oxon OX14 4SB. Telephone: (44) 01235 827720, Fax: (44) 01235 400454. Lines are open from 9.00–6.00, Monday to Saturday, with a 24 hour message answering service.
Email address: orders@bookpoint.co.uk

British Library Cataloguing in Publication Data
A catalogue record for this title is available from The British Library

ISBN 0 340 812621

First published 2003
Impression number   10 9 8 7 6 5 4 3 2 1
Year   2007 2006 2005 2004 2003

Typeset by SX Composing DTP, Rayleigh, Essex.
Printed in Great Britain for Hodder & Stoughton Educational, a division of Hodder Headline Plc, 338 Euston Road, London NW1 3BH by Cox & Wyman Ltd, Reading, Berkshire.

The leading organisation for professional management

As the champion of management, the Chartered Management Institute shapes and supports the managers of tomorrow. By sharing intelligent insights and setting standards in management development, the Institute helps to deliver results in a dynamic world.

Setting and raising standards

The Institute is a nationally accredited organisation, responsible for setting standards in management and recognising excellence through the award of professional qualifications.

Encouraging development, improving performance

The Institute has a vast range of development programmes, qualifications, information resources and career guidance to help managers and their organisations meet new challenges in a fast-changing environment.

Shaping opinion

With in-depth research and regular policy surveys of its 91,000 individual members and 520 corporate members, the Chartered Management Institute has a deep understanding of the key issues. Its view is informed, intelligent and respected.

For more information call 01536 204222 or visit www.managers.org.uk

CONTENTS

Week One: Project Management

Week Two: Negotiating

Week Three: Time Management

Week Four: Dealing with Difficult People

C O N T E N T S

Week Five: Presentation

Week Six: Memory Techniques

Mark Brown

Mark Brown is a management consultant and has a background in both technology and business. Being wheelchair-bound, he has a keen personal interest in a mobile world, which allows him to undertake his work wherever he is. As well as being able to give a view on M-commerce for business, he can also give a view of how it affects people, both as consumers and as individuals.

Peter Fleming

Peter Fleming is Managing Director of PFA International. With past experience in senior management in the public sector, training management roles in distribution, and buying exposure in retailing, he has had considerable experience of negotiating at all levels and roles. He is Training Consultant to a major UK Trade Association and visiting Training Consultant at the Henley College of Management, and has run many successful training programmes through the Chartered Management Institute.

Declan Treacy and Polly Bird

Declan Treacy was a business consultant specialising in helping organisations control their paperwork. The reviser, Polly Bird, is a professional writer of business and training books and has written over fourteen books for various publishers.

Brian Salter and Naomi Langford-Wood

Brian Salter and Naomi Langford-Wood are business and communication specialists, consultants and speakers on the international conference circuit. Together they have co-authored over eighteen business books.

Malcolm Peel and Jon Lamb

Malcom Peel was an experienced public speaker and designed and ran many training courses specialising in presentation and general communication skills. His chapter has been revised by Jon Lamb, a freelance consultant and business journalist.

Jonathan Hancock and Cheryl Buggy

Jonathan Hancock and Cheryl Buggy are regular broadcasters and writers who together offer workshops in Effective Learning and Memory Techniques to a wide range of businesses including the Chartered Management Institute. Jonathan is also a World Memory Champion.

Project
Management

MARK BROWN

C O N T E N T S

Week One

Acknowledgements

The author gratefully acknowledges Symantec (UK) Limited for permission to use TIMELINE to produce The Gantt Charts and Dependency Diagrams in this book.

■ I N T R O D U C T I O N ■

Project management has developed a reputation for being something of a black art – a skill which can only be practised by professionals who are well-versed in all sorts of odd-sounding disciplines and techniques.

There is no reason why this should be so. Project management is the application of good management practices in a structured manner and in choosing appropriate automated tools which can help you. The skill lies in identifying when the circumstances in which these practices should be applied, and the best way to do so.

This week looks at the main areas of project management. By understanding these areas and applying some of the techniques we can improve our chances of managing projects to a successful completion

The main areas of project management

- understanding the nature of a project
- the role of the project manager
- setting up a project
- planning a project
- controlling a project
- using automated tools
- the personal qualities of the Project Manager
- finishing a project successfully

The nature of a project

Today we will look at the nature of a project and what distinguishes it from other forms of activity.

> *The nature of the project*
>
> • distinguishing characteristics
> • a typical project life cycle
> • the role of the Project Manager
> • the benefits of a systematic approach

Before we can look at Project Management in any detail, we should understand what a project is and why Project Management is different from *routine* management activities.

To be given responsibility for a project can seem a daunting prospect. All too often your brief will have been given on a half page memorandum, or is the resolution of a committee meeting. It is for you to turn this into something concrete,

something which is readily identifiable and, more to the point, something which is under your control.

The most obvious characteristic of a project is that it has to achieve some particular purpose, and this is normally indicated in the project's name: The Channel Tunnel Project, the Airbus Project, the Canary Wharf Project, etc. This distinguishes it from routine activities which are part of an organisation's normal business, such as running the payroll, editing a daily newspaper or producing another ten thousand tins of beans.

We will discuss aims and objectives of projects as a particular subject later this week but for the time being it is probably most useful to think of a project as *an instrument of change*.

When the project is successfully completed it will have an impact on people's lives, by changing their working patterns or by changing their environment. Managing change is clearly different (and at times much harder) than managing the status quo and it is for this reason that projects are established to effect such change in a controlled manner.

Projects can vary hugely both in their subject and in their size. A project can range from putting someone onto the moon, to selecting a new coffee machine for the office. Projects exist in all sorts of different types of business, such as information systems, construction, finance, marketing, industrial research and local government.

Moreover, no two projects are the same. A project to develop this year's model family saloon may look suspiciously like last year's, but its objectives will be

different, the circumstances will have changed and it will
involve different people.

The main characteristics of a project are that it:

Main characteristics of a project

- is an instrument of change
- has a clearly identifiable start and finish
- has a specific aim
- results in something being delivered
- is unique
- is the responsibility of a single person or body
- involves cost, resources and time
- uses a wide variety of resources and skills

All of these characteristics will not necessarily be obvious
when a project is initiated. We may know the specific aim,
but we will be aware of hidden agendas. Even if we have
been given a budget and a deadline, we may still have little
idea of the real cost, resource and time considerations of the
project. All of these will have to be verified during the early
part of the project.

Perhaps the only thing that the Project Manager can be sure
of is that it is his/her responsibility and he/she will be
judged by its success or failure.

A typical project life cycle

To help us apply some form of structure to the project, it is
useful to think of all projects as having the same basic
underlying structure. Whatever the project, it will pass
through a number of distinct phases.

THE BUCK STOPS HERE

The nature of these phases will, of course, vary depending on the type of project. So too will the time taken to go through them, from minutes to years.

Typically, a project will begin as the result of a report or feasibility study. (The work to undertake the feasibility study may well itself have been run as an individual project.)

The feasibility study will have defined the problem which is being addressed (such as 'It takes too long to cross the Channel', or 'we cannot reconcile our month-end figures until six weeks after month-end'). It may have investigated what the real requirements are (e.g. 'We need to be able to cross the Channel in less than one hour'). It will have evaluated alternative solutions and recommended a course of action.

The remaining phases of the project are as follows:

Typical project phases

- initiation
- specification
- design
- build
- installation/implementation
- operation and review

Initiation

Initiation is the most important phase of any project. Unless it is carried out effectively, the project stands little chance of success.

Initiation covers such areas as defining the terms of reference, setting objectives, agreeing budgets and gaining project approval. We will discuss this in more detail tomorrow, but it is enough to say here that the initiation of a project represents its very foundation. The manner in which it is conducted will set the tone for the remainder of the project.

It can also be the most intense period for the Project Manager, and much of this book is devoted to the activities inherent in it.

Specification

Specification is the phase of a project where the detailed requirements are determined. It is a time when you will be in close contact with the ultimate users of the project deliverable.

The project team will be analysing the users' requirements in detail and these will be documented by a Requirements Specification, which will be signed-off by the user. This will form the definitive scope of the remainder of the project.

It is at this point that the user tells you in precise terms what he/she wants you to deliver. It is important to note, however, that at this stage we are only concerned with the 'what' and not with the 'how'. Here the user will say that he/she needs to be able to get a container from London to Paris in four hours; it is not until the Design phase that you start talking about tunnels and bridges, lorries and trains.

Because you have a clearer idea of what the project involves, you will also have a better idea of what the costs and time considerations are likely to be. Typically, you will return to the project sponsor – with more detailed information and more detailed plans – to seek approval to proceed further.

Design

It is at the *design* phase that the 'what' is translated into the 'how'. Gradually, the final deliverable is beginning to take shape. Armed with the agreed requirements, the technical experts – architects, systems analysts, engineers, physicists – will create a solution for the problem which had been expressed.

This design forms the blueprint for the next phase. It may come in a variety of forms; diagrammatic plans, a working model, a prototype, or a detailed specification.

As in the previous phase, the design is agreed with the user and more detailed plans are developed for the next phase.

▰▰▰▰▰ S U N D A Y ▰▰▰▰▰

Build

Finally something tangible is created: the tunnel is dug, the
building erected, or the system built. The *build* phase is the
period which is awaited with the most impatience. There
will always be a temptation to skimp on initiation,
specification and design, merely to be seen to be producing
something. *This is a temptation to be resisted.*

Implementation

The product has been designed and built and is now almost
ready to be put into operation. Although we will have
continually verified that what we're building is what the
user actually asked for, a final acceptance process will take
place during this phase.

Here we will also apply any transition procedures which
need to be effected. Remember, project management is
about the management of change. It is all very well
developing lead-free petrol, but cars have to be modified,
customers educated and prices set.

Operation

The operation phase is often overlooked as not being part of
the project itself. It should not, however, be neglected. Once
we are satisfied that the product works, that the ship didn't
sink when the bottle of champagne struck its bow, then the
project is over. As in the case of all the previous phases
something is delivered: a final report which details the
findings of a post implementation review.

Once your new product has been in use for a while – and
probably not a very long while at that – new problems and
requirements will emerge, and the whole cycle will begin again.

The role of the Project Manager

The role of a manager, any manager, is well understood to be as follows:

> *The role of the manager:*
>
> • to plan
> • to organise
> • to co-ordinate
> • to control
> • to lead

All this is equally applicable to a Project Manager. The distinction, however, is that he/she is fulfilling these roles in order to bring about change and not to preserve the status quo.

Planning, organisation, co-ordination and control outside of a project environment such as managing a department which operates in a functional role (e.g. sales, production or accounts) are frequently constrained by the process itself, by the activities of other departments, or by conflicting demands within the department.

Although no less true for project management, there is a shift of emphasis in which the above roles are all tightly focused on achieving the project's aim, and that the project is closely allied with the business objectives of the organisation.

A large part of this effort will manifest itself in the role of *communicator*.

▰▰▰▰ S U N D A Y ▰▰▰▰

Gaining and maintaining sponsorship
Project failure is frequently attributed to shortcomings in
communication and involvement at senior levels in the
organisation. Consider a breakfast of bacon and eggs
(vegetarians notwithstanding); the chicken is just involved,
but the pig is really comitted. You need a pig as your sponsor;
someone to champion your project with real passion!

Your project is likely to be competing for management
attention with a number of other projects and activities
within the organisation. An influential senior manager who
will champion both you and your project will ensure that
you receive appropriate senior management support. In this
way, when you need decisions to be made, approvals to be
granted, or resources to be made available, your project will
not always be bottom of the agenda.

Particularly in dynamic and rapidly changing organisations,
it is easy for the world to move faster than your project.
Whilst your project may have been flavour of the month
when it was initiated, it may no longer be so a year later –
even if the need for it genuinely remains the same – as
newer and more exciting projects appear.

Advertising the project
This is very closely related to gaining sponsorship, but applies to all levels of the organisation. The Project Manager has a responsibility to ensure that the credibility of his/her project is maintained at all times, and that the project maintains a high profile within the organisation throughout its lifetime.

The Project Manager is likely to be the main link between the project team and the outside world, and it is important that he/she makes a point of promoting the project.

Managing user expectations
It is inevitable on large projects – particularly long ones – that the users' perceptions of what you are going to deliver will differ from your own understanding. Regular reviews and control checkpoints (particularly at the end of each phase) will go a long way to avoiding this.

User expectations can vary enormously from complete cynicism to wild over-optimism about the way in which their lives will be enhanced when the project delivers.

It is vital to the success of the project that these excesses are curtailed. Users should be involved in all aspects of the project so that a relationship can be built that allows effective two-way communication.

Remember, in the end it is the users' reaction to what you deliver that is the prime determinant of whether your project was a success or failure.

A systematic approach

Having described projects as being fundamentally unique, varying in size, shape, time, cost and resources, it may seem odd that we should attempt to describe a standard project management approach which is universally applicable. But it is because of this variety that a systematic approach is necessary.

Benefits of a systematic approach

- It ensures that the product which the project is to deliver is clearly defined and understood by all parties.
- It enables the objectives of the project to be clearly defined and closely allied to the business objectives of the organisation.
- It allows responsibilities for different parts of the project to be understood, allocated and agreed.
- It promotes a logical approach to planning and encourages more accurate estimating.
- It provides a consistent means by which monitoring and control can be effected.
- It reassures senior management by demonstrating visible control.

Project initiation

Today we will look at the beginning of a proiect. As we discussed yesterday, the initiation phase of the project is the most important phase. Get this wrong and the project will almost certainly fail.

> *Project initiation*
>
> * setting objectives
> * defining the scope
> * establishing the strategy
> * deriving the work breakdown structure

The key to Project Initiation is the Terms of Reference document. This may manifest itself in a number of guises – such as the recommendations of a feasibility study or project definition report – but it is important that it is given proper attention.

In many ways, the Terms of Reference represents the Project Manager's contract with the users and with the project's sponsor. As such it serves to define the context of the project, what is expected and when.

The Terms of Reference is the first point at which a form of structure is applied to the project; it is given shape, size and direction, even if only in general terms.

Terms of Reference

Key elements of the Terms of Reference

- authority and project sponsor
- customer
- objectives
- scope
- constraints
- costs/budget
- resources
- deliverables
- project phases and timescales
- strategy
- risks
- roles and responsibilities

Authority and project sponsor

This needs to be no more than a simple statement describing who has asked that the project be carried out. Depending on the position of the project in the organisation – which we will discuss later – there may be times during the life of the project where you have to seek a decision from a higher authority, for example, to resolve conflicting priorities. It is as well to have this higher authority, and the authority which is delegated to the Project Manager, defined at the outset.

Customer

Over and above the Project Sponsor, it is important to be quite clear as to who you are doing this project for; who is the project's *customer*. This will usually be the final user of the product which you are delivering.

Objectives

Reasons for setting objectives

- to provide direction
- to focus on results
- to enable plans to be made
- to prioritise and organise work
- to motivate staff
- to communicate the purpose of the project
- to enable success to be recognised

M O N D A Y

We discussed on Sunday the role of the Project Manager in gaining and retaining sponsorship for the project. A key aspect of retaining the support of the organisation is to ensure that the objectives of the project coincide with the business objectives of the organisation. This alignment of objectives should be explicit, and describe precisely how the project will contribute to the business.

Objectives come in a variety of shapes and sizes: they can be strategic or tactical, technical or procedural, open or secret, long-term or short-term, applicable to the organisation or very personal, so it is difficult to generalise about them. However, here are some basic rules for the definition of project objectives:

M O N D A Y

Project objectives should:

- Be aligned to business objectives.
- Be measurable, in terms of
  - quality
  - quantity
  - time
  - cost
  - defined end product.
- Be achievable.
- Be consistent.
- Be readily understandable.
- Be few in number.
- Have the full support and commitment of senior management, project sponsor and users.

Project objectives should never suffer from vagueness or over-generalisation. If we are to know whether or not a project has been successful we must know whether our objectives have been achieved.

Measurable objectives

These measures of success are sometimes considered so important that you may find them as a separate section in the Terms of Reference. A project to develop a more fuel-efficient engine should state clearly *how much* more efficient that engine should be. A project to improve productivity should state *how many* extra widgets will be produced an hour, or what the cost savings will be.

▰▰▰ M O N D A Y ▰▰▰

Achievable objectives

It is clearly in the Project Manager's interests that the objectives are achievable and he/she should satisfy himself/ herself that this is so. If the objectives are not, then it suggests that the wrong project, perhaps in terms of scale or scope, has been selected.

Consistent objectives

It is not so obvious that we should think to ensure that our objectives are consistent. Business objectives often contain inherent inconsistencies – increasing shareholder return is not always consistent with a substantial R & D investment (at least in the short term) – and it is possible that your project objectives may suffer from similar inherent contradictions.

Where objectives appear inconsistent you should state what the priorities are, and what trade-offs are acceptable. All Project Managers must take a view on the relationships between their objectives relating to Time, Cost and Quality.

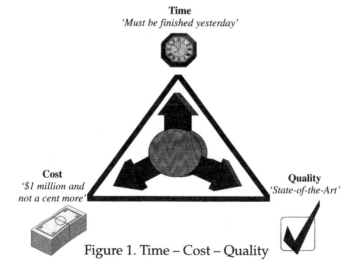

Figure 1. Time – Cost – Quality

This is the 'eternal triangle' of project management, and the Project Manager will constantly be engaged in some form of trade-off between these objectives. Where you position yourself within the triangle depends on the project: if you are producing commemorative plates for a particular event in six month's time you are likely to be near the top of the triangle, if you are developing safety-critical systems you may find yourself in the bottom right of the triangle.

Although it is useful to be able to say to yourself 'I am more concerned about time than cost', you should try to quantify this, if it has not already been imposed upon you; e.g. 'I have a budget of between £1,000,000 and £1,500,000, but come what may I have to deliver a working product in time for the Christmas sales drive.'

Scope

Unless clearly defined at the outset, an ill-defined scope is one of the areas likely to cause most trouble during the course of the project.

Scope can be defined in a number of ways and rarely can a single line be drawn to say what is inside and what is outside of the project. On Sunday, we discussed how project management is the management of change, so we must define our scope in terms of the things which we are going to change:

Scope can be defined in terms of:

- departments affected
- people affected
- locations or regions affected
- business processes affected
- products affected

▬▬▬ M O N D A Y ▬▬▬

This can be thought of as the 'Who, Where, When and What' of the project. A well-defined scope will stop you trying to solve the wrong problems, or wasting time on work which is not relevant.

A project to automate administration within a health authority may in the first instance cover only: 1) medical records departments; 2) hospitals in the south of the area; 3) admissions and appointments procedures; and 4) out-patients.

During the course of the project there will usually be pressures to change the scope. For this reason, your original scope should be clearly defined at the outset, and in this way you can more easily assess the impact of any change in the scope.

Constraints

Constraints are very similar to scope, but express what areas are outside of the scope, or what boundaries you may not cross. Time and cost limitations are common, and these invariably have an impact on the third factor, quality.

Constraints may also be the result of external forces over which you have no control: the law, geography, organisational etiquette, etc.

Costs

At this stage you may have little idea as to what the costs of the project will be. There may well, however, be a budget for the project, and this should be reflected in the Terms of Reference.

Resources

Again, you will not know precisely what resources will be required. You should, however, state from where you intend to staff the project – internally or externally, for which departments – and any particular resource or skill needs which are already apparent.

Deliverables

Project deliverables should be explicitly defined so that there is no doubt in the minds of senior management, users or the project staff what is expected. It is not enough, for example, to say that you will deliver a computer system: you will be delivering software, hardware, manuals, and training.

Additionally, there will usually be interim deliverables during the course of the project; documentation, research results, prototypes, designs and models.

Interim deliverables have the benefit of being tangible evidence of progress during the course of the project. As such, their production normally coincides with the end of a significant project phase or milestone.

M O N D A Y

Project phases and timescales

You should at this point be able to identify the main phases of the project, even if it is only at the level at which we described it on Sunday. You may choose to change the names of the phases, to make them more appropriate to your project or to your organisation's culture. But now, having given more thought to what the project is about, you should now be in a position to set some approximate timescales.

Phasing a project allows the work to be seen in more understandable components. Particularly in the case of long projects, it is easy for both project staff and senior management to lose their sense of commitment if the project end date is a very long way off.

It is, of course, difficult to say at this stage exactly how long any phase will take. The further down the road into the project the less information you have now, and the less reliable any estimate can be. Typically you will confine yourself to committing to a date for your first phase, and providing indicative dates for subsequent ones.

Strategy

Having defined your objectives, scope, deliverables, phases and timescales, your project is already beginning to take shape. However, you have yet to define how it is that you intend to pursue the project.

It is important that this is agreed in advance. Although you may be given a fairly free rein, senior management will need to have a degree of confidence in the approach that you are taking. Likewise, your own project staff (and other staff whose cooperation they will depend on) will require some high level guiding principles for the project.

Your strategy should include:

Strategic principles:

- The use of any particular techniques or methodologies.
- The adoption of any recognised standards.
- Relationships with other parts of the organisation.

Risks

The identification of *risks* in a Terms of Reference or Project Definition Statement is not intended as an opportunity for the Project Manager to say 'I told you so !' if his/her project fails.

It is, however an opportunity to consider what may be major problems in the project, and what can be done at this stage to ameliorate their impact or likelihood.

It may be that you are trying to do something particularly innovative, that you are adopting a new methodology, that you are subject to something totally out of your control (such as a stock market crash on the day you launch a rights issue, or the unexpected introduction of new legislation).

M O N D A Y

Risk analysis is a major subject in its own right. However, for the purposes of project initiation it should suffice to be able to do the following:

Risk analysis

- Identify the risks.
- Assess the chances of each occurring.
- Assess the impact on the project/organisation if the risks do occur.
- Identify measures which can be taken to prevent them occurring.
- Identify contingency arrangements which can ameliorate their effects if the risks do occur.

Assumptions
Any assumptions which are made at this stage should be clearly expressed as these are, in themselves, elements of risk.

Dependencies
You should include in your risk analysis any dependencies on external factors over which you have no or limited

control. This may be a dependency on another part of your organisation to provide a resource at a particular time, or a dependency on an external supplier to provide a product or part required for your project.

These dependencies will be detailed in the roles and responsibilities section of the Terms of Reference, but referring to them as risks can help to ensure that your project sponsor and senior management are aware of the impact of failing to ensure that other parts of the organisation are committed to your project.

Contingency
Contingency arrangements to allow for risks can be as simple as adding 10 per cent onto the expected project duration to allow for anything going wrong, or may be elaborate fall-back plans, or descoping of the project.

If contingency time is added onto plans – and it is not always appropriate to do so – great care must be taken as to who is aware of this. Clearly, it must be agreed with the project sponsor, but you must guard against the onset of Parkinson's Law (work filling available time) if it becomes common knowledge that 'no-one is really going to mind if the project is a month late'.

Roles and responsibilities

External resources
At this stage, you will have given little detailed thought to how the project will be staffed and organised – this comes later. It is important, though, to ensure that all external roles and responsibilities are made clear.

M O N D A Y

No project can exist in isolation and you will always require the cooperation of others, either within the organisation or from outside. Other people's involvement in your project can be to: execute specific pieces of work, provide information, take decisions or be available for consultation.

You should indicate when and how much involvement is required so that other people can plan to make the appropriate resources available when you need them. If you fail to do this you run the considerable risk of having those resources denied when you need them most.

Decision-making responsibilities

Establishing who decides what is a major prerequisite for any project. If clear decision-making responsibilities are not defined then either crucial decisions will not be made and the project will suffer from inertia, or the project team itself will take decisions, resulting in alienation and reduced commitment from the users.

As a general rule, decisions should be made by those who normally make them within the organisation, or have some accountability for the consequences. Accountants should make decisions about the accounts, technicians about technical problems, etc.

Levels of authority should also be defined, especially authority to spend money or deviate from the Terms of Reference. This should include escalation procedures to help resolve conflicts between irreconcilable decisions made by different decision-makers.

Project organisation

Having established what the project is and what it is setting out to do, we now have to consider *how* we are going to achieve it. Much of the work described in the previous two days has been concerned with establishing the appropriate environment for the project. Today we will look inward into the project itself and discuss organising the project and the first stage of the planning process. This is covered by the following topics:

> *Project organisation and high level planning*
>
> - work breakdown structure
> - project organisation
> - outline plan and milestones

Work breakdown structure

The Work Breakdown Structure (WBS) is a key document in the project and forms the basis of much of the subsequent work in planning, setting budgets, financial control, defining the organisation and assigning responsibilities.

Its development relies on the gradual decomposition of the project into units of work. We will already have mapped out the high level phases which the project will go through, and these represent the first level of breakdown.

Breaking the project down into manageable units is the key to being able to control it. Projects suffer from the 'Salami Syndrome'; i.e. when they are viewed as a whole they are rather unattractive, but when cut into fine slices they become quite appetising.

Through the process of gradually dividing a piece of work up into something more manageable we will finally arrive at discrete pieces of work which we will be able to estimate, plan and control.

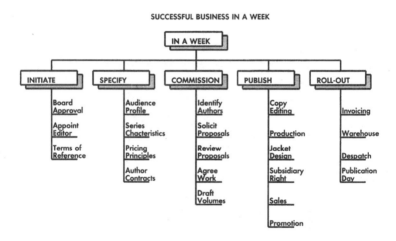

Figure 2. Work Breakdown Structure

Levels
Each different level of the WBS is often given a name such as phase, activity, or task. These names will vary between organisations, but it is important to be consistent when referring to them.

How many levels you arrive at will vary from project to project; generally the bigger the project the more levels you have. It is, therefore, difficult to be prescriptive: up to about five is fine, more than that and perhaps you should be thinking of initiating sub-projects to deal with different legs of the WBS. Anything over ten levels and the project scope is probably flawed.

Completeness
At this point the Project Manager will have to involve other people, who will probably end up as part of the project team. Except in the case of trivial projects, it is inconceivable that the Project Manager will be able to derive the WBS on his/her own as he/she will not have the necessary detailed knowledge of each area. Although we may consider ourselves to be experts in particular fields, generally no one individual should work on more than two levels.

T U E S D A Y

One of the main objectives of the WBS is to identify all the pieces of work which need to be undertaken to complete the project. It is important, therefore, that identification of the work to be done is carried out by those people who are most familiar with the processes involved. So the Project Manager might define the first two levels, heads of departments or team leaders the next, a senior engineer the next, and so on.

Occasionally you may be able to 'borrow' a WBS from a previous (similar) project. This will help, but should only be used as a final check-list to ensure that you haven't forgotten anything. Remember, *projects are unique*.

Projects fail more often because activities were not planned at the outset, than because activities were planned badly. Naturally, there will be changes during the course of the project, but there should not be any purely as a result of forgetting that something needed to be done.

Work unit characteristics
The nature of the work units will obviously differ as one works down the hierarchy; at the higher levels phases will appear which are probably discrete. These will result in major deliverables and constitute significant review points throughout the project.

At the lower levels they will be shorter in duration and be less 'self-standing'. What is produced by them will probably be an integral part of something else.

A great asset of this hierarchical levelling is that the WBS can be used as a communication tool at different levels in the hierarchy. The Managing Director may not be terribly interested in knowing when the wheels of the car are built, but he/she will certainly be interested in knowing when the overall design phase is finished.

We can, however, say that if we are to arrive at sensible tasks (particularly at the bottom level of the WBS) the tasks should conform to the following criteria. They should:

Task characteristics

- Be measurable in terms of cost, effort, resource and time.
- Result in a single (verifiable) end product.
- Have clear start and end dates.
- Be the responsibility of a single person.

The existence of the end product is sometimes a difficult thing to insist upon as this will not always be something tangible and, as a Project Manager, you will need to be able to satisfy yourself that a particular task has been completed.

On-going tasks such as management or administration should be included in the WBS as these will have an effect on the project budget, even if they will not obviously affect the project schedule.

You should also include tasks which are being undertaken outside of the immediate project area, such as reviewing of documentation by outsiders.

Whilst at this stage we are only interested in the existence of
the tasks, we should also be collecting as much information
about them as we can. This should include:

Task information

- description of task
- necessary inputs or preconditions
- deliverables
- particular resource requirements (with costs)
- particular skill requirements
- responsibilities
- estimated time

It is often convenient to have this information recorded on a
standardised form (see Figure 3) which can be maintained
on the Project File.

Project organisation

Having established the WBS you will now have a fairly
detailed view of what the project looks like; in particular,
what needs to be done.

The next stage is determining who is going to do it and how
they should be organised. Although it would be wrong to
suggest that correct organisation will solve all your
problems it is without doubt that a flawed organisation will
cause major problems on a project.

These will manifest themselves as difficulties in
communication, responsibility or commitment. The
organisation you select for your projects should, therefore,
try to address these issues.

TASK DEFINITION

WBS Code	TASK NAME

DELIVERABLE

Description	Quality Standard
Customer	Needed by date

DEPENDENCIES

Event/Deliverable	Dependency Type	Deliverer

START DATE		END DATE	

RESOURCING

Days Effort	Skills / Job Title	Optimum Staffing

COSTS		RESPONSIBILITIES	
Staff		Project Management	
External Suppliers		Delivery	
Professional Fees		Quality	
Fixed			
TOTAL			

ADDITIONAL INFORMATION / COMMENT

Author		Department	
Location		Tel.	

Figure 3. Task Definition Form

Logically, your WBS is your project organisation. We stated that for each work unit which appeared on the WBS there was a single person responsible for the delivery of the end product associated with it. We should, therefore, be able to map bottom level tasks onto individual workers, higher-level tasks onto their managers, and so on.

Function-based Organisation

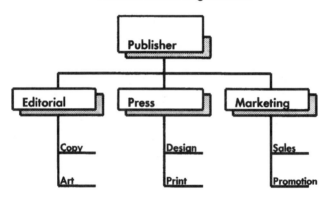

Work Breakdown Structure

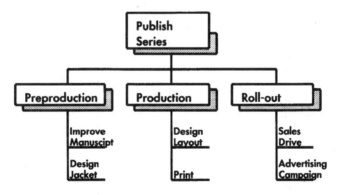

Figure 4. Hierarchical organisation structure

At first sight this implies a *hierarchical* project structure, and this is indeed a common means of organising projects. But it can also be applied to a *matrix* organisation.

Matrix project organisation

PROJECTS / DEPARTMENTS	PROJECT ALPHA	PROJECT BETA	PROJECT GAMMA
REQUIREMENTS	Jones	Jones	Brown
DESIGN	Williams	Smith	Smith
PROGRAMMING	Shannon	Black	Black
TESTING	O'Dee	O'Dee	O'Dee
IMPLEMENTATION	Thomas	Price	Philips

Figure 5. Matrix organisational structure

The matrix approach leaves staff working on the project within their own departmental structures. It allows the project to remain fully integrated with the mainstream organisation, and encourages decision-making to remain within the organisation, rather than isolated within the project.

In order to avoid a conflict of priorities and accountabilities there needs to be clear agreement between the project management and the departmental management about the amount of time and commitment that individual members of staff can spend on the project.

The Project Office

The role of a Project Office is to co-ordinate the activities which are being undertaken in functional departments for the project. It will therefore control:

Project Office co-ordination functions

- preparation of plans
- reporting of progress against plans and budgets
- resolution of dependencies and issues
- management of changes and enhancements
- preparation of standards and quality control
- tracking and resolution of issues

This is more than a simple administrative role, and should be fulfilled by a staff who see themselves as extensions of the Project Manager; acting as his/her eyes and ears and intervening where appropriate.

A certain amount of administration is, however, unavoidable. To avoid descending into a bureaucracy which stifles productivity,

administration should be kept as simple as possible. It is useful
to bring into the Project Office all those tasks which can be
usefully centralised. This might include time sheet keeping,
document control, project library, organising and minuting
meetings and maintaining the project diary.

You should, however, make the Project Office's
accountabilities clear; they can be responsible for facilitating
the resolution of issues, but cannot be held accountable if
issues remain unresolved.

The milestone plan

Having defined the structure of the project and the WBS, it
is important to begin to focus the project on results.

Particularly in the case of lengthy projects, the final delivery
of the end product will seem a long way off and it is,
therefore, difficult to instil a sense of urgency amongst
people working on the project. You should therefore define
intermediate targets, or *milestones*, towards the overall aim.

Defining milestones will assist the Project Manager in a
number of ways:

The purpose of milestones

- To provide a measure of progress on the project
  which is accessible to senior management.
- To provide a means of communication with people
  outside the project team.
- To focus project attention on results.
- To provide manageable stages of work.
- To enable responsibilities to be apportioned at a
  high level.

T U E S D A Y

The actual definition of milestones and the relationships between them – the dependencies – should be done by members of the project team working together. A 'brainstorming' session might be appropriate as this will encourage commitment to the plan by those involved.

By starting at the end of the project – the final deliverable – and working backwards, you should identify the major points through which you must pass.

Milestones represent particular points in the project, and as such should be expressed in the form *'When X has happened'*. This may be the production of the end product at the end of a phase, a major decision having been taken, or a document having been accepted.

Because they are a part of the project which the Project Manager will be controlling directly, and probably the most visible at that, milestones should be readily verifiable and there should be no doubt about whether or not the milestone has been reached.

It is easy to think that a document has been finished when the last word has been written, but in practice work will continue on it while it is reviewed, revised and agreed. Your milestones should recognise this.

The milestones do not represent a detailed plan of the project. Their number will depend on the size of the project but between 10 and 20 – corresponding to the second level of the WBS – will probably be enough to demonstrate the whole project adequately. These should be spaced at controllable intervals of between a fortnight and a month, again depending on the nature and size of the project.

Detailed planning

Today we will look at the more detailed aspects of planning and the tools which are available to help you with this.

Detailed planning stages

- estimating
- identifying dependencies
- constructing the dependency network
- assigning responsibilities
- allocating resources
- producing a Gantt Chart
- refining the plan

Planning requires a large amount of information, and the amount and quality of information which you will have is inversely proportional to the length of time between when you plan and when the tasks should be executed.

For anything but the very smallest of projects you will normally only provide a detailed plan for the project phase that you are about to enter. Typically, planning the next phase will be one of the last tasks of all phases of the project.

Estimating

Effective estimating is the key to a plan in which one can have a degree of confidence. It is also one of the hardest parts as it involves making judgements based on knowledge, understanding and experience. As such, different – and sometimes conflicting – interests come to the fore.

▄▄▄▄ W E D N E S D A Y ▄▄▄▄

Estimates will always be subject to human interpretation of these factors, and the Project Manager should ask himself/herself the following questions:

If estimates appear too long

- Is the estimator trying to give himself/herself more time than he/she really needs to make life easier?
- Is he/she unnessarily concerned (e.g. through lack of experience) about the complexity of the task?
- Is he/she planning to deliver what you would consider to be an over-engineered solution (e.g. a 200-page report when a one-page memorandum would suffice)?

If the estimates appear too short

- Is the estimator over-confident?
- Does he/she really appreciate the complexity?
- Does he/she fully appreciate what must be delivered?
- Has he/she made unreasonable assumptions?

To take account of the 'soft' human factors mentioned above, we should try to apply a degree of objectivity and empiricism to the process. No method of predicting the future is fail-safe, but by ensuring that we are taking *informed* judgements on the basis of sound data and reasonable assumptions we can reduce the risk.

There are many different techniques which can be used for estimating, each more or less appropriate to different circumstances. However, you should note that these can never be a substitute for judgement and experience.

Some of the main principles to be observed when estimating are described opposite:

Principles of estimating

- Estimates should be in terms of days effort. The elapsed time taken to complete a task is a product of the resources which can be applied to it and other constraints.
- Estimates should not include any allowance for contingency; that can be applied later at a global level.
- Estimates should be 'honest'.
- Individual commitment should be sought.

- The skill and experience levels of the available staff should be allowed for.
- The procedure used and any assumptions made should be documented.
- The process should be revisited throughout the project to ensure that assumptions and factors used in the derivation of estimates still hold true.
- Estimates should not be 'massaged'.
- Always apply a reasonableness check.

Estimating using historical data

Historical data about previous projects can be an invaluable source of base data for new projects. Generally, this data will only be available if your organisation has well-established planning and control procedures, which have faithfully recorded the time and effort spent on each task during previous projects.

Estimating using relative time

There is frequently a direct relationship between the time taken to do one task and the time taken to do a subsequent one. If it takes two months to design a particular type of product, then it might generally take four months to build it and a further two to test it.

Rules which specify these relationships may be well-known within your own industry.

Estimating using parameters

It is possible to derive formulae which can take into account the size of the deliverable and the complexity of the task. Some of these formulae are well-established in particular industries. In Information Technology there are well-known formulae based on the number of files a program will access, the number of decisions to be made within the program, and the language being used.

These formulae are often derived and refined using many years of historical data.

Dependencies

On any project some tasks will be performable concurrently and some must be done in a clear order. Defining dependencies is the process by which we identify the order in which things must be done.

Typically the way to do this is to start at the end of the project and work backwards, saying at each task 'What must be in place before I can begin this task'. Gradually you will establish predecessors for every task until you arrive at the beginning.

W E D N E S D A Y

This is not necessarily a straightforward exercise, as you will find tasks dependent on multiple predecessors, half-done predecessors and other complications.

There are four basic types of dependency relationship:

Types of dependency relationship

- Finish to start – in which the preceding task must be completed before the succeeding one can start.
- Start to finish – in which the preceding task must start before the succeeding one can finish.
- Finish to finish – in which both tasks must finish simultaneously.
- Start to start – in which both tasks must start simultaneously.

Because relationships are not always as clear cut as this, you should also be able to identify cases where there is a particular amount of overlap. Thus we might say that Task B might start one week into Task A.

All good planning tools will allow you to record this information.

FROM THE (Start/End) OF THE PREDECESSOR: Dig Foundations
(Add/Subtract) [0] (Minutes/Hours/Days/Weeks/Months)
THEN (Start/End) THE SUCCESSOR: Build Walls

Dependency networks

By establishing dependencies between predecessors and successors we can establish dependency networks. These are

also known as PERT (Program Evaluation and Review
Technique) charts.

Uses of dependency networks

- To determine the critical path.
- To determine the shortest time in which the project
  could be delivered.
- To identify tasks which represent particular risks.
- To identify periods when too much may be
  happening.
- To enhance your understanding of the project.

The minimum information shown on a network diagram is
the task and the dependency – we would normally add
other details, such as start and end dates – and these will be
represented as boxes connected with lines.

Except in the case of trivial proiects, most people would not
these days consider the manual production of a PERT chart,
preferring to use automated planning packages.

Automated planning tools will carry out much of the
laborious number-crunching involved in this process,
leaving you time to properly analyse the results.

Slack (float)
Slack is the amount of time which a task can be delayed
without affecting any other tasks or the end date of the
project. It occurs when one task is dependent on
predecessors which may finish at different times.

From the Project Manager's point of view the existence of
slack in a plan may be beneficial as it does allow a certain

amount of latitude for planning when tasks should be done. Too much slack and you might find yourself with undesirable peaks in resourcing.

The critical path
The critical path is established by tracing a line through those tasks on the dependency network which have no slack at all. This represents the path through the project where, if any slippage is incurred, the final end date will also slip.

Most importantly, however, it shows the shortest possible time in which the project can be achieved, and you can, therefore, use it to determine when the project (or phase) will be completed. Note, however, that to derive the genuine critical path it must be calculated using the *elapsed* time taken to complete a task, not the days effort.

The critical path (and those tasks near the critical path, i.e. those with very little slack) represent those areas of the project upon which the Project Manager must concentrate his/her efforts to ensure that everything goes well.

Responsibilities and resources

The Dependency Diagram at this point gives a strictly logical view of the project and in many ways represents what would happen in a perfect world.

Sadly, however, Project Managers operate in the real world of limited resources and fixed deadlines and the intrusion of these factors will change the view of the project. Where the network shows that a number of tasks can be executed in parallel, you may only have one person available to do them and they will, therefore, have to be done one after the other.

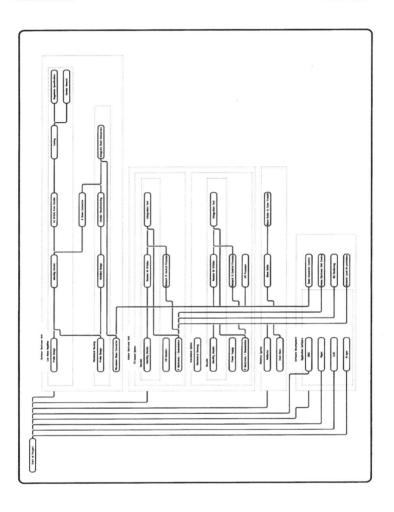

Figure 6. Dependency diagram

W E D N E S D A Y

At this stage we are ready to assign individual project staff to particular tasks.

Each task should be made the responsibility of one and only one person; shared responsibility means that responsibility tends to get bucked. If possible, tasks should only be carried out by one person.

Clearly, this is not always possible as some tasks will genuinely need more than one person, or you may wish a task which could be done single-handedly to be done by several people in order to get it finished quickly. You should begin, however, by determining the optimum number of people to execute a task in the most efficient manner.

Calculating elapsed time to complete a task

- Determining optimum number of staff required to efficiently execute the task.
- Determine the actual number of people available (and competent) to execute the task.
- Determine their availability (expressed as a percentage) taking into account other duties, training commitments, holidays, sickness, etc.

$$\text{Elapsed time} = \frac{\text{Days effort} \times \text{Staff availability}}{\text{Number of staff}}$$

You will also have to consider:

- the skill and experience levels of the staff assigned;
- their availability (it is normal to assume for estimating purposes that staff assigned full-time to a project are only productive four days a week at most to allow for sickness, administration, meetings, etc.);
- training, annual leave commitments and public holidays;
- 'unproductive' time spent in supervision; depending on the skill and experience of the staff being supervised, this could be as much as one day a week per person being supervised;
- the degree to which the optimum number of staff can be changed, some tasks simply cannot be completed any quicker no matter how much resource is applied.
- the constraints imposed by dependencies between tasks and externally imposed deadlines and milestones.

The Gantt Chart

The Gantt Chart is the primary tool which you will use for scheduling the project and then subsequently controlling it.

It is made up of a task information side (on the left) and a task bar side (on the right). The task information side holds such information as the name of the task, its WBS code, and who is responsible for it. The task bar is a line which graphically represents the period in time at which the task will be executed.

The precise content of a Gantt Chart should be determined by what you intend to use it for. As a communication tool to illustrate the project to senior management it would only be appropriate to include summary level tasks; if you are using it for your own purposes to monitor progress then more detail will be required.

A good planning tool will allow you to define the information you want displayed and the format in which it should appear.

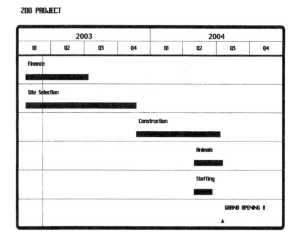

Figure 7. Simple Gantt Chart

W E D N E S D A Y

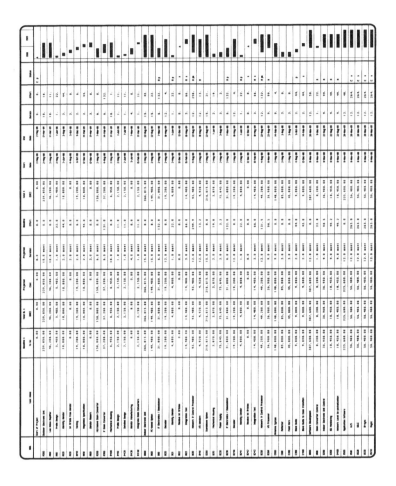

Figure 8. Complex Gantt Chart

The use of automated project management tools

Planning and control tools

The development of automated project management tools over the years has transformed the way in which Project Managers can work. Because of their ability to manipulate large amounts of complex information they are capable of relieving the Project Manager of many hours of tedious work.

Not only can they store and manipulate large amounts of information, they allow you to make changes to your plans very quickly. Planning is an iterative process in which one is continually changing variables to arrive at the optimum plan. By using an automated tool we can experiment with 'what-if' scenarios to see, for instance, what the impact of applying more resource at a particular point on the plan might be in a matter of minutes. This might take hours or even days using pencil and paper.

An additional major benefit is in the production of reports. Detailed information on budgets and costs can be produced almost at the press of a button. Presentations to management can include high quality visual graphics.

Using sophisticated planning tools is, however, no substitute for sound project management and will not of itself guarantee the success of any project.

Quite the contrary; there is a great danger – particularly on large projects – that maintaining the plan can become the be all and end all of the project. The Project Manager's attention becomes diverted from managing the real problems and issues facing the project and spends more and more time ensuring that the plan, with its great complexities is perfect.

A plan is only that – a statement of intent – and it is putting it into practice which is at the heart of the Project Manager's job. We have spent a lot of time discussing planning because it is an important distinguishing part of the Project Manager's role. However, like all managers, most of his time is actually spent managing the work.

Communication tools
The above has all been about automated planning tools and much of this week is about managing and controlling projects. An important key to this is communication, which should freely pass up and down your project team, and be with people and organisations outside it.

Automation has now provided us with a new channel for communication. It may not necessarily allow us to do new things but it will allow us to do things faster or more comprehensively. Everything described here remains true

but we should take advantage of new tools to help us. As
our projects grow larger and teams are spread across
countries, automation allows us to communicate with people
throughout the team, regardless of where they are. There are
many such tools around which enable project managers to
communicate with their teams and the wider population
involved in some way in the project.

The tools vary in sophistication and can be as simple as
email or grow to more complex applications such as
Microsoft's Outlook and Exchange products or Lotus Notes.
What you do is up to you and depends on how much you or
your organisation is prepared to invest (in time and money)
to implement a suitable communications infrastructure. Your
organisation may have embedded this infrastructure already.
If so, make full use of what is available. If not, you may have
a convincing case for acquiring them for your project. These
days it is hard to imagine a project without them.

You may want to start with something as simple as sending
SMS reminders to your staff's mobile phones reminding
them to complete time sheets. The more complex
applications have far greater facilities which will enable you
and the project team to:

• email
• maintain contact lists for people in and connected to the
  project
• manage diaries for everyone on the project
• arrange meetings
• record the outcome of meetings (decisions and actions)
• track actions and manage progress on their completion
• share documents, in their draft format, when they are out

for review or when they have been agreed
- maintain the document repository
- publish progress reports
- announce relevant news items
- manage issue resolution
- identify risks and manage their impact and resolution

Some of this information may be very sensitive and it is up to you to determine how much you want to make public. The technology should allow you to decide and govern who can and who cannot see each piece of information you publish.

■■■■■■T H U R S D A Y■■■■■

Controlling projects – monitoring

Although planning and organising have been fairly intensive activities for the Project Manager, it is controlling the project which consumes the most time. He/she must exercise control over the process from the moment that he/she is appointed to the time that the project is finally completed.

Controlling projects is about ensuring that the project objectives are met; specifically those objectives of:

- time
- cost
- quality

We must ensure that the project is completed on the planned end-date, is completed within the specified budget and delivers what it promised to deliver to an acceptable quality. What these objectives are were described at the outset of the project in the Terms of Reference.

Today we will look at the area of control with specific reference to those three objectives. Control is made up of two parts: monitoring and then taking action. Today we will concentrate on the first aspect, monitoring.

Why do we control?

Managing change
The awkward thing about projects is that they never quite turn out as you expect them to. No matter how thorough your planning, no matter how much senior management

commitment you have solicited, no matter how well
organised you have been . . . things go wrong.

Factors which change projects

- The planning assumptions may have been wrong
  - there may be more to do than you anticipated
  - it might be harder than you anticipated
  - resources you depend on might not be available.
- The requirements may change (very common).
- The deadline may change (usually earlier).
- The budget may be cut (try to complete projects
  within financial years).
- The priority of the project in the mind of senior
  mangement might change.
- Barriers/resistance to change.
- People make mistakes (usually large ones).
- Acts of God.

All of these things – and many more – will conspire against
your project and try to force it further and further away
from achieving its objectives.

Naturally, you do not know what will go wrong at the
outset of the project, although you will have allowed
yourself a certain amount of contingency in terms of time
and budget, simply because you know that *something* will go
wrong.

By maintaining a high degree of control on the project – and
this must extend beyond the immediate project team – you
will be able to spot these potential dangers early enough to
be able to do something about them.

T H U R S D A Y

Controlling projects is about identifying problems, working out what needs to be done to ameliorate them, and then doing it.

It is important that control is seen by the project team in this positive light. There is always a tendency to view control as merely an enormous chore for all those involved, whose only purpose is to give the Project Manager an opportunity to blame the guilty.

It should be portrayed as a process which is actually designed to help project staff in the work they do; to provide a mechanism by which they can flag problems they are suffering with, and through which solutions can be sought and implemented.

Pre-requisites for effective control

We will have already achieved a large part of the

prerequisites for control by the time we have invested in establishing the project. By progressing from the project objectives through to a detailed plan, we have broken the project up into controllable units.

Establishing a baseline
Deviations from the plan can only be measured and interpreted if we have a fixed view of what the original plan was. Fixing the original plan is known as 'setting the baseline'.

Establishing a formal control procedure
Control of projects should by and large be formalised. This is not to mean that it necessarily has to become a bureaucratic burden on all those involved. Merely that a regular and disciplined approach is taken to the control process.

As we mentioned above, project staff should understand the need for project control and they should also have a clear understanding of the process which is actually being used, and what in particular is being controlled.

What do we control?

As we said earlier, we will wish to control time, cost and quality. But what does that mean specifically?

Time
During the planning phase we will have established dates for major milestones on the project. These will have been widely publicised as part of raising the profile of the project. We have, therefore, a great interest in ensuring that these are adhered to.

▆▆▆▆▆▆ T H U R S D A Y ▆▆▆▆▆▆

We also defined start and end dates for all the activities
which contribute to the attaining of these milestones. These
also should be adhered to.

However, it is of little use to us if we get to our first major
milestone date and discover that we have not made it. By
recording basic data about the progress of tasks we can
derive considerable amounts of information to assist us in
its interpretation.

Time related progress data

- status (future, started or complete)
- elapsed time spent
- days effort spent
- estimate of days effort to go
- estimate of elapsed time to go

Most automated planning tools can compare this
information against your original plan (the baseline) and
derive the following statistics relating to time:

- proportional % achieved
- duration (projected)
- duration variance
- duration as % of baseline
- effort variance
- end date (projected)
- end date variance
- spent duration as % of baseline
- spent effort %
- to go duration
- to go effort
- To go duration as % of baseline

Here we are in severe danger of suffering from information overload, and you must choose carefully what is the minimum information you need to be able to answer the following questions:

- Have I made the progress I planned?
- Will I finish when I thought I would?

When determining progress it is important to remember that if you have spent half the time that you planned on a task it does not necessarily mean that you are halfway through it!

The most useful piece of information you can acquire about a task is how much longer (in terms of both effort and elapsed time) it will take to complete. By comparing this against your outstanding planned time to complete you can easily see if the task has slipped.

Cost

Control over costs is an area which is often neglected by Project Managers, particularly on projects whose only costs are staff costs and these are to a certain extent outside of the control of the project (e.g. where salaries are decided at a corporate level).

However, by managing costs the Project Manager will glean vital information about progress and the *value* of the work done. Costs can be used as a measure of progress.

From our planning exercises we will have determined resourcing profiles and therefore have a clear picture of how much the project will cost in staff terms overall, and what the profile of costs over time is. Other costs, such as for the acquisition of equipment, are usually fairly fixed. Do be aware, though, of costs which may be incurred in respect of services, consultancy, or cross-charges from other departments.

Remember, senior management tend to be particularly sensitive to costs, especially when things go wrong.

The degree of sophistication applied to the control of costs varies according to the type and size of project; it can be simple measurement of the number of people working on it, to complex accounting and control systems.

Some planning tools will go a long way to deriving statistics, but you should always remember that the quality of what you get out is directly proportional to the quality of what you put in.

The most important statistics are:

Estimated at Completion (EAC)
What the total cost of the project will be, as calculated by looking at the plan as it stands, i.e. costs incurred to date + scheduled costs
Budgeted at Completion (BAC)
The total cost derived from the plan before any work began
Actual Cost of Work Performed
The amount of money spent so far

Quality
Unlike time and cost, where we have units of measure such as days and pounds, the yardstick by which we measure quality is not so easy to find. Because it is difficult, it is often neglected.

The setting of quality standards involves having a clear specification of what the end product of the task should be, including whatever quality factors may be appropriate.

Views of quality are as varied as projects, but include such considerations as reliability, durability, accuracy, clarity and functionality.

Where quality factors are defined, then these should be measurable in some way. This might be the frequency of failures, the life-span, the number of corrections that have to be made to a document, or the number of comments made on a proposal.

Caution should be applied however, as statistics such as these can become distorted for perfectly sound reasons which are not necessarily a reflection on the quality.

Quality control is an important aspect – particularly in manufacturing processes – but a pre-requisite for it is quality assurance; establishing the right environment for quality to flourish.

Quality should be injected into the process from the outset. A common way of doing this is to develop a Quality Plan, which expresses your objectives for quality and how you will set about ensuring it.

This then becomes a key project document which is maintained to show when and how quality targets have been achieved, and any deviations from the Quality Plan.

The Quality Plan

- define working methods and procedures
- define standards for deliverables
- define standards for supervision and review
- define project checkpoints
- define user involvement

A commitment to quality from the project team is vital to achieving it. It should be inculcated amongst the staff as being an essential, not a luxury, and ingrained in the culture of the project.

Progress reporting

Monitoring of time, cost and quality requires the Project Manager to have detailed knowledge of the status of all the tasks currently being executed. There are a number of ways in which this information can be gathered:

Progress reporting

- progress reports
- one-to-one progress meetings
- group/project progress meetings
- wandering about

You should use **all four** of these techniques, as each will enable you to discover different pieces of information, or different perspectives on the same information.

Progress reports
The production of progress reports should be carried out on a strictly regular basis (usually weekly) by all those who are responsible for any planned activity. If this means that every single member of staff reports progress then so be it. The Project Manager does not necessarily have to read them all; they can be summarised by team leaders, junior managers and so on, to give overall progress reports for activities higher up the hierarchy on the WBS.

We have already mentioned that the whole area of control should be portrayed as genuinely being in the interests of the project staff.

Progress reports should, therefore, be as easy to complete as possible (which also helps you having to read them). A standardised form which shows the work done in a period, deviations from the plan, work for the next period, and any know problems, is ideal. An example is shown overleaf.

HERE – WEEK ONE'S REPORT

T H U R S D A Y

PROGRESS REPORT

Author	Mark Brown	Report Number	26
Dept	Publishing	Week Commencing	22-7-92

WBS Code	Task Name	Time Spent This Period	Estimate to Complete	Progress (Note 1)	Estimated Completion Date	Status (Note 2)
1.7.6	Receive "Report Writing in a Week"	0	0	0	22-7-92	Complete
1.7.7	Review "Report Writing" manuscript	3	4	-2	31-7-92	Started
7.1.3	Prepare monthly report for Board	1	0	+1	26-7-92	Complete
4.3.2	Paris Conference	1	0	0	25-7-92	Complete

Highlights this Period

1. Manuscript for "Successful Report Writing in a Week" delivered on time.

2. Monthly report to Board completed.

3. Paris conference a great success !

Problems Encountered this Period

Nature of Problem	Impact	Suggested Action
Report Writing- MS has been hand-written in green crayon and the author has adopted a prose style reminiscent of Marcel Proust.	1.7.7 will take an extra 2 days.	1. Send author on report writing course. 2. Warn graphics of delay.

Activities Planned for Next Period

1. Complete review of "Report Writing".

2. Presentation to Board.

3. Staff appraisals.

Note 1: Progress = Time Spent to Date + Estimate to Complete - Original Estimate
Note 2: Future/Started/Complete

Signed
Date

Figure 9. Progress report

You will notice that the report calls for the writer to make comparison with the Project Plan and to reconsider the estimates to complete the work.

Although you may often see it, asking people to give a 'percentage complete' figure is usually less than satisfactory as it is only too easy to give a figure which reflects the percentage of planned time spent. By forcing staff to actively reconsider how much more time is really needed you will get a much more accurate picture of the genuine progress.

Progress reporting is not, however, all one way. The Project Manager will be expected to report to a number of other people/bodies, including the Sponsor.

Like all reports, the frequency, style, amount of detail and actual content will be varied to suit the particular audience.

Remembering that one of the key roles of the Project Manager as a communicator is to maintain commitment to the project, it is often a good idea to give some of these reports (especially those to senior management) in the form of presentations.

One-to-one progress meetings
Meetings with individual members of the project team, although time-consuming, are probably the best means of assessing progress.

It is important, however, that these meetings are well-structured and reasonably formalised. The purpose of the meeting is to assess progress and discuss any problems; it is not to have a generalised chat about how things are going – save that for by the coffee machine!

T H U R S D A Y

The best vehicle for structuring the meeting is the progress report. Each activity on it should be discussed – even if there are no problems associated with it.

Particular problems which have been identified on the progress report should be discussed in more detail in order to gain a real understanding of why the problem has occurred and what can be done about it.

Adopting the right style for the meetings is crucial to their effectiveness. There should be no atmosphere of blame or recrimination. Staff should be encouraged to approach the meetings with an honest and open attitude and not in fear that they are to be hauled over the coals. Praise should be lavished generously when things have gone well.

One-to-one meetings are also the best opportunity for the Project Manager to inspect quality personally. A golden rule of project monitoring is 'Everyone will lie to you!'. This may sound a little harsh on your trusted team, but I would suggest that it is not a bad position from which to start.

It is very easy for tasks to be only 95% complete when you are told that they are finished, so ask to see the finished report, the user's sign-off, the testing certificate, or whatever. There is no substitute for seeing it yourself.

Group/project progress meetings
Meetings of the entire project team (or groups within it if the project is too large to bring it all together regularly) are useful, but need to be carefully managed.

Their primary purpose is to ensure that all parts of the project are aware of what other parts are doing, and any issues that have arisen.

Whilst it is important that team spirit is fostered, you should always be aware that people will show greater reluctance to disclose problems in their own areas in a large group. If there are problems to be discussed at this level, then these should have been identified and corrective action agreed between the relevant parties and the Project Manager *before* the meeting.

Using technology
Many organisations now make extensive use of electronic mail and groupware. These are immensely valuable tools to Project Managers, both for the transmission of information to you, and for the dissemination of information (including the project library) around the project team. In the case of projects which have geographically dispersed teams, particularly if they are operating in different time zones, these tools should be considered indispensable.

We spoke of automated planning and communication tools yesterday. The value of such applications becomes more apparent when we are thinking about monitoring projects. Tools such as Microsoft's Exchange 2000 and Lotus Notes 5 hugely increase the visibility of activities and their deliverables on the project.

We have never suggested that the role of a project manager is a dictatorial one and the real value of these tools is that they are collaborative applications. Leadership, from the Project Manager, is about building a team and nurturing it through sharing. Use of suitable technology can help in this respect. Technology will never be a substitute for such team-building activities as sharing a meal or a drink together and should only be used when an atmosphere of mutual trust

has already been engendered. It can, however, provide a
medium for open discussion and exchange of ideas where
such social forums cannot take place, for example, where
project teams are dispersed around the world across many
time-zones.

Obviously, this can help the formulation of creative ideas or
resolutions of problems, but this visibility can also help the
Project Manager to:

- measure progress quantitatively
- get a real feel for issues as they occur
- share possible resolutions widely

As we move towards a paperless office, retaining items such
as progress reports, deliverables and discussion threads on a
computer system can extend their audience much more
widely.

Wandering about
Do it ! You will find out more about the project by doing this
than any other way. By talking to your staff, especially the
ones doing the actual work in an informal environment you
will be able to grasp that intangible 'feel' of how well the
project is going, and you will also be able to pick up on
issues and problems as they arise, and before they have had
time to embed themselves.

Controlling projects – taking action

Yesterday we discussed the ways in which the Project Manager can gather information which will tell him/her the status of work being undertaken on the project. Today we will look at what we must do with all that information; how to keep the project on course and see it to a successful conclusion.

Controlling projects

- assessing the situation
- impact analysis
- resolving issues and problems
- controlling change
- completing the project

Control is the heart of what the Project Manager does – anyone can collate the information we discussed on Thursday, say 'what a shame' and file it, but it is up to the Project Manager to do something about it.

Assessing the situation

Prevention is, of course, better than cure, and this is why we have expended so much effort on producing a plan for time, cost and quality in which we have confidence. However, things will start happening differently from how you expected almost from the moment the project begins. Activities will start or complete late, costs will escalate and quality will fall.

You must be able to assess the impact of these occurrences on the overall project. To do this you must ask yourself a number of questions:

Assessing the situation

- How much will this effect other activities?
- What must I do to correct this particular problem?
- What must I do to put the project back on track?
- Why did it happen?
- What must I do to ensure that it does not happen again?

Most problems can be rectified provided that they are caught early enough. This is why we have emphasised the importance of regular and honest progress reporting.

Problems come in all sorts of shapes and sizes so it is hard to generalise about an approach to their resolution. A one-day slip on the plan may have no impact whatsoever if there is sufficient slack in the plan to cover it. On the other hand, there may be a one-day window in which something has to be done, and missing it might be disastrous.

Impact analysis

Establishing the impact of changes, whether brought about internally or through something happening outside of the project, cannot be done by the Project Manager single-handedly.

In the same way that the flap of a butterfly's wing in Brazil affects the climate in Europe, so the knock-on effect of change anywhere in the project is likely to be felt everywhere else. This rippling effect should not be underestimated, and – within reason and depending on the sensitivity of the circumstances – consultation should be as wide as possible.

You should note, however, that this will not only be people with 'downstream' tasks; changes – particularly changes in the specification of a product – could well have legal, health and safety, marketing, personnel and other implications.

■■■■■■ F R I D A Y ■■■■■■

Once again, it is not just a question of gathering information; we have to analyse it to assess its implications.

If it is taking twice as long as planned to define the specification of a product, does that mean that it will take twice as long to build it and twice as long to test it? Is this a one-off, or are all our estimates to do with specification suspect? Do we have the right staff working on specification? Is the approach wrong?

All of these questions and more need to be answered, and can only be answered on the basis of your own experience and knowledge, supplemented by the expertise of those in individual areas.

Where you can look for a degree of help, though, is in the impact of problems and changes on the plans. If you are using automated planning tools, into which you have recorded the dependencies between tasks, you can very quickly feed in the revised effort estimates from the Impact Analysis, and so calculate revised end dates for all tasks and the project itself.

The dependency network diagram which we constructed as part of the planning process can be used to see which tasks are directly affected by one particular task slipping its planned completion date.

The planning tool will also give you a clear picture on costs and how your resourcing profile is affected.

If it is a major change, you may be forced into some substantial replanning.

Resolving issues and problems

Although action to resolve issues will be as varied as the different types of problem that will occur as a project, it can be generalised into several basic categories:

Resolving problems and issues

- genuinely creative solutions to problems
- using contingency
- applying more resources
- slipping the completion dates
- de-scoping
- making sure it does not happen again

Note: there is no 'do nothing' option. Problems will not go away of their own accord, nor will they become more tolerable with time. They should be identified and resolved at the earliest possible opportunity.

Apart from the first and second approaches given above, resolving most problems implies a degree of compromise on your objectives of cost, time or quality.

Genuinely creative solutions

This is the ideal way to resolve a problem, but naturally the hardest. We can all lie awake at night seeking that flash of inspiration which will provide us with the answer to some acute problem; it rarely comes.

Re-examine the plan and particularly the planning assumptions. What may have appeared to be the only way to do something when you devised the plan might now be one of a number of ways, some of which may be better (and hopefully cheaper and faster).

Resource constraints may have forced you into doing things at certain times and in a particular order. Check if these resource constraints still exist as it might be possible to juggle some of the work.

On particularly long projects you may find that emergent technology or new techniques allow you to review your estimating assumptions.

Look again at the dependencies that are built in to the plan. Ask yourself if they really are finish-to-start dependencies, or if the second task can actually start with an incomplete input. (Apply caution here: it may impact quality and running tasks in parallel which are ideally done one after the other requires very careful management.)

Using contingency

You had the foresight to build contingency into the plans for this very eventuality, so use it! Be aware though that once it is all gone you cannot get it back again, and there might be times when your need of it will be greater. So use your contingency only when you really have no choice and monitor and control it carefully.

Applying more resources

Assigning more people to an activity which is running late is the most common means of rectifying a potential slippage. It is less desirable than whatever imaginative brainwaves we may have come up with earlier, but more so than the other two as it should not adversely affect your objectives of time and quality.

It will, of course, affect cost, but in the majority of projects time and quality tend to be considered more important.

Additional resource can be applied to tasks by moving staff off less important tasks (or at least tasks which are further away from the critical path). Be aware, though, that you may simply be deferring problems until later by doing this.

Alternatively, staff can be brought in from outside the project on a temporary basis, either from elsewhere in the organisation or by hiring contractors or consultants with specialist skills. Be aware, though, that this may be resented by the project staff who may see it as an unfavourable reflection on their own performance, and ensure that it is presented in a constructive and non-threatening manner.

Improvements in productivity tend to involve longer-term measures than you might be considering but you will always have the option of asking the staff to work additional hours, overtime and weekends. This must, however, be seen as a short-term solution of a recognisable crisis; in the long-term it will sap morale and probably reduce overall productivity.

F R I D A Y

Some further words of caution regarding applying additional resource:

Firstly, not all tasks can be completed more quickly simply by applying extra resource: two women cannot have a baby in four and a half months.

Secondly, bringing in staff from outside of the project may involve existing staff spending a lot of time teaching and supervising the newcomers. Do not underestimate either the amount of time it takes for people to get up to speed on the intricacies and issues of the project (no two projects are alike) and do not underestimate the impact it will have on other people's work.

Thirdly, beware of 'robbing Peter to pay Paul'. There is no point in moving staff onto a critical task if the first task is going to suffer as a result.

Slipping the completion dates

This is, of course, a highly undesirable course of action to have to take, although there may be times when you have no alternative.

This may mean that a particular task will be late, that a milestone will not be achieved on time, or even that the overall project will be delivered late.

Late achievement of published milestones or slippage of the overall project will usually require the authority of the project sponsor.

De-scoping

De-scoping means delivering less than you originally intended. It is a classic means of delivering something on time, and appropriate only if none of the above approaches will work and the project is in danger of being cancelled.

It is, of course, a serious compromising of the quality objective, but by delivering the minimum requirement on time, and leaving the 'nice-to-haves' until later (Phase 2 of the project), you at least preserve the organisation's investment in the work done to date.

Again, this should normally only be done with the consent of the project sponsor and in consultation with the users of the project's major deliverables.

F R I D A Y

Making sure it does not happen again

By and large the above approaches will involve taking tactical steps to resolve an immediate problem. It is equally important to ensure that the problem does not recur, either later on this project, or on other projects elsewhere in the organisation.

You should therefore examine – in a non-recriminatory manner – the root causes of the problem and what measures can be put in place to ameliorate them.

Areas worthy of review might be:

Causes of problems

- estimating procedures
- training policies
- recruitment policies
- quality control procedures
- management control practices
- the culture of the organisation
- staff motivational factors

Finding and implementing remedies to these sorts of problems is often outside of the immediate control of the Project Manager, but you should remember that as Project Manager you also have a duty to the organisation as a whole, and not just a single-minded devotion to your own project.

Furthermore, these may well be problems which are deeply embedded in the structure and culture of an organisation and will take a long period, possibly years, to change.

Controlling change

Ironically for the Project Manager, whose own role is to
effect change elsewhere, change is his worst enemy. It
destabilises all aspects of the project; the staff, the plan, the
budget and the final product itself.

It was for this reason that we placed so much emphasis
earlier in the week on clearly defining the scope of the
project and ensuring that all project phases involved review
and sign-off by the user.

But requirements will change during the course of a project,
particularly longer ones. We cannot freeze the outside world
during the course of a project and so we should not be too
dogmatic about resisting change.

What we can do, however, is ensure that change is properly
controlled. This operates at two levels: fundamental changes
to the project itself and detailed changes to the project
deliverables.

F R I D A Y

Project changes

Significant changes to the project will usually involve
amending the original Terms of Reference, usually the scope,
but sometimes the project objectives or the approach.

Requests for change, whether from outside or from within
the project team, should be subject to both Impact Analysis
and a degree of Cost-Benefit Analysis.

Departures from the original Terms of Reference can only be
made with the authority or consent of those who originally
agreed them; the project sponsor and the senior user
management.

So that an informed decision on whether or not to accept the
change can be made, the decision-makers must have a clear
understanding of what is involved.

Remember that the further a project progresses, the more
expensive change becomes and it is important to be able to
distinguish between what is absolutely necessary and what
would be nice to have.

At some point in the project you will have to 'freeze' the
specification. This is never popular with users, but is the
only way of ensuring that the project does not continue to
grow and grow as more features are requested.

Project deliverables

Apart from the final end product which the project is to
deliver, most of the project's deliverables will be paper – lots
of it; specifications, designs, reports, analyses, and plans.

These should all be closely controlled and this is often a
function of the Project Office. You should therefore establish

document control procedures which:

Document control procedures

- identify which documents are to be controlled
- specify the prime author of each document
- specify where the master copy is held
- list the names of copy recipients
- detail procedures for raising changes
- detail procedures for reviewing changes
- specify version numbering conventions

Completing the project

Finally the happy day has come. The work is done, the product has been accepted, implemented and is being used by thousands of satisfied customers.

Or are they ?

A *project review* should be conducted some time after project completion with the following objectives:

> **Project review objectives**
>
> - to measure the success of the project
> - to determine the need for further work
> - to identify any lessons learnt

Personal qualities of the Project Manager

Throughout the week we have been looking at the project very much in terms of its mechanics; thinking about the project, its tasks and the resources which will be used.

In many projects the main resource is **people** and so today we will look at some of the personal qualities which a Project Manager must bring to bear.

> *Personal qualities of the Project Manager*
>
> - motivating
> - delegating
> - communicating
> - leading

Successful management of people is a complex topic and by no means unique to project management. We must, however, recognise that project management is as much about handling people as anything else.

Unfortunately there are no prescriptive tools or techniques which can be applied to turn someone into a good people-manager.

Motivating

No matter how well planned and organised a project may be, its chances of success without the commitment of the project team are limited. It is largely up to the Project Manager to ensure that the project enjoys a culture and an atmosphere which is conducive to achieving the project objectives.

When you look for people to be on the team you will naturally look for people who are dynamic, committed, responsible, intelligent, forward-thinking, highly-skilled, and good team-players.

All admirable qualities, certainly, but qualities which require nurturing by the Project Manager. It may sound trite to say that a happy project team will result in a successful project – it won't. But we must nonetheless try to ensure that the project team actually *wants* to do the work and, moreover, wants to do it the way you want.

The key to motivating people is achieving a degree of
alignment between their personal objectives and the project
objectives. You must be able to show that people will
actually get what they want by doing what you want.

Of course working out what individual people want is a
tricky business and much has been written on the subject of
motivation in general.

Motivation theories

- *Maslow* – A hierarchy of needs ranging from
  physical to existential (see Leadership chapter for
  more details on this).
- *Herzberg* – Distinguishing between what motivates
  and what demotivates.
- *Pope* – 'Deadly Sin Theory'; people are motivated
  by pride, lust, anger, gluttony, envy, sloth and
  covetousness.

What these and other theories tell us is that different people
are motivated by different things. No surprise perhaps, but it
means that we must know and understand the individuals
we are trying to motivate if we are to be able to work out
what it is that drives them.

Pay and rations
Contrary to popular belief, pay is not a great motivator.
Large pay rises may induce a short-term sense of well-being,
but this quickly fades.

This is fortunate, as on many projects an individual's pay is not within the Project Manager's direct control. However, satisfactory pay is a pre-requisite for getting any work at all out of your staff, let alone high performance.

You should therefore ensure that the pay your project staff receive is competitive (to stop them from leaving) and fair (to prevent internal divisions). Pay is a quantifiable measure of how well the organisation thinks a member of staff is doing.

Bonuses for completing projects on time are, likewise, not terribly good motivators. They can be used, however, if you are suffering from debilitating turnover of staff and need to stabilise the situation at least for the duration of the project.

Non-financial incentives

Non-financial incentives are, however, within the direct control of the Project Manager. You should look for ways of meeting the following needs which people have:

Motivating factors

- quality of work (interesting, challenging and useful)
- sense of belonging (to project team)
- feeling of involvement
- sense of achievement
- recognition of success and effort
- opportunity for development and progression
- fulfilment of skills and abilities
- increased responsibility

Finding ways of fulfilling these needs varies from individual to individual, and it is clearly important that you get to know your staff well on a personal level.

Delegating

Not only does delegation, in the long run, make your own life easier, but it also enhances the working lives of your staff by making them feel involved in and responsible for the work being done.

Delegation is a delicate art and a balance must be drawn between complete abdication of your personal responsibilities and being dictatorial.

There is a natural reluctance in most people to delegate. This stems usually from a lack of trust or a belief that you could do the job better yourself. Even if this is the case it is no excuse not to delegate.

Some tasks should not be delegated (especially those involving personnel issues), but for many it is an efficient means of getting the work done and of developing the staff.

When delegating you should make clear what needs to be done and why, when it should be done by and how much authority you are giving the person.

Communicating

We discussed the need for the Project Manager to be a communicator when we described his/her role on Sunday. In a nutshell, we communicate in order to influence the behaviour of other people.

Differing circumstances dictate what is the appropriate style in which we should do this, and the Project Manager must be sensitive to both the nature of his/her message and its audience.

Above all he/she should be sufficiently flexible in his/her approach and pick the appropriate style in the broad range from ordering, through negotiating, persuading, advising and listening (for we must remember that effective communication is a two-way process).

Effective communication skills – in all circumstances – are vital to any Project Manager. Whereas the line manager can rely to a great extent on his/her position in the organisation to influence others, the Project Manager must fall back on his/her personality to do so.

Leadership

Leadership is one of the less easily taught aspects of management. To be effective, a manager must be able to lead, to inspire others to follow him/her. This need is all the stronger in project management because a project relies so much on the commitment and loyalty of those involved.

Unfortunately charisma cannot be bottled and applied in liberal doses every morning. See Week Two for greater detail on this subject.

Choosing a Project Manager

Project management is not something which can be done by anyone, and all too often there is an assumption that if someone can manage a department then that same person can manage a project.

The role of the Project Manager is an important one and fundamental to the success of any project. Organisations make large investments in projects and should make similar investments in the people they call upon to manage those projects.

It calls for additional skills and characteristics over and above those which are normally required for line management.

These are skills which can mostly be learnt through training and, above all, experience. Many organisations have now instituted project management development programmes which reflect its position as a professional discipline in its own right.

S U M M A R Y

Through this week we have concentrated on how the Project
Manager ensures that other people deliver for the project
within constraints of time, cost and quality. We should not
forget, however, that the Project Manager's own deliverables
are amongst the most important in the project.

Project Manager's deliverables

- Terms of Reference or project definition
- Milestone plan
- Budget
- Work Breakdown Structure
- Project Organisation chart
- Responsibility chart
- Task definitions
- Deliverable definitions
- Quality plan
- Dependency chart
- List of planning and estimating assumptions
- Gantt Chart
- Progress reporting standards
- Change control standards
- Progress reports
- End-of-phase reports
- Project review report

Negotiating

PETER RONALD FLEMING

WEEK TWO

C O N T E N T S

Week Two

■ I N T R O D U C T I O N ■

Negotiating an unrepeatable deal is the dream of many people – whether it is a multi-million pound agreement which enhances the firm's 'bottom line' or the house purchase and sale which is the envy of our friends.

When good bargains are within everyone's sights, why is it that some people obtain much better results than others?

The fact is that there are no magic answers! However, we can identify key skills and approaches – used by experienced negotiators – which should help achieve better deals for all parties.

This book covers ten steps:

Ten steps to successful negotiation

- create the right environment
- research your objectives
- decide who you are and who your 'opponent' is
- open the meeting
- talk and listen
- make proposals
- summarise
- close and confirm
- evaluate strengths and weaknesses
- continue your development

Remember that negotiating can be enjoyable. But there is no point in suggesting your opponents should negotiate – they may not have thought of it and are only too prepared to accept your first proposal!

Prologue

Our attitude to negotiation is critical because it can make a substantial difference to how we see:

- the solution
- our 'opponents'
- the outcome we would like to achieve.

'Super-deals' sometimes make the newspaper headlines but so too do disasters:

Unions flex muscles as bosses plan new pay round

'Multi-National' puts small supplier out of business

Super salesman sells 'dud' chemicals

Many people's reaction to such headlines is:

'If that is what it takes to be a negotiator, you can count me out!'

S U N D A Y

The fact is that, every day, many millions of deals are struck which do *not* lead to strikes, breaches of contract, high court actions, divorces or suicides!

There is always a possibility, though, that something could go wrong – and it is wise to ask yourself about this *before* setting up a negotiating meeting.

It is important to remember that negotiating may not be essential (or even desirable) in every situation. Alternative approaches or outcomes could include:

- Acceptance by the other party!
- Consulting them (this could result in erosion of possible objections).
- Selling the idea (a simple, but effective method of persuasion!).
- Imposition (not nice – but sometimes necessary as in a crisis situation!).
- Arbitration by another, mutually acceptable and appointed, party (result is usually binding).
- Mediation through a neutral third party (who provides an additional communication channel).
- Alternative dispute resolution – useful when all else fails and the parties want to avoid recourse to the law.

You will be more likely to be successful if you know how to create the right environment for negotiation to take place.

Creating the right environment

This is our first step in preparing for a negotiation.

It involves:

- creating the right **atmosphere**
- choosing the right **time** to negotiate
- selecting the best **place**

We must remember that we may have to negotiate at short notice and, although we may have had little or no time for preparation, it is still important to play by the rules!

Experienced negotiators recognise that there are four
possible outcomes to a negotiation:

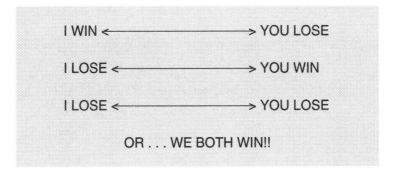

I WIN ⟵⟶ YOU LOSE

I LOSE ⟵⟶ YOU WIN

I LOSE ⟵⟶ YOU LOSE

OR . . . WE BOTH WIN!!

Most people would prefer not to be losers normally —
unless they have other motives — and the risk of 'losing',
divides negotiators into three categories – those who are:

- **Competitive** and want to win at everything.
- **Collaborative** and want to achieve the best deal for both
  or all parties.
- **Consensual** as they put the importance of maintaining
  good relationships above any issues which could threaten
  to divide the parties.

If your role or aim is the continuing development of your business, goodwill or relationships, the second style will bring better, long-lasting relationships and results!

So, the right atmosphere will be affected by:

- How you feel about the situation.
- How you feel about your 'opponent'.
- The relative power of the two parties.
- Your ability to cope with stressful situations.
- Your composure – especially with emotional pressure.
- How much you trust each other.
- Your degree of open-mindedness.
- Your aspirations.
  (Are you the sort of person who would wish to achieve better-than-average results?)
- How prepared you are to listen (as well as speak!).
- Your charisma.

Incidentally, our use of the word 'opponent' does not mean 'pistols at dawn'! It is simply a shorthand word to describe the person with whom we are negotiating!

Remember that, if you want to achieve a win/win deal, your opponent needs to **want** to arrive at a satisfactory agreement too.

You can influence this by the way you use the ten factors above.

Choosing the right time

The 'right time' to negotiate is probably when you have least need for a deal and your opponent's need is greater. However, collaborative negotiators minimise the 'fall-out' from such relationships. Otherwise, the opponent may feel 'beaten' and determined to beat you next time. Warfare of this kind can go on for years!

Skilled negotiators:

* choose their timing carefully
 (avoid the 'bull-in-a-china-shop' approach)

- patiently draw reluctant opponents to the negotiating table (it could take time)
- avoid spontaneous negotiation sessions (if at all possible!)
- prepare their case carefully
- weigh up what they think may be on their opponent's agenda
- know their own limitations and those of their opponents (for example – are you 'sharper' in the mornings or in the evenings?).

Selecting the best place

The right place to negotiate is any place where you feel most comfortable and, as important, most confident!

This comfort factor involves more than just feeling at home when your own 'home territory' could provide you with disadvantages as well as advantages.

For example, you would prefer not to:

- be distracted by minor queries while trying to concentrate on the negotiation
- be interrupted by telephone calls
- allow your opponents to see the state of your workplace (it could be chaotic or perhaps somewhat luxurious in their eyes! This might not impress them!)

These factors may help to heighten their confidence and lower yours.

On the other hand, witnessing these events on your opponents' ground may help you quite a lot.

'Neutral territory' is often suggested by negotiators as an appropriate way of avoiding any bias in the meeting.

However, you should beware of:

- neutral territory which subsequently turns out to be your opponents' home ground
- being 'landed' in a situation in which you are far from comfortable.

Social situations can put some negotiators at a disadvantage, for example being invited to a more up-market restaurant than they might ever have visited previously for a business negotiation – or vice versa!

Perhaps having to work in very cramped conditions, with very loud furnishings, might unsettle some people.

Summary

So, let's summarise our progress today:

- you should think carefully about how to build a partnership with your opponent
- look inside your heart and ask yourself:
  'Am I really seeking a win/win outcome?'
- when will be the best time to negotiate?
- are we/is our opponent in a hurry?
- how can we use time to our mutual benefit?
- what advantages are there in going to the other party to negotiate or asking them to come to us?

These questions may seem obvious but the art of negotiating lies in applying them to your own situation.

S U N D A Y

Try to relate them to a current project or need.

For example, you may be thinking of changing your car.

Which of these points might be of greatest help to you today?

ATMOSPHERE	TIME	PLACE
....	....	....
....	....	....
....	....	....
....	....	....

▮▮▮▮▮▮ M O N D A Y ▮▮▮▮▮▮

Research your objectives

Prologue

Have you ever considered when the worst time for the
week's food shopping might be?

Is it:

- When the store is busiest?
- When stock is running out?
- When you are in a hurry?

If concern about impulse purchasing is uppermost in your
mind, the answer has to be:

- When you are hungry!

Of course, you might always prepare a list before starting
the shopping expedition – some people do – but many
others don't. If you stand and observe your fellow shoppers
at the checkout, you can quickly identify those who
probably did not write or bring a shopping list!

M O N D A Y

There is nothing wrong with buying products we like, but was this a conscious decision, or was the final bill a shock? The objective shopper starts out with a checklist and then consciously buys items not on the list.

Similarly, the skilled negotiator always prepares a checklist of objectives – a 'shopping list' – and uses it to compare results from meetings with those expected. Any move away from the original plan is then a conscious decision and a target for trading-off concessions from the opponent.

Skilled negotiators rarely negotiate without any kind of plan – and most produce detailed plans on anything but the back of an envelope or cigarette packet!

M O N D A Y

Preparing your own 'shopping list'

Preparing for a dinner party you are going to host may involve some or all of the following:

- deciding on a menu
- preparing a list of ingredients
- making a list of jobs to be done (and by whom)
- drawing up a seating plan
- sending out invitations

Similarly, a decision to move house should lead us to prepare an objective plan. For example, you may have decided to move to a larger house – 3-bedroomed, semi-detached with a garage – from your present 2-bedroomed

terraced house. You will probably start with a 'wish list' for the 'new' house which might read as follows:

- 2 double bedrooms, 1 single
- 2 reception rooms downstairs
- a downstairs cloakroom
- separate garage – close to the house
- gas-fired central heating

Of course, these items are not negotiable – they either exist or they do not – but their priority may vary and your view may be very different from that of your partner!

We rarely find exactly what we want and this listing will probably provide an important basis for negotiation at home before you even visit a prospective vendor. The result of these discussions will be a base line of standards or objectives, against which various offers will be screened. Probably you will not then want to visit properties which do not come up to those expectations (although this is by no means certain – did your present accommodation exactly match your 'minimum' standards?).

Preparing your negotiation brief

Once you have selected a property which you find attractive, you will need to produce a negotiating brief both for your purchase and your sale (if you have a property to sell). This will be two-dimensional and encompass:

- your objectives and
- your best assessment of your opponent's objectives.

▇▇▇▇▇▇ M O N D A Y ▇▇▇▇▇▇

Planning your objectives

Establishing your own objectives will be relatively easy. Taking price as an example, the buyer's objective will be to obtain good value for money bearing in mind the need not to exceed 'market value'. The buyer's parameters for price will be determined by:

At the 'top end':

- available funds – from the sale of a current property
- any bridging finance available (e.g. from your firm)
- a personal loan from your favourite Aunt
- how much you really want the property.

At the 'lower end':

- the lowest price you feel the vendor might consider without insulting him/her and causing the withdrawal of the property
- the price which you feel correctly matches current market activity
- a price which enables the vendor to meet his/her plans.

Assessing your opponent's objectives

Assessing your opponent's objectives means carrying out some research – at best; and guessing – at worst!

The process requires the ability of putting yourself in your opponent's position. For example, a vendor may have chosen to advertise a property at £180,000. It would be surprising (and unusual) if this did not include a 'fall-back position' which would allow for the agent's advice and the fact that some (if not all) potential buyers may make a lower offer.

So, the parameters for **the sale** may vary between:

(a) Price

Base Limit   Ideal Position

£ 162,000 ⟵————————————————⟶ £180,000

The 'base limit' here represents 10% discount on the asking price and could be lower if the vendor is desperate to sell, or if some fault is discovered in the building survey.

(b) Timing

Base Limit   Ideal Position

5–14th April ⟵————————————————⟶ 3–31st May

(This would allow for a holiday between 16th and 30th April)

Of course, there is a lot more at stake when we buy a house
– e.g. how well our own furniture will fit into it and what it
will 'feel' like when we are living there. Vendors are often
keen to sell items of furnishings such as carpets and
curtains and this can be very helpful if the move is a strictly
budgetted affair. Expensive mistakes can be made here too:

(c)   Furnishing and fittings

Bottom Line   Ideal Position

Vendor 'gives'   Buyer pays vendor's
contents away ⟵———————⟶ valuation of £10,000
with agreed house   for contents
purchase

As we shall see later, goodwill between buyer and seller
may have quite an effect in arriving at the most appropriate
point of 'balance' between the two extremes on the chart.
Any breakdown or loss of confidence between the parties
can lead to a Lose/Lose outcome.

Examples of Lose/Lose results could be:

• Either party changing their mind and withdrawing from
  the transaction (leaving one party, or possibly both,
  considerable professional fees to pay – and nothing to
  show for them).
• Carpets and curtains (etc.) put into store rather than
  given away (leading to increased costs for the vendor).
• Some items 'taken' by the vendor when the buyer
  expected them to be included in the price (leading to a
  rearguard action for restitution).

M O N D A Y

The effect of time

Time can have a crucial effect on the negotiation process as we shall see later in the week. However, suffice to say here that a vendor who is being moved by his company (with a tight deadline) may be prepared to consider a lower offer if he is convinced that the contract can be speeded up (e.g. by a cash sale).

Equally, the vendor who can arrange to put his house contents into store (and is prepared to – bearing in mind his firm's preparedness to pay the bill) may be prepared to meet the buyer's timetable – especially when sales activity is depressed.

How do you find out about such levers?

At its simplest – you need to ask!

- Friends and family, etc.
- Professional advisers (e.g. solicitors, agents etc.).
- People who have moved recently.
- Your opponent/his family/staff, etc.

My opponent? 'Surely he will not tell you the truth,' you may say. That may be so, but exaggerations or understatements can easily be checked and, if proved to be 'economical with the truth', may risk the breaching of all trust between the parties.

The broader the issue on which you are likely to negotiate, the more valuable it is to consult a wide range of people. In commercial negotiations the following consulting checklist may prove useful:

M O N D A Y

- past users of the product/service
- other experienced buyers/sellers
- present referees
- comparison agencies/publications
- advisers
- other people in your own organisation (the Japanese use this method to great effect – especially with new business contacts)
- your opponent's own staff

So, your negotiation brief should include:

- an agenda of issues to discuss
- your objectives expressed in terms of parameters
- questions to ask to reveal information about the negotiation or your opponent's position.

This is not paper for the sake of paper – a systematic approach will pay for itself over and over again!

Week Two

M O N D A Y

Pre-Meeting planning

The following checklist may help you avoid any loose ends:

OPENING

- How should I open the meeting?
- How interested are they in the meeting?
- What needs might exist?
  - Theirs
  - Ours
- What areas of common ground exist between us?

AUTHORITY

- Who am I meeting?
- What is the history/track record of the relationship?
- How much authority does my opponent have?

POWER AND INFLUENCE

- What is their 'power' over us and/or our competitors?
- What is our power in this situation?
- How can we exploit our strength for mutual benefit?

COMMITMENT

- How interested are they in the meeting?
- How badly do they need an agreement?
- Do we want/need agreement today?
- Will a negotiated agreement stick?

COMPETITION/EXCLUSIVITY

- How might market forces effect the negotiation?
- What leverage might be used?

M O N D A Y

INNOVATION AND PROMOTION

- What concessions are we likely to have to make to ensure the deal is successful?
- How innovative are the proposals under discussion?
- Who will contribute what to help?

Now that you have worked through Monday's text, why not try out your own plans for a car change, a house move or perhaps where you would prefer to spend your Summer holidays.

M O N D A Y

Planning your objectives

Your objectives   **'Opponent's position'**

1. ....
2. ....
3. ....
4. ....
5. ....

Concessions you   **Concessions you**
can give   **seek**

1. ....
2. ....
3. ....
4. ....
5. ....

Questions I need to ask

1. ....
2. ....
3. ....
4. ....
5. ....

People and places

Prologue

How able are you to persuade other people?

Some people are dismissive of sales people and would certainly not wish to sell as a career. Apart from the fact that the market economy depends upon a healthy marketing function for its success as an economic system, most of what we buy as consumers would not be available if it had not been for the efforts of salespeople in the distribution chain.

Negotiation is not about having blazing rows with your opponents – nor creating an icy atmosphere (although this might provide a possible tactic in certain circumstances!). The fact is that success in negotiation is really dependent on our ability to persuade other people and, in this respect, the sales person has a head start!

Think about your circle of friends and acquaintances. Do you know people with 'irresistible' personalities? People who always seem to be the centre of attention with no shortage of people wanting to support them, their ideas, be in their company, and do what they want? **Charisma** is a special quality but, sadly, it is rather rare and most of us have to manage without it. Furthermore, it is a gift and not necessarily enhanced by wearing designer clothes, the best aftershave or perfume!

Actually, persuading others is a skill which we use every day, with our families, our staff, our friends and colleagues, and (most important of all) our bosses!

Who am I?

Success in negotiation is affected by our ability to carry out the following skills and attributes. Rate yourself on this checklist:

T U E S D A Y

FACTOR	LOW				HIGH	
I am the kind of person who:						
1 presents myself as a person who likes people	1	2	3	4	5	6
2 is positive	1	2	3	4	5	6
(who wants to work with a negative person?)						
3 is persistent	1	2	3	4	5	6
('No' can nearly always be turned into 'Maybe' and 'Maybe' into 'Yes')						
4 is open-minded	1	2	3	4	5	6
(there is always more than one way of achieving an objective)						
5 develops a good sense of timing and tact	1	2	3	4	5	6
6 develops high aspirations for deals	1	2	3	4	5	6
(skilled negotiators have high aspiration levels and tend to search for above-average agreements)						
7 presents the case assertively	1	2	3	4	5	6
(i.e. without waffle)						
8 chooses the most persuasive words	1	2	3	4	5	6
(use of vocabulary)						
9 thinks clearly under stress	1	2	3	4	5	6
10 influences the emotional atmosphere of meetings	1	2	3	4	5	6
11 maintains self-control	1	2	3	4	5	6
12 is decisive	1	2	3	4	5	6

On the above table, rate yourself against the factors by circling the figure which you feel represents your present skills.

We may not be good at **all** these things but, as this week
progresses, awareness may encourage experimentation, and
practice makes perfect! But, be careful not to experiment on
live negotiations which could make a significant effect on
your organisation's objectives – well, not yet, anyway!

Today's topic is about our personal effectiveness in relations
with others and how to identify the strengths and
weaknesses of your opponents.

Personal communications and negotiations

One facet of personal effectiveness, when it is applied in
negotiations, is the use of an appropriate communications
style. There are two specific styles which are used by us all
in everyday communication:

- the extrovert style
- the inductive style.

T U E S D A Y

As may be readily deduced from the names, the first style is about our attempts to persuade the person to do something by giving lots of information – in effect, seeking to persuade by 'pushing' your opponent into a position.

The inductive style is concerned with trying to encourage your opponent to do something, by 'pulling' them towards that position. Clearly, this approach is more about manipulation and is more subtle than the extrovert style.

The extrovert style

Obvious characteristics of this style are shown below. This person:

- always has a say
- produces lots of ideas and suggestions
- may enjoy a discussion and argument
- quite likes to stir things up in discussion
- may reveal inner thoughts regardless of the circumstances
- frequently gets his/her own way in conversations

The style also has a 'down side' which may dilute its effectiveness – especially in extreme cases! If opponents are to be *persuaded* rather than bludgeoned into submission, these factors need to be kept under control. The person may:

- take an aggressive approach to others
- call a 'spade a spade'
- give as good as he/she gets in an argument
- stick to a point of view having once expressed it
- criticise others
- look for all the snags and problems in new ideas

This style will be most successful, in the short-term, when negotiators are working in a powerful situation (i.e. power is on their side) and in a competitive climate. However, if the relationship is dependent on goodwill for its continuing success, there may be a greater likelihood of bruised feelings resulting from the negotiation. This, in turn, may lead to more aggressive tactics being used by the opponent next time (i.e. 'tit for tat') and the possibility of special 'favours' being offered to someone else if and when they become available!

Characters of the 'old school' who have developed a reputation of being strong negotiators – with a measure of charisma in their personal make-up – may attract a high level of respect from other people. This is particularly noticeable in competitive organisations and in sales oriented negotiations.

However, the style may not always transfer readily into non-aggressive environments and may lead to the isolation of the negotiator if the style is not appreciated by staff, senior managers, trade unionists or, indeed, customers!

The inductive style
As we have seen, this is the opposite communications style and, as such, tends to be rather less predictable than the extrovert style.

Its relative success is based on the principle that the more you are able to test out the attitudes and arguments of your opponents, the more likely you will be able to pinpoint weaknesses in their arguments. Indeed, the weaknesses may become clearer to them, thus enabling you to induce them to move towards your position!

Conversationally, the skills will involve the following:

- putting others at ease
- encouraging them to come up with lots of ideas
- being able to extend and develop those ideas
- encouraging a warm and friendly atmosphere
- giving credit and praise to others
- taking care to avoid upsetting others

T U E S D A Y

Do you know someone like this? How do you feel about being in discussions with them? Can you imagine your probable response if they were to ask for your help? Most of us would probably be pre-disposed to help them.

This effect is enhanced still further if you are also able to use clarifying behaviour in interactions with others, to ensure that there is a minimum of misunderstandings! This will involve:

- listening carefully to what others say
- checking that you have understood what they have been saying
- finding out what others are saying

and all this is possible if you

- ask lots of open questions!
  (These are the ones which start with What? When? Who? Why? Where? and How?)

These effects will be further enhanced if you are the sort of person who:

- admits to mistakes readily
- conciliates when things get heated
- admits to your weaknesses!

Finally, these skills should enable you to:

- obtain the information from others which you need in any negotiation situation

and all this will demonstrate the advantages of co-operating rather than competing with others!

Choosing a style

There is no perfect style which will work in every situation. Both styles listed will have advantages – for example, a sales representative will need to be reasonably *extrovert* to survive the various 'knocks' from clients, especially when involved with canvassing!

Similarly, a negotiator involved in a much 'longer game', spread over, say, several months (e.g. the purchase of natural gas from the Norwegians), will need to adopt a softer, *inductive* role.

We should also bear in mind two other influences:

1 Making the relationship work
If your opponent is a natural extrovert who fills the time with lots of communication you may find yourself in competition for 'air time'. If this were to continue unabated,

it could lead to increasing frustration, over-talking each other and, eventually, conflict!

If two negotiators, whose natural styles lie in the extreme areas of the inductive style, were to meet to discuss a case there could be many questions asked by one party only to be met with more questions from the other!

In practice, styles tend to be a mix of both styles, with plenty of 'give and take'. In fact, the skilled negotiator will aim to develop expertise in both areas, so that he or she has complete flexibility and can move in and out of either approach depending on the needs of the opponent.

2 General cultural influences
Over the past decade in the UK, there has been a general move towards the inductive style in management and society in general. This may be attributable to a variety of influences:

- political neutralising of some of the aggressive influences in the industrial relations field
- increased awareness of the importance of meeting the needs of others
- effect of the human relations school of management theory
- increased effects and support of management training

Negotiators who are working in other cultures – perhaps in the Middle or Far East – need to adapt their style to suit the local customs and culture.

Who is my opponent?

We have seen that knowing something about your opponent before the meeting will be an advantage to any negotiator. So, having met the person before will enable us to be able to predict some of the possible levers and arguments which might be successful in the next round of discussions.

Aspects of communication style have already been discussed above and we will now consider possible 'pressure points' which could be applied to the debate.

All negotiations take place against an atmosphere of 'needs'; if needs did not exist then there would be little point in meeting to negotiate. To help you prepare for the meeting it would be helpful to consider the needs of your opponent in more depth. There may be a 'hidden agenda' which will help you select a negotiation strategy.

The famous Industrial Psychologist, Abraham Maslow, identified a **Hierarchy of Needs** to explain why people work in a modern industrialised environment:

The broad concept of the triangle is that we all have the
need to survive, by satisfying the needs at the base of the
triangle. Having satisfied these *physiological* needs our
attention turns to the need for *security*, satisfied through the
provision of adequate housing/accommodation. Both these
factors may be satisfied through the earning of money but
the higher motivators such as *social needs*, *status* and *self-
fulfilment* are not normally satisfied in this way.

The model is shown as a triangle to illustrate the fact that
not everybody reaches the higher needs – indeed some
people become hooked on one particular need – or their ego
just likes to be flattered under one of the headings.

For example your opponent may have a particularly 'soft
spot' for good food and therefore may be a lot more
malleable after a good meal (at your expense of course!).
Others may be especially 'hooked' on status symbols and
quickly identify your deal as one way in which they can be
successful and earn a bigger company car or a status jump
in the firm's hierarchy.

Equally manipulative is the industrial relations negotiator who holds a little in reserve to allow an opponent to feel victorious – just as the Union Branch is about to re-elect its representatives, or the Management is to consider the re-grading of Personnel Professionals!

So where should we meet?

At first sight this is a common sense matter. Sales representatives might say they always expect to go to visit the buyer and the Management side of a Joint Industrial Council might always expect to hold meetings in the Boardroom.

Actually, the place of the meeting can make quite a difference to its 'comfort factor'. Some people seem to be able to fit into any environment and still behave confidently in business meetings. Others are intimidated by the very thought of having to negotiate on the opponent's ground!

T U E S D A Y

So, playing 'home' or 'away' may have advantages to you and your opponent.

'Home' advantages

- You may feel more in control.
- You can control interruptions.
- You can orchestrate recesses.
- Back-up support is available should you need it.
- You can choose your office/location/layout to suit you.
- You may have the moral advantage in cases of late arrivals etc.

'Away' advantages

- You have the chance of assessing your opponent's workplace.
- Your opponent may make allowances as you are not on home ground.
- You can pressurise your opponent by suggesting senior staff get involved to break any deadlocks.

Another alternative is to choose 'neutral territory'. But, once again there may be some hidden advantages. For example the lobby of a hotel may appear to be neutral until you discover that your opponent is a regular visitor there and is personally known to the manager, the restaurant manager, the head porter, the barman and even the waitress. This can be most impressive – and is intended to be!!

Will any of this make any difference to the meeting? It could do. After all, if you are dependent on your opponent for a crucial piece of information on which to base the negotiated agreement, would you mistrust someone who is so obviously credible in this sophisticated environment?

Plan your style and negotiation venue

What do you know about your opponents?

WHO WILL BE INVOLVED? ....

THEIR PREFERRED STYLE **YOUR PREFERRED STYLE**

....

....

POSSIBLE VENUES

Home: .... **Away:** ....

Neutral Ground: ....

PEOPLE NEEDING A BRIEFING

....

....

....

....

Opening the meeting, and talking and listening

Now that we are half-way through the week it is time to meet our opponent!

Today we will consider how to open the meeting, and how to talk with impact, and develop our listening skills.

Prologue

We have now seen that good preparation is essential for effective negotiation meetings but it would be surprising if good presentation did not also play a major part in achieving good results!

Charismatic negotiators can be tempted to achieve their results solely through their force of personality and interpersonal skills. Most of us, however, need to be good at both!

W E D N E S D A Y

Today introduces our opponent and the early stages of the meeting:

- Opening the meeting.
- Talking and listening.

As with our earlier days' work, we will find that a common sense approach to these two areas is sometimes overlooked by less experienced negotiators. Later parts of the meeting may well be affected by this so it is important to establish the meeting on the right footing, at the start.

Results from the opening, and the development of the early stages of the meeting, will be affected by the following factors. Before working through today's pages, you might like to rate your current skills in each of these areas. Please circle the rating which you feel applies:

Factor	Rarely used				Always used
• Establishing rapport – verbal and non-verbal	1	2	3	4	5
• Establishing common ground	1	2	3	4	5
• Exploring mutual objectives for the meeting	1	2	3	4	5
• Building a joint agenda	1	2	3	4	5
• Getting comfortable	1	2	3	4	5
• Clarity of speech	1	2	3	4	5
• Assertive behaviour	1	2	3	4	5
• Avoidance of bias and 'tunnel-vision'	1	2	3	4	5
• Maintaining flexibility	1	2	3	4	5
• Listening for overtones and signals	1	2	3	4	5
• Questioning skills	1	2	3	4	5
• Controlling and reading body language	1	2	3	4	5

Your performance in each of these areas can be improved and will affect your results!

W E D N E S D A Y

Opening the meeting

Creating the right atmosphere for the meeting will be important if later parts of the meeting are to end in agreement. Tough issues can be sorted out without necessarily establishing an ice-cold atmosphere at the start; equally, if the players have not met before and the stakes are high, quite a time may be allocated to establishing an atmosphere of trust.

Two parties of two negotiators from businesses in the finance sector met recently for the first time to discuss transfer charges between their two organisations. Millions of pounds were at stake and, from the start, it was obvious that both sides were nervous about the possibility of making expensive mistakes!

To the surprise of both teams when they met in the hotel room, all the participants looked similar, were of similar ages, had dressed alike, and came from similar backgrounds. All this became increasingly evident in the first 45 minutes of the meeting which covered almost any topic except that which the meeting was about!

At this point, almost instinctively, the parties felt they had built up a feeling of trust, and they started on the agenda! Progress was then rapid and, to everyone's surprise, the meeting concluded in 1.5 hours with a Win/Win agreement and a celebratory lunch! The agreement endured for a year and provided a sound basis for subsequent renewals.

Establishing rapport
Meeting people for the first time – or indeed greeting
someone we have met before – is normally accompanied by
an appropriate choice of words and actions.

However, how these things are carried out can be
significant.

Passing the time of day and, as important, using your
opponent's name, is an accepted custom in greeting – just as
shaking hands provides an acceptable way of expressing

warmth to the other person. We make some hidden judgements on the basis of these greetings:

- The firmness of the handshake – the 'crusher'or the 'wet fish'!
- The distance of the parties when they shake hands.
- The formality or informality of the greeting – varying from 'Good morning' to 'Hi' or 'G'day'!
- The warmth of the facial expression when meeting e.g. smiles can be open or, perhaps, cynical.
- The extent of eye contact – open and level, or hooded and uncertain.
- There is also the appearance of the parties – the manner of dress, etc.

The golden rule in the areas of appearance – for the best results – is to try not to breach any areas of preference on the part of your opponent! This is not to say that there is no room for individuals in negotiation – but, breaching areas of known inhibition can be dangerous and expensive (as many employees will know from the experience of asking the boss for a rise!).

Common ground
It is always easier negotiating with someone you have met before because you will have some knowledge of that person's domestic circumstances, leisure interests, last holiday and/or drive or motivation. The early stages of a meeting provide an excellent opportunity to 'catch up' with what has been happening with your various lives – domestically and, probably more importantly (from the point of view of the negotiation), recent business activities – since you last met.

This episode should help either party to re-build common ground between you which may be especially valuable if (or when) the going gets tough later in the meeting.

Obviously, a new contact needs careful nurturing – and the opportunity should be taken to find out a little about each other – without creating the impression of being either nosy or pushy!

The agenda

It is surprising how often negotiators meet together – with a mutual interest in meeting – but without having established a common agenda at the start. This is probably because each negotiator tends to think of his own agenda as of paramount importance and superior to the other person's interests.

If the meeting is to be collaborative,then it is important to provide the opportunity for *both* participants to air their own agenda. Apart from anything else it is quite a challenge to check your opponent's agenda against the items you *expected* him to raise when you prepared for the meeting!

This does not mean that every agenda item or objective *has* to be revealed at the start of the meeting, but failure to do so in a collaborative atmosphere will invite the question 'Why was this item concealed? Was it really a slip of the memory or has some advantage been sought by failing to reveal the topic?'

Physical comfort

Physical conditions of the meeting will also influence how comfortable (and possibly how co-operative) either party may feel and this can be readily transferred to comfort with the deal itself. A variety of tactics may be adopted to win 'unfair' advantage over the opponent. Mostly these only work when they are not too obvious and, by virtue of their exposure, they tend to become decreasingly effective.

Examples are:

- Your opponent's chair set at a lower level to yours.
- Your opponent having to look into the sun (or bright light).
- Orchestrating interruptions when the going gets rough.
- Manipulating the temperature of the meeting room.
- Choosing a venue for the meeting which has distracting furnishings (e.g. walls decorated in, say, a vivid blue can affect some people and may account for an opponent's preparedness to agree to proposals).
- The rather prominent positioning of a clock which may give discussions a sense of time pressure.

How should you deal with these tricks if and when they arise?

In short, the best method is to let your opponent see that you have noticed the tactic and seek his/her approval to remove the influence. This may be achieved by correcting or neutralising the influence and commenting on it to allow the opponent to understand that you have noticed the use of the tactic!

Talking and listening

The most obvious skills are sometimes those which cause
most difficulty in meetings. The effect of the talking and
listening process is affected by a variety of factors:

- self-discipline in being prepared to allow your opponent
  some 'air-time'
- the actual style we use in speaking (e.g. not too biased or
  self-opinionated)
- quality of listening – which is affected by factors such as
  interpretation and concentration
- our body language

W E D N E S D A Y

Talking

From our earliest years, talking is essential to our well-being but how we talk in a negotiation meeting can have quite an effect on how we are perceived by those we meet. For example the following request to the boss:

'I suppose it wouldn't be possible – I know this is probably not the best time to ask – to maybe find five minutes to get together to see if you could find your way clear to, perhaps, pay me an extra £5 per week?'

would probably be greeted by a simple . . .

. . . 'No!'

▰▰▰ W E D N E S D A Y ▰▰▰

A great deal of work has been done recently on helping people develop assertiveness skills and this was a good example of non-assertive behaviour . . . waffly, vague, apologetic and almost defeatist! Few skilled negotiators would contemplate using this approach!

Equally, making the following demand:

> 'If you don't pay the yard staff an extra £10 per week, you will be looking for a new team!'

could result in the response

> 'If that's your attitude then perhaps that is the best thing for us to do!'

Skilled negotiators are more likely to use the following approach:

1 Q: 'When will the Board be looking at this year's pay review?'

2 A: 'It is scheduled for consideration in March'

1 Q: 'How much are you proposing to include in the budget?'

2 A: 'We will be under great pressure to find anything – given the present state of the market; how could the staff side make a contribution?'

1 A: 'If you are talking about productivity improvement – the staff need money on the table! However, if you have something to offer there may be scope for discussion.'

Assertive expression is based on our needs; and the use of *we* is better than *I*. In fact, self-opinionated negotiators who use an egotistical approach often find it difficult to persuade others to change their minds or adopt their proposals.

Similarly, emotional responses are best kept under control. The use of anger, for example, can make a short-term point in a meeting but, if it is over-used it can obstruct a negotiated settlement – with a 'lose/lose' result. The golden rule is to keep cool, avoid rhetoric and provocative language and maintain self-control. This can be difficult if the opponent is hyped-up and determined to cause maximum disruption as a deliberate tactic. In such cases, a good defence is to slow interaction down, make a conscious effort to avoid reaction and concentrate on non-controversial language!

HEY, WOLF! LET'S LOOK AT SOME ALTERNATIVE STRATEGIES!

Listening

To say that it is essential to listen to interaction in negotiation meetings is to state the obvious. However, this can be harder than it seems. For a start, the process in any conversation can be difficult for some people; and when we are seeking a negotiated bargain it is complicated by the additional demands on our brain in the meeting.

Put simply, negotiator 1 makes a proposal to negotiator 2 who listens carefully to the point. However, as the statement is unfolding, negotiator 2 seeks to comprehend the point made – checking it against prior knowledge and experience and listening for the overtones in the expression – whilst also beginning to form a suitable reply and appropriate method (e.g. 'Shall I ask a question, make a statement or what?'). It is hardly surprising that points are missed in such circumstances – and sometimes our response may be totally irrelevant! (How well do you listen to your partner at home?)

W E D N E S D A Y

Why else can it go wrong? People have a habit of 'tuning out' – especially if they do not want to hear what is being said (try telling your teenage children to tidy their bedrooms, for example!). Others turn a deaf ear, making the right sounds but their brain is really in 'neutral' and there is no real commitment to change!

And, lastly, we take the power of vocabulary for granted – especially the importance of using comprehensible language. Jargon, for example, needs to be avoided and it is essential that any which is *not* understood by the opponent is immediately clarified. Here, again, is another valuable use of assertive questioning.

Recipes for improving your listening skills include the following:

- watching your opponent's lips while they are talking (and watching their eyes while you are talking – to gauge their reaction to what you are saying)
- try concentrating on the over-riding message in their contributions – rather than becoming bogged-down or distracted by individual words
- take notes to aid your concentration
- avoid trying to second-guess your opponent's statements or trying to finish off their statements (even in unison!)
- categorising contributions received from your opponent (e.g. is this contribution a question, summary, or proposal – and planning an appropriate response)

■ W E D N E S D A Y ■

These approaches will help your concentration and enable you to spot opportunities for discussion and for bargaining. For example, an innocuous discussion during the earlier part of a meeting with a client might reveal that . . .

1 '...yes, things have been pretty busy – we have just changed our computer'

2 'What kind of pressures has this brought? Strings of noughts on pay-slips?'

1 'No, but our bought ledger system has come to a halt'

If you are proposing to supply this customer with a service or goods, then be careful. You could decide on a contract easily enough but you may have a job to encourage the client to pay up! So, this signal should be followed up when it comes to agree terms of the contract at the end of the meeting.

There are many ways of communicating:

Non-verbal communication

Body language, and the skills of reading it, has recently become a very popular topic amongst the business community. 'If we could read the minds of our opponents and be able to work out exactly what they are thinking and planning, we could achieve much better deals!' Unfortunately, it is not as easy as that because the analysing body language is an imprecise science!

However, there are some simple signals which are useful to observe in negotiation, although the novice should be careful *not* to apply the meanings in a literal sense in every situation.

Face touches

It is said that in conversation about, say, the price of a service or goods, if the speaker accompanies a price quotation with a typical statement such as 'This is my best offer' with a rub of the nose, a scratch of the chin, a wipe of the eye or a tug at the collar, it may be an untruth! The chances of this will increase if a chain of these actions occur together. However, it should always be remembered that the speaker may have a cold (causing a constant nose irritation), or be feeling uncomfortable in a hot environment (hence the tug at the collar!).

The moral here is that, whilst it is sensible to observe and try to read your opponent's body language, it is best not to allow your hands too near your face whilst negotiating!

W E D N E S D A Y

Mirroring

Two people who are anxious to make a good impression on each other with the aim of a win/win deal, may mirror each other's body position and movements. The explanation for this is that each party is sending signals to convince its opponent that both people are very similar in terms of attitudes, values and aims.

This approach can have a significant effect, although it may only be sub-conscious! So, if your meeting is rather cold and you wish to try to relax your opponent, mirroring his/her body positioning may have a helpful effect.

Eye gaze

We saw earlier that level eye contact is often taken as an indication of honesty and, therefore, an interpretation could be that the negotiator may be trusted. However, eye gaze cannot be constant in one direction, or it will be interpreted as staring! Negotiators need to vary their use of eye contact but an essential use is to look for reaction to ideas or trial proposals. Failure to do this may protract a meeting – simply because the signals of possible progress in persuading the opponent to accept your position may go unnoticed. What signals? The occasional frown or flicker of a smile; the raising of an eyebrow or even the sharp return of a glance. We take many of these points for granted, but, if observed, they may help us interpret progress in the negotiation.

Hand movements

Many people talk with their hands and, whilst this is quite natural, it is important that such movements should not become extravagant or distracting to your opponent. A pen or pencil can provide a useful means of underlining a point – especially if the meeting has become emotional – but aggressive movements should be eliminated. Anything which causes irritation in an opponent is to be avoided as this may otherwise lead to non-acceptance of your proposals.

In general, open-handed expressions may be taken to underpin the sincerity of the speaker, whereas pointing or closed fists may reveal aggressive undertones in your opponent.

Review

Now that you have worked through Wednesday's chapter, go back to the checklist on page 148 and look again at those items which you marked lower than 4 or 5. Place a cross against the scores you would aim for in future negotiation meetings.

T H U R S D A Y

Proposing

Prologue

Negotiation meetings are about mutual needs. For example:

• You need a new car and the dealer needs to sell one.

or

• You need to obtain the re-instatement of a suspended work colleague and the management needs to obtain staff support for overtime to meet a rush order.

Wednesday's session showed that meeting discussions provide the opportunity for us to present *our* side of the case – to promote and defend our interests – to sell our position and the advantages of accepting it to the other side.

We will also have tried to draw from our opponent a description of their position so that we can begin to debate it, undermine it and make it seem impossible or unreasonable. Whilst this is going on, our opponent may be trying the same tactic on us!

For example, a standard tactic when surveying a secondhand car is to fault the car by referring to the high mileage, worn tyres or rust-marked body. This softening-up process is designed to precede the making of a proposal (often a rather low one!) but this tactic may be easily rebuffed if the vendor is prepared to claim the 'large number' of other potential buyers who have been in touch about the car! Is the buyer really interested, or not?

kick!

Assertive questions such as 'How can you justify this position?' may draw your opponent to reveal his or her arguments and aims in the negotiation. With persistent questions, difficulties in arriving at a mutually agreed strategy on his or her side may be revealed, thus enabling you to take the high moral ground or express the stronger (more persuasive) argument! Dividing your opponent from his or her side is easier once you know that there may have been some difficulty on their part in arriving at an agreed negotiating strategy.

Of course, such debating points are reversible and you must be careful not to lay yourself open to the use of this approach by your opponent. So, any attempts by the vendor of the car to sell it to your partner – who is loudly proclaiming enthusiasm for the vehicle – may cause you some difficulty when it comes to obtaining the best price or terms.

In reality, it is unlikely that your opponent will make any major moves for nothing, so you will have needed to demonstrate your preparedness to move in some way – as a means of obtaining movement on your opponent's side. These signals should have been sent and received before beginning to form the proposals which will lead to the final bargain.

Today's session describes how to maintain this process through the making of appropriate proposals. We will consider:

- timing
- encouraging proposals
- the best formula
- defending principles
- meeting inhibitions

> All your preparation will prove its value in this vitally important stage.

Timing

There is a right time for proposals in a negotiation meeting and experienced negotiators sense when the moment is right. This sense of timing is akin to the sales person's ability to choose the right moment to close the sale. How we find this out, other than by trial and error, is analysed below.

Exhausting every avenue of discussion will leave you with a need to achieve progress in the meeting, and making proposals is the next obvious step. However, this stance can feel over-cautious and pedestrian, and may lead your opponent to become exasperated through lack of progress. (This can, of course, be turned to an advantage if your opponent is very anxious to conclude the meeting – a process which might be quicker if he or she makes some quick and major concessions.)

When your meeting concerns an urgent issue and either or
both negotiators have a strong sense of destiny, there will be
an irresistible force moving the discussion towards
agreement – especially if the parties have already expressed
a strong desire to reach an agreement. In such a situation,
proposals will flow naturally almost as a summary of each
party's position.

The reverse of this natural progression rests in the truism described by Professor Parkinson (ref: Parkinson's Law) – that time taken for decisions is in inverse proportion to the costs incurred. Committees have been known to spend hours taking decisions about the replacement of canteen cups but only minutes on major decisions which few members understand! The same can be true of negotiation, when small issues combine with ready quantities of time, progress in the meeting can be very slow – with as much attention given to the social objectives as the deal itself!

Finally, beware of the use of time as a major tactic in the meeting. Logical movement through the early stages of the meeting may be positively unattractive to so-called skilled negotiators and this fact may lead to one of them suggesting a jump from base square to final square in one move. A simple, innocuous question might be asked:

> 'We are both busy people and I am sure we could close this deal very quickly – if you agree, of course?'
> 'Yes, that seems a good idea.'
> 'So, what is your bottom line?'

Revealing this position may make it difficult for the opponent to trade movement once the base position has been revealed. There will then be little alternative to agreeing to the initiator's proposals – without breaking off negotiations altogether!

■■■■■■■■**T H U R S D A Y**■■■■■■■■

Encouraging proposals

If you feel that the time is right for proposals to be made but are not sure whether this feeling is mutual, you can always ask! Hand-holding skills are valuable in negotiation, i.e. encouraging the opponent to feel that you are trustworthy, and are not trying to lay a trap. Apart from giving the other side the opportunity to drive the meeting, encouraging them to make leading proposals in an open atmosphere will help progress to be made.

Such a step needs to be accompanied with appropriate non-verbal signals – warm smiles, gentle nods and a high level of attention (eye contact and slightly laid-back body position but facing the opponent).

Who should make the first proposal – and what that should be – is an issue which can give the inexperienced negotiator some concern. After all, there is little pleasure in feeling that your first 'bid' was too high and, through speed of acceptance by the other party, you sense that you are paying more than you needed to have done!

A major aim of the early discussion stage in the meeting is to tease out the other party's position on each agenda item – and the arguments used to defend them. This may well indicate that, say, the vendor's preferred price is going to be totally beyond the resources of the buyer and some concessionary proposal is necessary to keep the buyer in the meeting. (A similar argument can be advanced for the buyer who tries to introduce a very low offer – risking insulting the vendor!).

So, the opening stance is recognised as the position that would bring most benefit for the proposer's party – the debate will doubtless seek movement towards the opponent's position – and the best format for this is when both parties move towards each other – trading concessions.

The best formula

Phrasing for proposals is quite crucial. The best formula is to present your proposals using a conditional approach. For example –

'If you will give us payment terms of 30 days, *then* we will meet your price request.'

Now, this proposal may seem rather bald – especially without examples of the earlier conversation! When a bridge is needed between the discussion part of the meeting and concluding the bargain, either party may introduce *trial proposals*. These will suggest tentative ways forward without necessarily burning our boats and risking earlier agreement by suggesting something which is not acceptable to the opponent.

A typical example would be:

'I'll tell you what we might be able to arrange, *if perhaps* you could find a way of speeding up payment – say, in 30 days – *then we might* be able to find a way of reducing the price.'

If this approach brings a constructive response, then it is likely to be followed swiftly by a formalised proposal along the lines of the first example above.

Defending principles and meeting inhibitions

It is at this stage that you may find your bottom line under attack or in threat of being compromised. For example, HM Government made it clear after the Falklands War that sovereignty was not even on the agenda for peace negotiations with Argentina and this would be a pre-condition for any future discussions.

There could be a risk that, whilst such a condition might be agreed, your opponent may reintroduce that element in the meeting itself, with the expectation that the constructive atmosphere might persuade negotiators to allow discussion of the issue. This clearly should not be accepted and the team would have to make it clear that approaches to put the subject on the agenda would jeopardise agreements on other issues.

At the same time, you must remember that your opponent is not an entirely free agent. He or she is representing another organisation or party, with interests which may be different from your own. These interests will overlap – or there will be no point in attending the meeting – but it is obviously in his or her interests to persuade you to move from your ideal position.

For example, a client may complain about one of your service engineers whose behaviour on his premises had been the source of complaint from several of his staff. His initial approach may be to demand the withdrawal of that person ('Never send him here again!') and this may be readily countered with an apology and a convincing promise to hold a full and thorough internal inquiry.

However, if we were to think through our opponent's position we would see that his organisation has in it several people who would also like to see the back of the engineer! Failure on his part to sort out the issue could lead to a significant loss of face and credibility for your opponent. Such inhibitions can lead to apparent obstinacy and may make a win/win agreement more difficult to achieve if the client's inhibitions are not addressed.

F R I D A Y

Summarising, closing & confirming

Prologue

There is little point in investing time in negotiation meetings if we cannot close them with satisfactory agreements. However, there are many people in the commercial world who make presentations with a view to sell a product or service, or buyers who invest time in meeting with sales representatives and those meetings do not result in a contract!

The question is, do those involved ever discover why their closing rate is not higher? And can they do anything about it? In staff relations meetings there is less priority given to immediate results – often meetings are broken by recesses and adjournments – and consultations between staff representatives and their members and personnel staff and their managers. But the same disciplines apply here – if time is invested in meetings, then agreement must be the ultimate objective.

So, what are the skills we need to develop in closing off a negotiation meeting satisfactorily? The following checklist may provide useful insights:

- summarising progress
- resurrecting earlier issues for agreement
- using concessions to improve the agreement
- choosing appropriate persuasion strategies
- linking issues in the agreement
- listening for concessions
- using appropriate closing techniques

Mistakes at the 'last fence' can be very expensive and frustrating! Make sure you are able to clear the last few hurdles cleanly so that you are satisfied with your performance!

F R I D A Y

Summarising

One little word!

It is not possible to do too much summarising in a meeting; the fact is that many people become confused during negotiations and, even though one party has a clear belief on what has been agreed, it often happens that the opponent has a very different view of that same agreement! Both people were at the same meeting and yet there is still confusion and little unanimity – and this is very dangerous when the agreement is actually implemented!

Examples of things going wrong, after the negotiations have stopped, are legion. Buyers select colours of merchandise and plainly state the colours they do not want – and yet, somehow, those colours still arrive in deliveries! Similarly,

F R I D A Y

sales representatives inform buyers about discount terms and yet they still claim they have not been told about these points after the invoice arrives.

Summaries help to clarify proposals and the terms of agreement. You cannot do too much of it! Remember the one little word which provides the signal of a summary – 'so', ... and try to use it:

- whenever the progress of the meeting is stuck
- when you are not sure what has been said or agreed
- when you feel that the time is ready to begin to close the meeting

Accuracy in summaries

When summaries are used in a meeting they can have an extraordinary effect! Firstly, a summary often seems to fix the points stated and agreed – even though both sides know that the discussion is not yet finished. This can be very helpful when seeking to make speedy progress but it is important for the summary to be accurate. If you include in your summary something which has *not* been agreed – even if you feel that you are taking artistic licence – there is a risk that the relationship between the two parties will be broken and trust breached.

Similarly, it is very important to listen to summaries given by your opponent. There is always a risk that something you believe has been agreed is left out or changed in the opponent's summary. If this should occur it is important that the party who spots the error speaks out straight away.

F R I D A Y

Otherwise the change may be accepted into the agreement by default, and could cause a major disruption towards the end of the meeting with a possible emotional effect on both parties. This might not affect the ultimate agreement but it might leave either or both parties with a bad taste in the mouth, with a knock-on effect on future meetings.

Resurrection

By virtue of the fact that a strategic summary will be seen as a means of bringing the meeting towards a close, it provides a last opportunity to raise any items on which no progress was made earlier.

F R I D A Y

Remember on Tuesday we talked about persistence being an important quality for negotiators? The fact is that people who refuse to move earlier in a meeting may be a little more flexible when the end of the meeting is in sight. Also, the presentation of your case and the subtle temptation of concessions may encourage your opponent to be more flexible on issues which were sticking points before.

Linking

Linking one item with another is a further method of obtaining movement on difficult issues. Most negotiators see their agenda as consisting of a variety of separate issues or objectives – indeed many commercial deals involve the sale and purchase of several products or items, each of which needs to have been negotiated. It would be quite normal for the negotiators to achieve different deals on each item on the list but it is also likely that either side may resist giving way on one particular item. A way out of this is to link one issue with another.

For example, a buyer may have agreed to pay a wholesaler £11.00 for a box of 5 reams of photocopying paper with an order of 100 boxes. He is pleased with this agreement as the price agreed is 50p a box less than he had expected to have to pay. Another item on his shopping list is some specialised bond paper for use in preparing and presenting reports. The wholesaler has offered a price of £18.00 a box which the buyer is unprepared to agree – his counter offer is £16.00. On the basis of negotiating the same quantity of paper, the buyer offers to increase the price on the copy paper by 25p per box if the vendor will agree to a price of £16.00 for the bond.

F R I D A Y

Remember that everything is negotiable and you just need to persuade the other side to accept this to make progress with issues on which your opponent has inhibitions!

Using concessions

Concessions may provide a way of obtaining additional
movement towards the end of the meeting. Skilled
negotiators know to keep additional concessions up their
sleeves to use in closing the meeting. These will be most
effective where the concessions are cheap for you to give
but very valuable to your opponent.

For example, if you have just sold your car – and therefore
have cleared the cheque – you may be able to persuade your
garage to extend the warranty on a new car for the all-in
price which you agreed earlier, but now with the additional
concession of a cash transaction.

Closing

Sales people are frequently trained to close the sale and a
variety of methods exist to help achieve just that! However,
if negotiators have done their job well the meeting will close
itself. The best resolution of the meeting is when both
parties have achieved what they set out to achieve (i.e.
within the parameters of their objectives) and all that is left
to do is to formalise the agreement.

This may not always happen so it is sometimes necessary
for the meeting to be nudged towards closure. The
following checklist shows some common ways of achieving
this:

- calling a recess
- imposing a deadline
- threats to pull out or call time
- asking for agreement
- the summary close

Calling a recess

The forming of a decision about, and therefore a commitment to, the agreement which has been discussed often requires a little time and space. Reluctance for your opponent to agree to the deal may be overcome by planting the seeds of satisfaction in his or her mind and then allowing time for thought (with a view to allowing the seed to mature and flourish). If you have covered the ground well and summarised the areas of agreement, a short recess at this stage should bring a positive decision.

Imposing a deadline

If there is any doubt about the result of the recess it might be prudent to lay down some rules about the time for which the current offer will be valid. Clearly this approach may be viewed as pressurising your opponent – but is quite justifiable when the time period is fair.

A typical example could be a quotation for a construction task which is dependent on the supply of the materials – and the quotation assumes no price rises for the materials – therefore the quoted price can only be valid for, say, one month.

Threats to pull out

If one party believes that the other party *needs* the agreement, then a bluff to pull out of the meeting may work. However, such orchestrated tactics can easily rebound on the bluffer if the timing or style of the threat is tactless. You might easily find that you are allowed to go and not called back!

On the other hand, it has been known for creative answers to be found to situations where the time has run out on the negotiating.

For example, when international negotiators spent 18 months trying to negotiate a Strategic Arms Limitation Treaty, and the self-imposed deadline was reached, the parties agreed to stop the clock for 36 hours – just sufficient time for the final agreement to be transacted. When they finished, the agreement was back-dated to fit the original deadline!

F R I D A Y

Asking for agreement

A simple way of closing the deal is to ask for your opponent's agreement! At first sight this is such an obvious approach that it may be unclear why everyone doesn't use it all the time. 'Asking for the order' is a classic technique taught on most sales training courses. However, sales people do not often use the approach, simply because of the risks of being turned down.

Actually, a turn-down may not be the disaster it may seem. It may be possible to rescue the deal even at a late stage simply by asking 'Why?'. The answer may clarify your opponent's objections giving you one last chance to bring the negotiation to a satisfactory conclusion.

The summary close

Finally, the closing point for the meeting should be summarised. The skills for this have been described earlier today.

A cautionary note!
Don't forget that your opponent enjoys a free will to agree
or not to agree! Even though you may have worked hard
and concluded a good deal, your opponent is still acting for
his or her reasons not yours. This may be worth bearing in
mind if you are feeling euphoric when you start to evaluate
the deal!

Confirming

Even when your meeting seems to have closed with a full-
hearted agreement, there are still risks that the
implementation of the agreement is faulty. The success of
the negotiation lies in this process and it is probably hard –
with the euphoria of a successful outcome – to turn our
minds to what can go wrong.

However, things *do* go wrong, often for no sinister reason.
The parties' recollection of what was agreed may be
inadequate but if the performance of the agreement does
not meet either sides' expectations it would be quite
understandable if underlying motives were questioned.

F R I D A Y

Solutions to avoiding these problems include:

- taking and exchanging notes
- getting the agreement in writing
- checking that minutes and opponent's notes agree with your notes
- taking care with the small print

Taking and exchanging notes
It isn't easy to contribute to a negotiation meeting – talking, listening *and* making notes, but working notes of the meeting will be an essential foundation for any subsequent agreement or contract. In the commercial world, it is quite usual for a representative's memorandum of sale and a buyer's order to be drafted during the meeting, and exchanged at the end. This provides the first check that both sides have a common understanding of what has been agreed and, with experience and trust built up over time, one side may be prepared to accept the other's notes.

In staff relations meetings it is common for both parties to nominate their own secretary to take minutes of the meeting and the notes are then used to form the ultimate record of the meeting.

Get it in writing!
Even when notes have been exchanged at the end of the meeting it is still important for a *formal record* of the agreement to be exchanged. Most negotiations commit two organisations as well as the various players and formal records will need to be exchanged.

Confirmations may take the form of:

- purchase requisitions
- sales order notes
- letters of confirmation
- revised proposals (bringing letters of acceptance)
- formal contracts
- joint communiqués or treaties
- procedural agreements and bargains

A cautionary check is to ask yourself:

> 'Am I covered in law if anything should go wrong?
> Who could I sue?'

This is not to say that you would wish to – most disputes between contractors are resolved by negotiation. But skilled negotiators will not put themselves into a position where they have no recourse if the opponent should renege on the agreement.

Check confirmations agree with your notes
How often have you attended meetings and failed to recognise the minutes when they have been released some time later? Unfortunately, those who have the responsibility to prepare the notes are sometimes tempted to misuse that power to rewrite them to suit their preferred position – subsequent to the meeting. Even if this is not intended, subtle changes may take place to meet the political inhibitions of the boss, the organisation or even some of the people present. Where changes have been noted, and where these affect the letter or spirit of the agreement, a loud complaint should be made, officially. Any apathy here may be taken as acceptance of the new situation!

F R I D A Y

Take care with the small print

One major company in the North of England employs a whole department of lawyers whose main task is to check buying agreements and ensure that their own terms and conditions are supreme over those of their suppliers. The consequence of this is that any small supplier is unlikely to be able to achieve any variation to those terms and may be faced with the stark choice of contracting on the buyer's terms or not at all.

We would all prefer that breakdowns do not lead to recourse to the law – this could be very expensive in time and money – but the larger the contract the better it would be to ensure that the worst consequences of failure do not leave you totally exposed to losses as a result. For this reason, penalty clauses are often found in construction contracts, restraint of trade in personal contracts and even clauses allowing actions for damages against trade union bodies where the continuity of supply of a service is affected by a trade dispute.

Evaluating performance and continuing to grow

Whilst there is little point in crying over spilt milk, there is no doubt that we can learn from past mistakes. Indeed, it is likely that all negotiators have made mistakes at some time or other – what is unforgivable is to make the same mistakes over again!

Consider the following checklist which may help you pin-point your own strengths and weaknesses:

Preparation
1   Do I spend enough time preparing to negotiate?
2   Have I discussed the case with other people in my organisation?
3   Have I researched my opponent's case?
4   Is there any additional information I may be able to collect from my opponent's organisation?
5   Which outcome do I really want:

Win/Win, Win/Lose or Lose/Lose?

6   Have I prepared a negotiation plan/brief?
7   What is on my objectives/shopping list?
     What are the parameters for each objective?
8   Have I prioritised my objectives?
9   What concessions can I give?
10   Where will we meet?
11   Have I analysed relative power positions of our two organisations?
12   When will be the best time to meet?

▆▆▆▆ S A T U R D A Y ▆▆▆▆

Know yourself

13   In what circumstances am I:
- most comfortable?

- least comfortable?

14   How easy do I find it to:
- take decisions?

- persuade others?

- be positive and persistent?

- choose the most persuasive words?

- think clearly under stress?

- control myself?

15   What motivates me?
      What 'Achilles Heels' might exist in me?

16   Am I a disciplined listener?

17   Am I tempted by a win/lose opportunity if I will be the winner?

Opening the meeting

18   How good am I at putting others at ease?

19   How good are my presentation skills?

20   Can I control and read body language?

21   How able am I at probing others for information?

22   Can I respond to others' probing without giving away anything of value?

23   How well am I able to develop a collaborative atmosphere in the meeting?

24   Have we established a common agenda and identified common ground?

████ S A T U R D A Y ████

The meeting

25   How well can I balance talking and listening?
26   How can I make the meeting layout work for me?
27   How good are my concentration and listening skills?
28   When might a recess be useful?
29   How can I make good use of interruptions?
30   Who is in control in the meeting?
31   Have I identified the best time to make proposals?
32   How good am I at introducing trial proposals?
33   How can I formulate counter-proposals to overtake opponent's proposals?
34   Am I using 'If...then' and 'So' successfully?
35   When my opponent blocks my proposals, am I able to unblock them again?
36   How able am I in using closing skills:
     • hand-holding?
     • summarising?
     • using late concessions?
     • linking?

Don't forget that the real test of your negotiation meeting lies in the results and that . . .

. . . Skilled negotiators have:

• a track record of significant success
• a low incidence of failure in the implementation of their agreements
• high ratings for effectiveness by both sides

▬▬▬▬▬ S A T U R D A Y ▬▬▬▬▬

Continuing to grow

Negotiation is a practical skill. It is subject to the same characteristics as other skills – it gets rusty if it is not used – and improves, and is sharper, when used frequently. So, there are a number of steps which the negotiator can take to increase these skills:

- Take every opportunity to negotiate.
- Talk about negotiation with experienced people both inside and outside your organisation.
- Read about negotiation – look at:
  - newspaper articles for recent cases
  - trade magazines for technical sources
  - books and articles.
- Review your deals carefully and thoroughly.
- Attend a training course which enables you to obtain some feedback about your style and skills (preferably through the use of cctv).

The truth is rarely pleasant and the review process will be pointless if you indulge in a form of self-kidology! Check your objectives and those known about your opponent – and make sure you do not make the same mistakes twice! Happy and successful negotiating!

Time
Management

DECLAN TREACY
Revised by Polly Bird

WEEK THREE

C O N T E N T S

Week Three

▆ I N T R O D U C T I O N ▆

It's been a hectic day as usual. The phone has rung at least a dozen times, we've attended three meetings, we've spent an hour answering emails, we couldn't begin to count the pieces of paper we've handled, we've dealt with five queries from colleagues who unexpectedly arrived in our office, and there have been two major crises to sort out. We've been so busy but we don't really feel as if we have achieved anything. Even with the wonders of modern technology to help us such as fax machines and mobile phones the work seems to pile up. There seems to be too much to do and just not enough time!

There are 86,400 seconds in each day. Why is it that some people can run large organisations or even countries within that time while others seem to get bogged down in the simplest of jobs? The secret lies in effective time management.

Over the next week you are going to fine tune your time management skills step by step. Each day, you will explore a new topic and after reviewing the theory, the checklists and exercises will encourage us to apply the principles to our own work situation. All the time management

■ I N T R O D U C T I O N ■

techniques recommended here are already being practised by successful managers. You only have to look around to see.

Our agenda for the week is as follows:

Sunday	– Self-assessment
Monday	– Masterin
paperwork	
Tuesday	– Planning
Wednesday	– Controlling IT
Thursday	– Taming th
telephone	
Friday	–
Managing meetings	
Saturday	– Managin
projects	

To get the most out of this week, you will need to set aside one hour a day to work through it. Approximately 45 minutes should be spent reviewing each chapter and completing the exercises, and 15 minutes reviewing your performance at the end of each day. You should start as you mean to go on by blocking off these time periods in your diary now!

For many of its readers, this book will serve as a catalyst for a dramatic change in their working lives; for others, it will serve only to pass a few hours with little real benefit. Only you can determine which category we will fit into. If you choose to change, the benefits of good time management are immediate and substantial. You will:

■ I N T R O D U C T I O N ■

- Achieve better results.
- Improve the quality of your work.
- Work faster.
- Lower your stress levels.
- Make fewer mistakes.
- Reduce the number of crises faced.
- Increase your salary.
- Improve your work satisfaction.
- Improve the quality of your non-working life.

Remember: *it is what you do during the 86,400 seconds of each day that will ultimately determine how successful you are in your chosen career.*

Involving your colleagues

You need to involve your colleagues in your efforts to manage your time better. As managers you are responsible for the performance of the people around you. If one of your colleagues is buried under a mountain of paperwork the chaos will have a negative effect upon the rest of the office. If someone else consistently fails to plan their projects, everyone else will suffer when the ensuing crisis materialises. Everyone in your department and throughout the company should be encouraged to learn how to manage their time effectively. You should encourage all our colleagues to read this book. If you demonstrate how effective its advice is by our own example we will encourage them to improve their own time management skills. If possible, you should arrange for a time management expert to talk to our department and perhaps set aside a day or two for putting some of the ideas in this week into practice.

You should ask your colleagues to tell you their own ideas for saving time. It is the people who do the work who understand the problems. They might come up with ideas that not only improve their own time management but also help other people in the department. When everyone in a department or company becomes involved in improving their time management skills everyone is motivated to become more productive. If one person slips back into old habits other members of the department can bring them back on to the right track.

Self-assessment

Today, we are going to evaluate our current time
management skills. This is a very important exercise and
will form the foundation of our future success. By the end of
today, you will have completed a time log, made a list of
your top 12 timewasters and explored the process by which
you will develop timesaving habits.

Self-assessment
- analysing your current use of time
- identifying the timewasters
- changing your habits

Analysing your current use of time

The first step in improving your time management skills is
to analyse how you currently spend your time. Research has
shown that managers constantly need to change the focus of
their attention, and spend an average of only 10 minutes on
each task throughout the day. We can easily get swept along
in the cut and thrust of daily office life without appreciating
where our time goes.

In this section we will complete a self-assessment
questionnaire and compile a time log. Both exercises give us
the opportunity to stand back and evaluate our
performance objectively. A special notebook should be
obtained and used for these exercises.

The self-assessment questionnaire:

S U N D A Y

	Yes	No
I tend not to tackle paperwork the first time I see it	☐	☐
I face more crises than I need to because of poor planning	☐	☐
I sometimes have to be chased by others to get things done	☐	☐
I have a vague idea of what my priorities are	☐	☐
I spend more than 30 minutes a day looking for things	☐	☐
My meetings tend to last longer than necessary	☐	☐
I allow others to negatively influence how I spend my time	☐	☐
I start a lot more projects than I finish	☐	☐
I am always busy but not always productive	☐	☐
I hang on to tasks that should really be delegated	☐	☐

If you have answered 'Yes' to five or more of the statements above then the week ahead will provide you with some much needed insights and solutions to your time management problems. If you have scored less than three on the questionnaire you have probably not been ruthless enough in your self-assessment. Improving your time management skills can only come about through an appreciation of what is currently going wrong. Regardless of your score you should come back to the questionnaire at the end of the week and complete it again.

S U N D A Y

Compiling a time log will provide you with some additional insights. A time log as shown overleaf should be made up and completed for Thursday and Friday of last week. Each task completed during the day should be written down, along with an estimate of its duration: telephone calls, correspondence, meetings, interruptions, memos, junk mail and so on. You should note down whether the task was planned or not, and then estimate its pay-off. This exercise might also be carried out on Monday and Tuesday of this week to give you a further insight into your time management, and then periodically every few months to gauge your improvement.

S U N D A Y

Time log

Time	Activity	Pay-off	Duration	Planned
9.00	coffee/chatted with colleagues	low	15 mins	no
9.15	processed mail	med	25 mins	yes
9.40	sales call	low	5 mins	no
9.45	fax arrived	high	20 mins	no
10.05	follow-up call	high	10 mins	no
10.15	colleague dropped by to talk about contract	med	15 mins	no
10.30	sales meeting	med	85 mins	yes
11.55	dealt with telephone messages	med	20 mins	no
12.15	browsed through leaflets left in in-tray	low	10 mins	no
:	:	:	:	:
:	:	:	:	:
:	:	:	:	:
:	:	:	:	:
4.00	draft report for MD	high	70 mins	yes

S U N D A Y

After completing the time log you should ask yourself the following questions:

- What proportion of my tasks were planned?
- Was there any real structure to my day?
- Did planned tasks take longer than expected?
- Why did I spend so long on the low pay-off tasks?
- How many interruptions did I face?
- Do I allow others to dictate how I spend my time?
- During what part of the day was I most productive?
- Have I been productive, or just busy?
- What can I do to gain greater control over my time?
- What proportion of my time could I realistically plan for?
- On a scale of 1–10 how would I rate my effectiveness?

Identifying the timewasters

When completing a time log, many people are shocked at the amount of time that is wasted during the day. People we don't need to talk to are on the phone, colleagues are constantly dropping by for a chat, bits of paper are mislaid, meetings last longer than expected. Our days seem to be saturated with timewasters: low pay-off activities that deflect us from the important work .

The list overleaf outlines the 12 most common timewasters. After considering each item on the list we should compile a list of your own top 12 timewasters.

S U N D A Y

The 12 most common timewasters

1   Losing things
2   Meetings
3   Telephone
4   Interruptions
5   Procrastination
6   Junk paperwork
7   Crises
8   Reverse delegation
9   Perfectionism
10 Distractions
11 Emails
12 Surfing the Internet

Let's look at these timewasters in more detail.

Losing things

How much time is spent rummaging amongst the pile of papers on the desk in the typical week? If you spend just 30 seconds every five minutes extracting an item from the bottom of the in-tray, looking for a telephone number you scribbled down on a loose piece of paper, or locating a misfiled document, it adds up to four hours a week. Time you can't really afford to waste. How often do you have to do things twice because you lost the original?

Meetings

How much of your time is spent in meetings every week? What proportion of that time is wasted due to meetings that should never have been held in the first place? How much time do you waste because meetings start late or overrun?

S U N D A Y

Do you often have to sit through long meetings and find that only five minutes are relevant to you?

Telephone

How many times a day are you distracted from important work by the telephone ringing? What proportion of these calls are unexpected? What is the average length of each call? What proportion of these calls are really necessary? Do you allow your calls to drag on for longer than they should? Do you ever find yourself ringing someone back because there was something you forgot to discuss during the first call?

Interruptions

How many times a day are you interrupted by colleagues arriving at the desk? Are these interruptions really necessary? Does the location of your desk mean that you always catch people's eye as they walk past? Do these interruptions have a negative effect on your performance? Do you encourage social interruptions by always stopping what you are doing and chatting to people?

Procrastination

What tasks have you been avoiding over the past few weeks? What excuses have been used to delay action? What is usually the end result of our procrastination?

Junk paperwork

Are you as ruthless as you should be about getting rid of junk mail or obsolete documents? Do you resist delegating certain tasks because you enjoy doing them? Do you find yourself browsing through magazines, newsletters and brochures when there is higher pay-off work to be done?

Crises

Do you spend your days rushing around dealing with one crisis after another? Is every crisis you deal with really a crisis? Is every crisis that you deal with really your problem? If you were more pro-active would you have avoided some of these crises?

Reverse delegation

Do you respond to requests for help by saying, 'leave it with me, I'll tackle it later?'. Is there work on the desk that your

S U N D A Y

subordinates have left for your input?

Perfectionism

Do you spend extra time getting things 100% right when 95% would do? Does your attention to detail on one project mean that something else more important doesn't get done?

Distractions

In the middle of one task, do you often find your attention being grabbed by other work around you on the desk? How do these distractions affect your workflow?

Emails

Do you answer your emails as soon as they arrive? Do you read through all your emails regardless of how many there are and how many are junk and should be deleted unread? Do you print your emails instead of storing them? Do you send emails when a phone call or note would be more appropriate? Do you write long emails when a short one would do?

Surfing the Internet

How many times do you search the Internet for information that could be obtained more quickly and easily by looking in a book or asking somebody? Do you use the Internet as a way of avoiding other work? When surfing the Internet do you get side-tracked by interesting or irrelevant sites?

Working through your own personal list of timewasters, you should ask yourself how much time you waste in each category during the typical week.

Telephone	48 mins
Crisis management	45 mins
Meetings	25 mins
Interruptions	19 mins
:	:
:	:
:	:
:	:
Surfing the Internet	65 mins

Changing your habits

The identification of your timewasters has been a major step forward. You now need to concentrate on eliminating those time-wasting habits and substituting timesaving habits in their place.

Many of these timewasters will have become a natural part of your work style: allowing meetings to drag on, retaining junk mail, procrastination. The first time you organised a meeting that was running over time you probably looked impatiently at your watch and shuffled your papers but

decided to say nothing. The next time it happened, you might have noted that the meeting was running late, again without commenting. Day after day, week after week, you allowed your meetings to overrun. The timewasting behaviour was repeated so often that it gradually became an unconscious habit. Now your meetings don't finish until everyone has stopped talking. You expect them to drag on and therefore don't even set a finishing time when arranging them.

Now is the time to change; to reverse the process.

Reading this book alone will not help you to alter your timewasting habits; it will take time and effort. If you were learning to play a musical instrument you would not be able to read a book and step straight on to the concert platform to give a virtuoso performance. The psychologists say it takes approximately 21 days to change a work habit. At first, you will have to make a conscious effort to keep your meetings on track and if things are dragging on, you need to stand up and indicate that the meeting is over. It will of course be difficult at first but once you have done it a few times it will become easier. From time to time, you will lapse back into your old habits, but perseverance will bring rewards in the long run. The decision to change is yours alone and the best time to change is now! Twenty years from now, many of this book's readers will be attending seminars and buying books on managing meetings.

The four-step process of change
The four-step process below should be applied to each of our timewasters. Procrastination will be used as an example.

If procrastination is one of your major timewasters, we probably put off things using excuses such as, 'I'm too busy right now', 'I need to wait for more information', or 'I'll do it tomorrow'. You might start off at the beginning of the day by pushing aside just one item, but it is soon joined by other documents. As more and more unfinished papers join the pile at the bottom of the action tray, you resist approaching that part of the desk. If you tackle one item, you will have to face everything, causing an immediate flood of guilt and stress. Subconsciously, you say to yourself, 'Now what can I do instead?'

1 Write down the timewaster
On the top of a new page in our time management notebook we should write down the timewaster you wish to tackle: Procrastination.

2 List the problems caused by the timewasting habit
Next you need to list the problems faced as a result of procrastination: constantly feeling guilty about unfinished work, increased stress levels, spending too much time on the enjoyable things which bring few rewards, a reputation around the office as someone who is unreliable.

3 Visualise the timesaving habit
All thoughts of procrastination should be removed from your mind and you should visualise yourself as a 'doer'. What would things be like in the office if you had the reputation for getting things done, rather than for procrastinating? How would you handle your correspondence? How would you approach difficult reports? How much unfinished work would there be lying in the in-tray? The benefits of being a 'doer' should be written down.

4 Develop the timesaving habit
Next you need to write down the steps that are necessary to change your timewasting habit:

a I will stop using phoney excuses like, 'I need to wait for more information';

b I will have to remove tempting distractions such as brochures and magazines from my line of sight;

c I need to spend more time planning my day;

d I need to break down large projects into more manageable tasks;

e I will finish the uncomfortable items first and then reward myself with more enjoyable tasks.

This four-step process should be followed for each of your top 12 timewasters. One page in your time management notebook should be devoted to each timewaster: listing the problems it causes, visualising the way you want things to be in future and writing down the steps you need to take to change your timewaster to a timesaver. Every day during the coming week, a few minutes should be spent reviewing your notebook to remind yourself of the things that need to change.

Adapt to suit the environment

No matter how effectively you plan, you must always be prepared to adapt to changing circumstances. Often you can predict likely changes in advance. If you get a lot of phone calls in the morning, you should not schedule an urgent task for that time. If your boss delegates work late in the day, you should try to get your 'A' priority work done before then so that you are not swamped with work. If you face a lot of genuine crises, then you should only plan a small proportion of the day.

The KISS principle

The KISS (Keep It Short and Simple) principle should be applied to everything you do. It is a waste of time holding a meeting if the matter can be resolved by a quick phone call. There is little value in writing a 10-page report where two pages are all that is necessary. There is no need to send a memo to someone when you bump into them several times a day. Introducing a form is unnecessary if the information asked for can be obtained elsewhere. You should go back and look at the time logs you completed on Sunday and ask yourself which activities would not have been undertaken if the KISS principle was used.

Adopt a positive outlook on life

A positive outlook on life can only increase your chances of being successful. Excuses can always be found for the problems that confront us. With a negative outlook we spend our time complaining and blaming others for our problems instead of working to find a solution. Of course, it is not always easy to be positive, but in the long term you will be rewarded. A positive outlook will also motivate the people around us to get things done. Looking back over the past week, you should mentally list all the time management problems that we blamed on others, rather than asking what you could do to eliminate them.

Perfectionism can be dangerous

In some cases, it is wise to pay attention to detail but in many cases it can be counterproductive. To get something 90% right will often suffice. If you spend time getting internal memos, reports, presentations or projects 100% right it often means that something more important is left in the in-tray. Furthermore, the extra time you spend on any one task is rarely worth the extra pay-off. The law of diminishing returns comes into play. If you are preparing something for someone else, you should agree on a level of performance that is acceptable. There is absolutely no benefit to the company if you spend an extra 30 minutes printing an internal report again to correct a few spelling mistakes. If others are drafting letters or reports for you, you should try to avoid editing their work. You have to appreciate that others may say things in a slightly different way to you, but which is no less valid.

Tomorrow, you will focus on conquering the paper mountain. You cannot begin to manage your time effectively until you have gained control of the paper flow.

Mastering paperwork

Despite predictions about the move towards the paperless office, you still seem to be drowning in a sea of paper, much of it unnecessary. Today, you are going to look at ways of controlling the constant flow of paperwork arriving on the desk. By the end of the day, the desk will be clear of paperwork, you will have implemented techniques for reducing the inflow of unnecessary paperwork, and you will have streamlined and reorganised your files. This is necessary because it is essential to create the right physical environment before you can begin to manage your time effectively.

Mastering paperwork

- paperwork reduction campaign
- effective paper handling
- effective filing

Paperwork reduction campaign

Low pay-off paperwork is costly to generate and it deflects attention away from what is important. If we examine all the memos, reports, faxes, letters, magazines, invoices, junk mail and other bits of paper that arrive on a daily basis, it becomes clear that most of it should never have been generated in the first place.

We frequently blame others for our paperwork problems, but it is often our own work style that causes the heavy inflow of paper. How often can we be heard to say to

M O N D A Y

colleagues, 'Send me a copy for my files', 'Could you confirm that in writing?', 'Write me a report on it', 'Send a memo around to everyone', or 'I can't act on that unless I have it in writing'? Before asking others to send paperwork, you should ask yourself if the information is really necessary. If you need the information, you should try to obtain it by word of mouth or email. Paper should be your last resort. We also complain about the amount of junk mail we receive but then deal with unwanted telesales callers by saying, 'Send me some information'.

And what about the paper that you create and keep? Do you really need to print a hard copy of each email you send and receive or every computer file you create? They all add to the piles of paper on your desk or clutter up your files. You can surely delete most of them or store them on your computer.

As well as reducing the inflow of paperwork, you need to cut down the outflow from the desk. If you are constantly distributing forms, memos and photocopies to others, you can expect nothing less than an avalanche of paperwork in return. You should spend 30 minutes today devising and implementing strategies for reducing paperwork. The checklist below serves as a useful starting point.

Paperwork reduction checklist

- have name removed from external mailing lists
- remove name from internal circulation lists
- ask colleagues to be concise
- where necessary have paperwork rerouted
- talk to people instead of writing
- ask colleagues to report by exception
- reduce the volume of paperwork leaving the desk
- return unnecessary paperwork to sender

You should set a definite target for reducing paper in the office over the next few months and enlist the help of your colleagues. Less paper means lower costs, improved productivity, improved morale, improved communications and a better service for your customers.

Effective paper handling

Ideally, each piece of paper that arrives on the desk should be handled only once. Few of us can afford the luxury of picking up the same piece of paper again and again without actioning it. If you are handling the same bits of paper over and over again you will be extremely busy but at the end of the day you will not have actually achieved anything extra.

M O N D A Y

The measles test

An exercise that will encourage you to handle paperwork
the first time you see it is the measles test. For the next
week, every time you pick up a piece of paper to deal with
it, you should use a red marker and place a red dot on the
page. If by the end of the week most of the paperwork on
the desk has had an outbreak of measles, then you know
you need to change your habits.

The lack of a system for processing incoming paperwork,
combined with our natural tendency to be indecisive,
results in stacks of unfinished paperwork building up on
the desk. Many of us work in chaotic environments and
rationalise it with statements such as, 'I know where
everything is!', 'It suits my personality!' or 'It's organised
chaos!'

We can always find an excuse, but research and common
sense tells us that the chaotic desk leads to:

- low productivity
- missed opportunities and deadlines
- frantic searches for lost information

- long working hours
- high stress levels
- low morale
- unwanted distractions
- unexpected crises

If you think back over the past week you will have experienced many of the problems on the list because of your desktop chaos.

Before you can begin to process the flow of paperwork efficiently, you need to clear the desk. The clear-out should start today, with all the junk you have accumulated on your desk: glossy brochures, obsolete reports, magazines you will never read, memos you will never look at again. These items will have accumulated because they looked interesting at first glance and you put them aside telling yourself you will look at them again when you have more time.

Once the desk has been cleared, it should remain clear.
Many people say, 'I know I have lots of paper on the desk
but it's only junk it's not real work!' This junk however
hides the important paperwork; it constantly distracts us
and when we are procrastinating about an item of real
work, this junk becomes infinitely more attractive and
worthwhile. Operating a clear-desk policy does not mean
that you will never be seen with paperwork on the desk
again. It means that you should restrict your workspace to
one project at a time. You should also try to avoid having a
clear desk whilst having every other available space in the
office piled high with paper.

The RAFT technique
The RAFT technique should be used to keep us afloat on the
sea of paperwork. As soon as a piece of paper arrives you
should make a definite decision about what to do with it
and move on. There are in fact only four things you can do
with a piece of paper that lands on the desk: refer it, act on
it, file it or throw it away.

▬▬▬▬ M O N D A Y ▬▬▬

Your referred paperwork should go straight in the out-tray, filing paperwork belongs in the filing system, junk should go straight in the bin and, where possible, your action paperwork should be dealt with straight away. Any 'act on' paperwork not dealt with immediately should go in a bring-forward file. You should have a place for everything and everything should go in its place.

Paperwork management checklist

- be decisive when dealing with incoming paperwork
- try to handle each piece of paper only once
- avoid using a plethora of diaries and notepads
- restrict the workspace to one project at a time
- try to avoid high-rise trays on the desk
- avoid using the in-tray as a storage space
- use the RAFT technique
- set up a bring-forward file for tracking unfinished paperwork
- sort out the papers in your briefcase every day

Effective filing

The filing system, whether paper or electronic, is one of the most important management tools we have. You will concentrate on your paper files today, but the same general principles should be applied to computer files.

Unfortunately, filing is often seen as a clerical activity and not worthy of management attention. As a result, our filing systems tend to be poorly organised. Stacks of 'to file' paper build up on the desk, increasing the chances of items being mislaid. When we do file paperwork, it tends to be done in a haphazard fashion with the focus on getting the documents out of sight. We rarely give any thought to the question of finding them again.

To win back control of your filing system, you are first going to look at overcoming your tendency to hoard too much information. Then you will reorganise your files to make things easier to find.

De-junking the filing system
If you take a brief look through your files, you will probably find that most of their contents are obsolete: abandoned projects, glossy brochures, out-of-date reports, untouched reading material. In fact, studies have shown that approximately 85% of the information we keep will never be looked at again and 45% are already stored somewhere else.

You should try to set aside 90 minutes today for purging your files. Working through the folders one by one you should consign to the bin all those items that:

a you will never get the time to look at;
b can easily be located elsewhere if needed;
c have a low pay-off attached to them.

If you are sufficiently ruthless, then the contents of your filing systems should be reduced by more than 50%. One rule that is adopted in many bureaucratic organisations is, 'Before throwing anything out, make a copy of it just in case you might need it again'. The rule should be taken with a pinch of salt, but it identifies the fear that many people have when throwing things away. We tell ourselves that someone is bound to need the document at some time in the future. If we talk to people who are ruthless about binning things,

M O N D A Y

they will say that junked items are very rarely needed again and when that happens there is always a copy somewhere else.

Once the clear-out is complete, you should try to keep the quantity of files down by:

- purging your files as you use them on a daily basis
- asking others to retain copies of documents they send you
- marking items with a discard date
- never keeping copies of the same document in different files
- asking others to keep paperwork concise
- transferring infrequently-used files to archives

Reorganising the files

The better organised your files, the more likely you are to make use of the information you keep. There is an important filing maxim which states, 'If you don't know you have it, or you can't find it, then it's of absolutely no use to you'.

M O N D A Y

Very few of us have ever sat down and considered setting up a logical filing system. Our file headings are usually created with little thought and file folders are usually arranged at random in the drawer. We only have to watch ourselves and others trying to retrieve mislaid items from the filing cabinet to realise the importance of a good classification system.

There are six main ways of classifying information:

- by subject category
- alphabetically
- by date
- by colour
- geographically
- numerically

You should experiment with different combinations of the above classifications until you develop a system that suits your way of working. Once you have decided on a suitable system, you will need physically to reorganise the files. The file management checklist below will help you in that endeavour.

> *File management checklist*
>
> • use simple file headings
> • subdivide bulging folders
> • separate active files from infrequently-used records
> • put the filing cabinet within reach of the desk
> • don't allow stacks of filing to build up on the desk
> • use a classification system that can be trusted
> • purge files regularly

Filing on computers

Now that computers have become standard office machines we can use them to our advantage to keep our emails and computer document files under control. The techniques are similar to filing paper. You need to decide which files to delete, which to pass on and which to keep so that you can easily retrieve the ones you need to work with. Before you save any computer file you must decide whether it can be safely deleted or whether it should be saved. If the file should be saved the next question is where to file it.

Sorting into folders
Word processing documents, spreadsheets, emails and other computer files can all be sorted into folders and sub-folders. The computer manual and on-line help will show how your applications save files. Choose obvious names for your

main folders such as Project A, Staff or Book. Then subdivide these into relevant folders. So, for example, you could divide the Project A folder into folders for project outline, control and folders for the input of individual staff members Tom's Section. Or the folder for the best selling book you are writing in your lunch break could be divided into folders for each chapter, the outline, character descriptions and letters from publishers. You can then move each computer document into the relevant sub-folder. You can also scan paper documents into your computer and save them in the relevant folders.

Setting up filtering systems
Incoming emails can be filtered into relevant folders. Your email help box will tell you how to do this. For example, you can filter all emails with $ or £ signs or the word 'win' in the subject line to a folder marked 'junk'. You can then periodically delete this folder without reading the contents. You can also filter emails from particular people or groups into separate folders. So all emails from your boss can be filtered into one folder and dealt with first.

Once you have your paperwork under control, you free up your time for more productive pursuits.

Tomorrow we shall concentrate on planning.

Planning

Today, we will look at planning on three levels. We will start
off by looking into the future to set long-term business and
personal goals. Next we will devise the action plans which
provide the blueprint for turning our dreams into reality.
Finally we will look at planning on a daily basis.

> *Planning*
>
> * setting goals
> * devising action plans
> * daily plans

Planning is one of the most important time management
skills. Our goals give us a sense of direction in both our
personal and business lives. Those people who lack a clear
vision of where they are going, spend a large proportion of
their time reacting to the demands of others: urgent faxes,
emergency telephone calls, asap memos and crisis meetings.
No matter how efficient we are in dealing with those short-
term demands it is difficult to be successful in the long term
without plans. Accidental success is quite rare.

Setting goals

Successful companies have goals: to achieve the highest
market share, for instance or to have the most efficient
production line. Without these goals things would be
chaotic. Successful athletes have goals: to break the world
record, or to win a gold medal at the Olympics. Athletes

would not get up to train at 5 a.m. on a cold winter's morning unless they had a clear vision of standing on the podium receiving a trophy. Successful managers also have clear goals.

Creative visualisation

Half an hour should be set aside today for an exercise in creative visualisation. You are going to sit back and dream of the future, banishing all negative thoughts from your mind. It is easy to be self-critical and to tell yourself, 'I could never achieve that'. Long-term goals, such as running our own business, initially appear to be beyond our reach. In the next section you will look at breaking down your goals into manageable action plans. Once you have completed an action plan, all you have to do is concentrate on one step at a time. Before starting the creative visualisation process, you should ensure that you won't be disturbed.

Your look into the future should focus on both your work and your family life. You should try to see yourself in one, five, 10, 15 and 20 years from now. The questions overleaf will help you in that process.

Business goals

- What would I like to have achieved by the time I retire?
- What salary would I like to earn?
- Would I like to run my own business or become a senior manager in a large organisation?
- Should I remain in this country or work abroad?
- Would I benefit from further education?
- What business skills do I need to develop?
- What industry would I really like to work in?
- What is my ideal job?
- What professional organisations should I join?

Once we have visualised a successful future in our working lives we need to consider our personal lives and aim to achieve a healthy balance between the two.

■■■■■ T U E S D A Y ■■■■■

Personal goals

- What hobbies/special interests would I like to pursue?
- Where would I like to live?
- Do I need to spend more time with the family?
- What parts of the world would I like to see?
- Should I learn a new language?
- Do I need to adopt a healthier diet?
- Could I improve my level of fitness?
- What sort of home would I like to live in?

As you visualise your future achievements you should write them down as goals in your time management notebook.

You should hold a creative visualisation session every six months because certain goals may have been reached or, due to circumstances beyond your control, certain goals may have changed slightly. Each time you achieve a goal, you should set another one so that you are always working towards a more fulfilling business and personal life.

Devising action plans

Unless you make definite plans you cannot hope to turn your dreams into reality. The action plans you devise for each of your goals will provide step-by-step guidelines for achieving those goals.

The benefits of action plans are clear to all those who use them.

Action plans:

- Break down daunting goals into achievable steps.
- Motivate us to achieve our goals.
- Make implementation of ideas easier.
- Provide us with a useful overview.
- Enable us to focus on the important rather than the urgent.
- Provide a benchmark against which we can judge progress.
- Help us to anticipate problems.

The steps you need to take to achieve each of your goals should be written down on the relevant page in your time management notebook. If you have a goal to be MD of a large company you should work back from the goal and ask yourself, 'What do I need to do to get there?' Any major steps you need to take should be broken down into smaller more achievable steps. You should also set a deadline for achieving your goal and deadlines for achieving each step along the way.

An important question you need to ask yourself is, 'What will it cost to achieve the goal?' There may be a substantial financial cost involved, such as investing in an MBA programme. There may also be a personal cost involved. If you are going to set up your own business, it may mean you have less time to spend with family and friends. So, you need to weigh up the cost of achieving your goals against their pay-off.

■■■■■■ T U E S D A Y ■■■■■■

Daily plans

Once your action plans are complete, you need to shorten the time frame and look at compiling daily plans or 'to-do' lists.

Daily plans:

- enable us to plan our work sensibly
- act as reminders
- unclutter the mind
- help us to keep track of deadlines
- motivate us to get things done
- help us to focus on priorities

Eight steps to effective daily plans
We are now going to look at a straightforward process for compiling daily plans. The medium on which you capture your plans is not as important as the process. Electronic to-do lists, index card systems, personal organisers, or desk diaries can all be used effectively.

T U E S D A Y

1 Five minute planning period
At the end of each day you should spend five minutes
planning the next day. As you turn the page of your diary
there should already be a number of things to do,
commitments and action plan steps which have been
carried forward from previous days. For example:

To do	Priority	Completed	Delegate	Time
Call John				
Finish marketing report				
Read article				
Arrange meeting with M.G.				

2 Carry forward today's unfinished activities
If there are any activities on today's to-do list they should
be carried forward to tomorrow or another suitable date. If
you frequently find yourself with a large number of
unfinished tasks at the end of the day, you are probably
trying to squeeze too much into the day. You should
therefore leave more room in the day for unplanned events.

To do	Priority	Completed	Delegate	Time
Call John				
Finish marketing report				
Read article				
Arrange meeting with M.G.				

T U E S D A Y

To do	Priority	Completed	Delegate	Time
Call T.D.				
Reply to B.C.G letter				
Finalise budgets				
Send file to A.C.				

3 Plan tomorrow's activities
Taking account of your scheduled activities such as
meetings and appointments, list the activities to tackle
tomorrow.

To do	Priority	Completed	Delegate	Time
Call John				
Finish marketing report				
Read article				
Arrange meeting with M.G.				
Call T.D.				
Reply to B.C.G letter				
Finalise budgets				
Send file to A.C.				
Copy for brochure				
Check travel arrangements				
Send slides to bureau				
Prepare mailshot				
Read next chapter of this book				

▬▬▬▬▬ T U E S D A Y ▬▬▬▬▬

4 Include goal-related activities
You should always include activities that will help you to
achieve your long-term goals. When busy you tend to react
to the urgent items rather than the items that will benefit
you in the long run. It is important therefore to always
include goal related activities on your to-do list.

To do	Priority	Completed	Delegate	Time
Call John				
Finish marketing				
report				
Read article				
Arrange meeting				
with M.G.				
Call T.D.				
Reply to B.C.G letter				
Finalise budgets				
Send file to A.C.				
Copy for brochure				
Check travel				
arrangements				
Send slides to				
bureau				
Prepare mailshot				
Read next chapter				
of this book				
Co. MBA sponsorship?				
Buy French tapes				

5 Prioritise things to do
Working through the list, you should prioritise each activity.
Your goal-related activities should always be assigned an

T U E S D A Y

'A' priority; items with associated deadlines are the same, as
are items with high pay-offs. 'B' priorities will include those
items you would like to get done but which can be delayed
if you don't have the time. Anything you think should be
assigned a 'C' priority should be crossed off the list – you
have better things to do with your time.

To do	Priority	Completed	Delegate	Time
Call John	B			
Finish marketing report	B			
Read article	B			
Arrange meeting with M.G.	A			
Call T.D.	B			
Reply to B.C.G letter	B			
Finalise budgets	A			
Send file to A.C.	B			
Copy for brochure	A			
Check travel arrangements	B			
Send slides to bureau	A			
Prepare mailshot	B			
Read next chapter of this book	A			
Co. MBA sponsorship ?	A			
Buy French tapes	A			

T U E S D A Y

6 Delegate activities

No manager should ever get bogged down in a mountain of paperwork because it can always be delegated. Working through your to-do list you should ask yourself who the best person is to deal with each item. In delegating, you should be seeking to develop the skills of the people around you rather than dumping work on them.

To do	Priority	Completed	Delegate	Time
Call John	B			
Finish marketing report	B		J.D.	
Read article	B			
Arrange meeting with M.G.	A			
Call T.D.	B			
Reply to B.C.G letter	B			
Finalise budgets	A		J.D.	
Send file to A.C.	B			
Copy for brochure	A			
Check travel arrangements	B		A.H.	
Send slides to bureau	A			
Prepare mailshot	B			
Read next chapter of this book	A			
Co. MBA sponsorship?	A			
Buy French tapes	A			

T U E S D A Y

7 Estimate the length of time each task requires
This process is difficult until you get used to it. When you
have totalled up your estimates along with your scheduled
activities they should not add up to more than 75% of the
working day. It is important not to try to plan every minute;
you need to be flexible in order to accommodate the
unexpected.

To do	Priority	Completed	Delegate	Time
Call John	B			10
Finish marketing report	B		J.D.	60
Read article	B			15
Arrange meeting with M.G.	A			5
Call T.D.	B			10
Reply to B.C.G letter	B			20
Finalise budgets	A		J.D.	5
Send file to A.C.	B			5
Copy for brochure	A			30
Check travel arrangements	B		A.H.	5
Send slides to bureau	A			10
Prepare mailshot	B			20
Read next chapter of this book	A			60
Co. MBA sponsorship?	A			10
Buy French tapes	A			5

T U E S D A Y

8 Work through mail and make additions to list
Tomorrow morning your mail will invariably throw up a number of important things to do. These should be added to your list.

To do	Priority	Completed	Delegate	Time
Call John	B			10
Finish marketing report	B		J.D.	60
Read article	B			15
Arrange meeting with M.G.	A			5
Call T.D.	B			10
Reply to B.C.G letter	B			20
Finalise budgets	A		J.D.	5
Send file to A.C.	B			5
Copy for brochure	A			30
Check travel arrangements	B		A.H.	5
Send slides to bureau	A			10
Prepare mailshot	B			20
Read next chapter of this book	A			60
Co. MBA sponsorship?	A			10
Buy French tapes	A			5
Check invoice	*B*			*10*
Discuss complaint with sales	*A*			*20*
				295

Once tomorrow's to-do list is complete we are ready to
attack the day. The temptation is often to start on the quick
and easy activities, ticking off many items on the list. The
only effective way to work however, is to tackle our
activities in order of priority. As a general rule, you should
not tackle a B priority item unless all your A priorities have
been completed. It can be useful to set aside a 'quiet hour'
in the day when you know you will not be disturbed for
tackling important items. Where possible, similar activities
should be grouped together: telephone calls,
correspondence, or delegation to secretary.

The realities of prioritising

In an ideal world we would move from one task to another
in the order we prioritised them. Unfortunately, life isn't
like that. Just because we have prioritised actions does not
mean that we can always complete them in order. New
instructions from our boss or the problems associated with
dealing with crises mean that priorities get changed. The
importance of prioritising our daily plan is that it keeps us

focused when we need to get back on track. Once we have
dealt with the immediate demands from our boss or solved
a crisis we can see from our plan immediately what other
work we need to do and which work should be completed
first. You may never get to the end of your daily list but you
can be reasonably sure that you are dealing with your most
important work.

The manager's emergency prioritising trick:

Take all your papers and quickly sort them into three
piles:

- now
- later
- unimportant

Take the first pile only and quickly sort it according to
the order in which tasks must be done that day.
Concentrate only on that pile and work through it
steadily, starting with the task you have prioritised as
the most important.

Time and travel

Executives are spending more and more of their time
travelling, both nationally and internationally. The time
spent travelling can eat into your productive working time.
Careful preparation before major trips is essential. Some
time should be spent writing down a list of objectives for

T U E S D A Y

the trip and then collecting together all the necessary paperwork. You should keep a travel file for collecting together all your travel documents, and prepare a special file containing the background information for meetings you will be attending. During the trip, it is essential to keep all your papers under control, because the chaos is very difficult to unravel when you get back to the office. At the end of each day, you should review your paperwork for the day, try to deal with any action points on the spot, and discard any unnecessary documents.

On long or short trips, you can always make use of your travel time. It is an ideal opportunity to catch up on your reading. Magazines, newsletters, reports, routine correspondence should be collected in a reading file so that you can catch up when travelling. If you find it difficult to read while travelling, you can substitute the spoken word; most of the business bestsellers are now available in audio format. Use your laptop if you have one to catch up on correspondence or writing reports.

Using computers for planning

Computers and electronic organisers are now common planning tools. Used effectively they can make planning easier and save time. Many organisers can be connected to a desk top computer. This means you need not write out your diaries or plans more than once. You can record details away from the office on your laptop or organiser and then later transfer them to your desk top machine.

Co-ordinating diaries

Whether you use a paper diary or an electronic organiser
you need to ensure that you co-ordinate them with your
secretary's diary or whoever else needs to be informed. This
should be done at least at the beginning and end of each
day.

The pay-off from our long-term plans is never immediate
and that is why many people adopt a reactive approach to
time management. Urgent and immediate tasks will always
give us an instant pay-off whereas a longer term, pro-active
approach will delay the pay-off but it will always be much
greater. A useful principle to bear in mind when working
through our to-do list is the 80:20 rule: 80% of our results
come from 20% of our activities. Thus 80% of our sales come
from 20% of our customers, 80% of our achievements will
come from 20% of our paperwork and conversely 20% of
that report we have to read will give us 80% of the
information we need.

Tomorrow, we will look at controlling IT.

Controlling IT

The Information Technology (IT) we use is faster and more powerful than ever before and the use of computers is widespread and vital in today's modern business world. This should mean that we become more productive and work more efficiently. However, it can also encourage us to waste time unless we use it effectively. Today we will look at the technology we use and discover how to get the best use from it.

Getting the most from computers

The computer is undoubtedly the main office took of today. Used effectively it can be a powerful means of communication and an effective planning tool. Modern computer applications and powerful computers mean that they can make time management quicker and easier. But they are only as effective as the software they use and the people who use them. No matter how large and expensive a computer might be, unless the person using it knows how to get the most out of it, it might remain an expensive office toy. Computer planning applications include on-screen organisers, diaries, calendars and forms and these, as well as the standard office applications, can make time management easier.

A computer can also be an efficient way of gathering information when connected to the web through the Internet. Office computers are often connected to an intranet which is a kind of private Internet restricted to users within one company. It enables communication between individuals and departments in a company. It is easy to confuse the Internet and intranet.

The difference between the Internet, the web and intranet:

Internet
- The worldwide physical networks of computers that communicate using common protocols.

The web
- The content of the Internet consisting of many pages on different sites usually containing text and graphics.

Intranet
- A self-contained Internet with a website that can only be used within an internal company network.

Using the intranet

The company intranet is largely a library of information that is accessible to all staff. Because it is designed for internal use only we may need a password to access it. We should not assume that everyone will see everything we post on the intranet. It may be necessary to use a brief email to alert staff to any new information posted. On the other hand we should be careful what we post on our intranet because everyone in the company could read it.

W E D N E S D A Y

> *Do not use the intranet to:*
>
> - Post personal information for everyone to see.
> - Write long rambling pieces.
> - Post personal remarks about other staff.
> - Give information that should be presented in person or in a personal memo.

Using the Internet

The Internet is a world-wide source of information but it can be frustrating and time-wasting if we don't know how to use it. You should remember that basic information is often quicker and easier to obtain from a book, a phone call or a question to colleague. Information on the Internet and the web can be posted by anyone so when you find a page that looks useful you need to check the source and see if it mentions when the pages were last updated to judge whether it is reliable. A recently updated page posted by a government agency, for example, is likely to be more reliable than one several years old posted by an individual. Each website has a unique web address known as an URL (Uniform Resource Locator). When you find a reliable and useful website you should make sure you can reach it again by saving it in your favourites list on your computer. To save time when searching for information you should make your request as specific as possible.

W E D N E S D A Y

Online time-saving tips

Going online whether to the Internet or an intranet can be
addictive. A great deal of time is wasted by people who
play games online, transact personal business or spend
hours 'surfing the net' unnecessarily. You must not use the
web as an excuse for not getting on with other work. The
Internet should not be accessed during office hours without
the employers' permission. Some companies severely
restrict employees' use of the Internet as opposed to the
company intranet. Using the Internet for personal business
or playing games is usually forbidden.

Save time when online by:

1 Restricting your searches to specific pieces of information.

2 Making your search request as specific as possible.

3 Only going online for information that cannot be
obtained more quickly and easily from traditional sources –
or by asking a colleague.

4 Asking your secretary or administrative support person
to make searches for you.

5 Setting a personal time limit for searches – e.g. ten
minutes maximum.

6 Make a list of information you need and search for them
in order allowing three attempts only for each question.

W E D N E S D A Y

Other timesaving machines

There are many other useful machines that help to make our work easier and save us time. By eliminating paper and enabling us to work wherever we are they reduce the amount of time we have to spend on filing or hunting for information.

Laptop computers
Although a desk top computer is standard office machinery some companies provide their staff with laptops or employees may have laptop computers of their own. Laptop computers can often be connected to a desk top machine via a port or infra red connection. This makes it easy to transfer work done away from the office. We should not be like the business people who use laptops on trains and who are more often than not playing solitaire or patience on them. Keep game playing for weekends.

Advantages and disadvantages of laptop computers:

For
- easy to transport out of the office
- can be used to work at home
- can be connected to a desk top computer
- can be used to give off-site presentations

Against
- more vulnerable to theft
- can be heavy to carry

▬▬▬ W E D N E S D A Y ▬▬▬

Laptop computers can be useful for giving off-site presentations. The presentation can be prepared in the office using a graphics program and transferred to a laptop either directly or by disk. The laptop can then be carried to the presentation site and be used to give a presentation on the spot. Laptops may have batteries that only last for a couple of hours so a mains lead should be kept with it and used whenever possible.

Electronic organiser PDAs
Electronic organisers or PDAs (Personal Digital Assistants) store contact details and notes and some have word processing or spreadsheet programs. They are small enough to fit into a briefcase, handbag or pocket and can be used to keep contact details to hand. The versions of word processing and spreadsheet programs installed may be scaled down versions of the main applications. Some PDAs can be connected to mobile phones for email and Internet use. Make the best use of them by:

- using short cut keys for frequently used numbers
- using a PDA that has the same applications as your desk top computer
- keep personal and work contacts in separate files

Scanners
Scanners save time by reducing paperwork because scanned documents, business cards, invoices etc. can be stored on a computer. Scanned documents can be sent straight from a computer by fax or as an email attachment. The original document can be destroyed once it has been scanned into a computer.

Fax

Faxes can be sent from stand alone fax machines or straight from a computer either as scanned documents or written directly into the computer's fax template. Faxes are particularly useful for image based documents or those with a signature. Have a standard cover sheet prepared with your own and your company contact details clearly printed on it.

Getting the most from the software

Computers usually come with standard applications such as spreadsheet, word processing programs, a graphics package, a database and an organiser. We often underuse these programs because we don't know their full capabilities and only learn how to use them by trial and error. You should ensure that you ask for training in how to use these efficiently or consult the handbooks. Libraries often have training CDs or videos about how to use the well-known brands available for borrowing. Applications might be easier to use if they resemble paper products that we are used to. Other applications should be investigated and used if they increase productivity. To save time you can:

- print out pages from your computer organiser only when you require them to save carrying a large paper organiser
- set up your organiser to automatically record regular dates and move forward ongoing commitments
- send database, spreadsheet or word processing documents to colleagues online

W E D N E S D A Y

Email

Emails make corresponding quicker and cheaper. But some managers can receive up to 200 emails every day. If we spend all day answering our emails we will not have time to do any other work. Most of the time wasted by emails is caused by sending unnecessary correspondence. Our friends and colleagues do not need a copy of the latest round robin email joke nor attachments of photos of the office party. We must resist the temptation to copy emails to everyone in our address book or send long personal messages. There are some simple way to reduce the time taken to answer emails.

1 Delete unwanted emails.
It is usually easy to spot the junk (spam) emails by their subject headings. Delete them unread.

2 Answer emails at set times.
Decide to answer emails twice a day, perhaps once in the morning and once in the afternoon. Do not read emails between times.

3 Prioritise emails.
Answer important emails immediately and leave the rest until a convenient later time.

4 Use standard replies.
Prepare standard replies to common questions and paste these into emails when appropriate.

5 Deflecting emails.
Ask staff to copy emails to other people only if they require action from those people.

W E D N E S D A Y

> *Email etiquette:*
>
> * don't write or pass on unsuitable or irrelevant emails
> * don't write in CAPITALS – it's like shouting
> * keep emails short and succinct
> * put the main point of the email in the subject line
> * don't send personal emails from work

Voicemail

Many office computers can accept and send voicemail. This can save time but only if you set up your voicemail efficiently. Make sure that the message the callers hear is up-to-date and relevant. Listen to voicemail twice a day and reply to important messages as soon as possible. As voicemail is sometimes turned off during working hours you must check that voicemail is on when you leave the office and arrange for it to be transferred to your mobile if you are out of the office during the day.

Viruses

Computer viruses can destroy a computer's entire hard disk and all the programs and work that are on it. It is easy to install and use a virus checker. The company technical department should help. Once it is installed use it regularly – once a week is the absolute minimum. Never download unknown programs from another computer or disk nor allow staff to do so. If a new program is necessary the company technical staff should be consulted. The time taken to do a regular virus check is small compared to the hours or days that would be lost if a virus attacked your computer.

Tips on saving work:

- save work at frequent intervals throughout the day
- download work regularly on to removable disks, preferably at the end of each day
- make a back-up copy of start-up disks and programs
- keep dated back-up copies of work in a safe place

Tomorrow we look at how to keep phone calls under control.

Taming the telephone

Today we are going to look at ways of taming the telephone. First of all we will look at telephone mismanagement and the traits of the telephone junkie. We will then look at techniques for controlling our incoming calls and for making our outgoing calls more productive.

Taming the telephone

- the telephone trap
- the telephone junkie
- incoming calls
- outgoing calls

The telephone trap

Many of us make and receive dozens of calls every day of
our working lives. The telephone is an invaluable
management tool. It allows us to communicate instantly
with people anywhere in the world. It is more cost-effective
than travelling to a meeting and quicker than written
communications. There is a downside, however, in that we
are instantly accessible to anyone who wishes to speak to us
regardless of how unimportant the issue or inconvenient the
time. Our use of mobile phones has also made us more
accessible and encourages us to chat. We can say 'no' to a
meeting and throw a low pay-off letter in the bin but as
soon as we pick up the telephone and hear, 'Let me tell you
about our new photocopier', 'About the letter I sent you', or
'I just rang to see how things are going', we are trapped.
Someone else is determining how we spend our time.

The secret of good telephone management lies in
eliminating, or cutting short, the junk calls while getting the
most from the important ones.

The telephone junkie

Telephone junkies have a detrimental effect on everyone in
the office: too many unnecessary calls are made, too much
time is spent on each call, important calls are not returned,
items agreed upon during calls are not followed up... the list
is endless. We all exhibit the traits of the telephone junkie
from time to time. The following questionnaire will help
you to determine how often.

▬▬▬▬▬ T H U R S D A Y ▬▬▬▬▬

Telephone junkie questionnaire

Do I:

	Sometimes	Always	Never
rush to answer the phone as soon as it rings?	☐	☐	☐
spend longer on calls than is really necessary?	☐	☐	☐
have to make calls twice because there was something I forgot to say?	☐	☐	☐
allow telephone calls to interrupt my meetings?	☐	☐	☐
dial numbers and then forget who I called?	☐	☐	☐
drop what I'm doing when I remember a call I need to make?	☐	☐	☐
not screen my calls even when there is someone available to do so?	☐	☐	☐
spend more than 30 seconds dealing with unsolicited sales callers?	☐	☐	☐
finish calls without covering the topics I want to discuss?	☐	☐	☐
scatter my outgoing calls randomly throughout the day?	☐	☐	☐
write down messages on the handiest piece of paper at the time?	☐	☐	☐
forget to pass telephone messages on to others?	☐	☐	☐

Scoring the questionnaire:

For each 'sometimes' answer, you should score yourself 1 point; for each 'always' answer, 3 points, and 0 points for each 'never' answer. A score of 16 or more puts you into the telephone junkie category and you need to sit back and evaluate how you are using the telephone. Why are you not

using it productively? What needs to change before you can gain control over the telephone? Even a score of less than 16 means that the telephone probably rules your life from time to time. The questionnaire will have helped in identifying those areas you specifically need to work on today and in the future. You should use your score as a benchmark to gauge your improvement over the coming weeks and months.

Incoming calls

The telephone rings continuously during the day. A certain proportion of our incoming calls bring good news or provide useful information, while the remainder are unnecessary. Unfortunately we cannot tell before picking up the phone which calls are important. Managing incoming calls is therefore partly a damage limitation exercise. You need to keep the unwanted calls brief, and the important calls productive.

You should not give your phone number to everybody because that increases unwanted calls. You also need to be aware of the security problems of using phones in public places. Private business information may be overheard or a mobile phone could be stolen together with any private contacts saved on it.

Most of us underestimate the length of time we spend on the phone during the day. Setting up a telephone log, as shown below, will therefore be a revealing exercise. Every call you receive today should be noted along with its duration and pay-off. Your time management notebook should be used for this exercise.

Telephone log: incoming calls

Date:

Time	From	Re:	Duration	Pay-off
9.20	sales	photocopier	5 mins	low
9.50	S. West	set up sales meeting	17 mins	med
10.30	D. Martin	in meeting, asked to call back	2 mins	low
11.00	M. George	query on memo	11 mins	low
11.20	client	sales order	13 mins	high
11.48	sales	training course	4 mins	low
:	:	:	:	:
:	:	:	:	:
4.50	A. Smith	tennis game	15 mins	low

Total time spent on incoming calls: 2 hrs 5 mins

Looking back at your telephone log at the end of the day you will undoubtedly be shocked at the number of calls you have received and their duration. You should set aside five minutes to analyse your calls and ask yourself the following questions:

- How many unexpected calls did I receive?
- How many unwanted calls did I receive?
- How many calls lasted longer than necessary?
- How many calls could have been dealt with by someone else?
- How many calls interrupted me when I was busy with a high pay-off item?
- How many calls could have been screened out?

It pays to practise techniques for keeping your junk calls brief. In your time management notebook, you should note down at least three excuses you can use, such as, 'I'm in the middle of a meeting right now can you tell me very quickly what you want', 'I have a taxi waiting for me', or 'I have a conference call booked in about two minutes'.

When the telephone interrupts our work, many of us have a tendency to scribble notes on the nearest piece of paper, whether it is a letter or an open report. This habit creates problems for us when we need to go back and find someone's telephone number or check on the price we quoted. Which bit of paper were we using at the time? Where did it go? For important colleagues or contacts, you should set up an index card or a page in your personal organiser. Each time they ring, you can turn to their page and immediately see what the last conversation was about or if there are any items we need to discuss with them. The key points of the current conversation can be captured and retrieved quickly if you need to refer to them.

The checklist below outlines 10 important techniques for managing incoming calls. You should try to use them all throughout the day. If you have problems with any of the techniques you should develop strategies for overcoming them.

Techniques for managing incoming calls

- Put phone on divert or DND when busy.
- Set aside a quiet hour during which you will not take calls.
- Ask for all calls to be put on hold during meetings.
- Be polite, firm and brief with unwanted sales callers.
- Ask people to call at particular times when you are less busy.
- Avoid tackling peripheral tasks while on the phone.
- Avoid taking notes on loose bits of paper.
- Arrange for calls to be screened whenever possible.
- Ask the receptionist not to give out names to cold callers.
- Make a list of excuses for keeping calls short.

Outgoing calls

Outgoing calls are more manageable. We can decide who
we wish to speak to, when we make the call, what we want
to say, and we also have greater control over its duration. A
telephone log should be set up for outgoing calls in your
time management notebook.

Telephone log: outgoing calls

Date:

Time	To	Re:	Duration	Pay-off
10.20	Personnel	job advert	8 mins	med
12.00	Personnel	forgot to ask about salary details	3 mins	low
:	:	:	:	:
:	:	:	:	:
3.20	J. Coates	arrange meeting	24 mins	med

Total time spent on outgoing calls: 1 hr 38 mins

Towards the end of the day, when your outgoing calls
telephone log has been completed, you should ask yourself
the following questions for each call:

- Was the telephone the best way of getting the message across?
- Did I achieve my objective?
- Did I waste too much time on small-talk?
- Did the call drift into low pay-off areas?
- Did the call last longer than anticipated?
- Was there anything I forgot to say?

■■■■■■■T H U R S D A Y■■■■■■

Planning the call

Most outgoing calls are made on the spur of the moment. We are sitting at the desk and we suddenly remember we have to call someone. We pick up the phone without thinking and launch into the call. As a result we forget things we want to say, we put things across badly, and we fail to get the information we need.

Before making any call you should ask yourself: what information do I need to pass on? What information do I need to obtain? What is the best way to get the message across? What papers do I need to have to hand for the call?

Making the call

You should treat each call as a mini-meeting. You should ensure that you get your own message across, and that you capture the other person's ideas. It is a good idea to summarise quickly the points made during the call, to make sure there is no confusion. You should block off time in your diary once or twice a day and make our outgoing calls together. Grouping your calls will motivate you to be brief and to the point. Your calls should also be prioritised and then made in order of priority. You should also create a sense of urgency with your lower pay-off calls by setting a definite time limit.

After the call

Any action points that arise as a result of your discussions should be followed up immediately or written down on a to-do list.

The checklist below provides guidelines which should be followed for each outgoing call made. You should block off

T H U R S D A Y

time in your diary for tomorrow and make a list of all the calls you need to make.

Checklist for managing outgoing calls

- plan calls as if attending a meeting
- make outgoing calls in blocks
- prioritise calls
- set limits on the duration of each call
- collect relevant documents before the call
- summarise discussions before the end of the call

Mobiles phones

The time management techniques in this chapter also apply to mobile phones. But although mobile phones can save us time by enabling us to keep in contact with the office, they can also be great time wasters. Just because we can get football results or listen to music on our mobile phones does not mean we should. Nor do we need to spend time sending and receiving text messages from our friends. We should switch our phone off during meetings and use its voicemail facility so that we can decide when to respond. We should not use our mobile phones for personal calls during office hours.

Most people reading this chapter at work will have been constantly interrupted by unnecessary telephone calls. The techniques in this chapter should help to reduce this problem and make the telephone a more productive management tool.

Tomorrow, we will look at managing meetings.

F R I D A Y

Managing meetings

Most managers spend somewhere between 30 and 50% of their working lives in meetings: drop-in visitors, committee meetings, recruitment interviews, brainstorming sessions, crisis meetings and conferences. We all know that an unacceptable proportion of the time spent in meetings is wasted.

Today, therefore, we are going to explore ways of maximising that time investment. First of all we will try to identify some of the factors behind unproductive meetings. Then, starting afresh, we will look at what should be done before, during and after our meetings, whether as chairperson or attendee, to make them more productive. We will examine checklists that can be followed for all meetings, whether they are one-to-one discussions or more formal gatherings.

F R I D A Y

Managing meetings

- Why do meetings go wrong?
- What to do before meetings.
- What to do during meetings.
- What to do after meetings.

As a means of communicating, meetings can prove very useful. They enable you to:

- transfer information and receive feedback
- generate new ideas
- build consensus for a decision or course of action
- combine expertise to solve problems

Things can go wrong, however, as hinted at in the business adage, 'In all your parks and all your cities you'll find no statues of committees'.

Why do meetings go wrong?

You should set aside about 20 minutes to evaluate your current meeting management skills. The first question you need to ask yourself is, 'What proportion of my time is spent in meetings?' Next, you should ask yourself, 'What proportion of that time is wasted?' Thinking back over the meetings you have attended in the past few weeks you should explore the following areas:

F R I D A Y

- How much did the meetings cost?
- Were the costs of attending the meetings greater than the benefits gained?
- Were the meetings adequately planned?
- How many meetings were delayed because of late-comers ?
- Did the meetings frequently last longer than expected?
- Were there problems with equipment and facilities?
- Did I make worthwhile contributions to the meetings?
- Did other participants make worthwhile contributions?
- Did the meetings tend to wander away from the agenda?
- Were decisions, taken during the meeting, followed up?

Now that you have identified the potential pitfalls, we will turn our attention to making our meetings more productive. We will start with the meeting preparations.

What to do before the meeting as chairperson

Whether guiding a formal meeting or arranging an informal chat, it is your responsibility to make sure that the right people are in the right place at the right time and have received the relevant background information. The checklist below should be followed before each meeting that you organise. Preparation is the key to success!

F R I D A Y

Chairperson's checklist
- Is the meeting really necessary?
- What are the alternatives to meeting face to face?
- What are the objectives of the meeting?
- Who is needed to ensure that these objectives are achieved?
- What will be the pay-off from achieving the objectives?
- What will the meeting cost?
- What equipment/facilities are needed for the meeting?
- If an agenda is required has it been prepared/distributed?
- Are all the attendees clear about the start time and location of the meeting?
- Have attendees received all the relevant background information?
- Do all the participants need to be present for the whole meeting?

At first, you may find working through the checklist a bit laborious, especially for smaller meetings, but over time, the questions will become ingrained in your memory. Running through the questions mentally will become a matter of habit and as a result your meetings will become more productive.

What are the alternatives to a meeting?
How many of the meetings you attended in the past week could have been replaced by a brief chat, a memo, a quick telephone call, a decision by the person in charge? Could the issues have been added to the agenda of another meeting? Before arranging any meeting you should look at all the other alternatives.

The meeting's purpose
You should clearly define the the meeting's objectives, and communicate them to participants when arranging the meeting. This gives others the chance to prepare in advance and ensures that people do not have to sit through an irrelevant meeting because they thought it was going to be about something else.

The meeting pay-off
Once you have set the objectives for the meeting, you need to ask what the pay-off from achieving each objective will be. The pay-offs will enable you to prioritise the agenda and focus on the important items. The total meeting pay-off should be weighed against the meeting cost to see if it is a worthwhile exercise.

Preparing the agenda

As the number of participants in a meeting increases, so the need for an agenda grows. The agenda should be kept brief and uncluttered. The agenda items should be positive and achievement oriented, i.e. 'To find a solution to the distribution problem', rather than 'To discuss distribution problems'. The highest pay-off items should be placed at the top of the agenda so that if you run out of time, the major issues will have been covered.

What to do before the meeting as attendee

As meeting participants, you need to evaluate the necessity of attending the meeting and to be well prepared. There is nothing more infuriating than sitting through a meeting which, with the benefit of hindsight, you know you should not have attended. You should learn to guard the precious asset, your time, more carefully. Instead of attending, you can save time by talking to people who have attended or by looking at the minutes afterwards.

■■■■■■■■■ **F R I D A Y** ■■■■■■■

- Do I really need to attend the meeting?
- Is there an alternative to the meeting?
- Am I sure of the correct time/location of the meeting?
- Have I arranged my schedule so that I will get to the meeting on time?
- What do I want to contribute to the meeting?
- What do I want to get out of the meeting?
- What background paperwork do I need to tackle?
- Do I need to attend all of the meeting or just part of it?

What to do during the meeting as chairperson

As chairperson, you need to be aware of the destructive forces that can make meetings unproductive. You will look at some of the more common forces, along with strategies for coping with them.

Late-comers
You should never reward the late-comers and punish the punctual participants by holding meetings back until everyone is present. If you are lax about start times, you give participants licence to make extra phone calls or to chat with colleagues in the corridor before the meeting. You should, without exception, start your meetings on time. As soon as the meeting starts, the door should be closed. As

F R I D A Y

late-comers arrive, we should never interrupt the meeting
to bring them up to date on what has been discussed.

Hidden agendas

At the start of the meeting, attendees should be asked what
they personally want to get out of the meeting. We will then
get the hidden issues and concerns out into the open where
they can be addressed. Participants hi-jacking the meeting
to promote their own agendas should always be interrupted
and reminded of the true purpose of the meeting.

Rambling discussions

The only way to stop long-winded or irrelevant
contributions is to interrupt. You should wait for someone
to take a breath, jump in, briefly summarise the point being
made, and move on.

Low participation

You should actively try to encourage the participation of
attendees by reacting positively to contributions. There is no
quicker way to silence a group than to be over critical. If
someone with potentially useful contributions is silent, you

should ask them directly for their ideas. Asking people to confer in pairs or smaller groups is another useful technique for getting things started.

Interruptions

There is a famous story about a US senator in a meeting with the President. The phone was ringing continuously and the President was getting involved in a protracted conversation each time he picked it up. Eventually, the senator left the room and called the oval office extension. He immediately got the President's attention.

You should arrange for all calls to be put on hold for the duration of your meetings. 'Do not disturb' signs should also be used for office doors indicating the time that the meeting will be over. If someone does break through your initial barriers, you should arrange a time when you can get back to them.

Arguments

If people are arguing unproductively during meetings, you should suggest that their discussions be continued outside the meeting. If that is not possible, you should acknowledge the differing points of view and ask participants to focus on a solution. In larger meetings, you can bring arguments to an end by asking for a show of hands on the issue.

Group indecisiveness

There is no point having meetings where lots of things are discussed but nothing is decided. After each item on the agenda has been discussed, you need to summarise the decision taken, any follow-up actions and deadlines. If

F R I D A Y

possible, you should produce an instant action summary during the meeting and distribute photocopies to participants as they leave.

Decision/action to be taken	Person responsible	Deadline
Letter to be sent	J.D.	12/5
Report on product launch	G.H.	22/5
Sales conference details	J.D.	22/5
New computer system	M.G.	28/5

On paper, many of the suggestions for controlling meetings look straightforward. In the middle of a meeting however, they will appear a lot more difficult, and the easiest option is to do nothing. You need to practise these techniques, meeting after meeting, until you get them right. A start can be made by analysing the effectiveness of your next five meetings and making a checklist of areas in which improvement is needed. If you learn how to control destructive forces, your meetings will be dynamic, productive and enjoyable.

■■■■■ **F R I D A Y** ■■■■■

Chairperson's checklist

- always start on time
- set out the objectives for the meeting
- stay positive throughout the meeting
- follow up actions from the last meeting
- decide who will take the minutes
- encourage participation from reserved attendees
- silence sidetrackers
- keep the discussion focused on the agenda
- adhere strictly to the agenda timetable
- summarise decisions/actions to be taken as the meeting progresses, and again at the end
- ensure that all the items on the agenda are covered
- finish the meeting on time.

What to do during meetings as attendee

As participants at meetings, you should always try to be constructive. If you act counterproductively, you are wasting your own time as well as that of the other participants.

Attendee's checklist

- contribute constructively to the meeting
- restrict contributions to agenda items
- focus on the meeting's objectives
- be clear about any follow-up steps to take
- avoid private discussions during the meeting

F R I D A Y

What to do after meetings as chairperson

What happens after the meeting, ultimately determines whether or not the meeting has been a success.

As soon as the meeting is over the chairperson should quickly work through the questions below. In certain circumstances it can be useful to evaluate the meeting with the participants.

Chairperson's checklist

- Has the meeting been a success?
- Were the right participants present?
- Were all the items on the agenda covered?
- How should unfinished items be dealt with?
- Do I need to distribute meeting minutes?
- What should I do differently next time?
- Could we have achieved the same results without a meeting?

What to do after meetings as attendee

The meeting we have just attended is worthless unless actions are taken as a result of the discussions. After the meeting has finished, you should transfer any follow-up actions into your to-do list and ask yourself the questions below.

Attendee's checklist

- Was my participation in the meeting really necessary?
- Am I clear about any follow-up actions I need to take?
- Did I contribute constructively to the meeting?
- What should I do differently next time?

Holding virtual meetings

Now that business is conducted nationwide and worldwide it is not always possible for individuals to attend all the meetings they need to because of the time and cost of travel. Virtual meetings are therefore becoming more commonplace. Meetings can be held by video link, telephone or on the web.

What happens at a virtual meeting?
The link is set up beforehand and booked with the supplier if necessary. The meeting takes place at a prearranged time and the participants in each place assemble beforehand in a special room. At the arranged time the link is opened and participants can communicate by phone or video link even though they are not in the same place.

Rules for a successful virtual meeting:

- ensure everybody is assembled on time
- arrange for a secretary or colleague to refuse entry to anyone once the meeting has started
- make sure everyone is seated where they can head, see and be heard
- allow for a time delay

Meetings can be a productive way of getting things done but they can also be an unnecessary drain on your time. If you pay attention to getting things right, the rewards throughout your careers will be enormous.

Tomorrow, we shall take a look at project management.

Managing projects

Today, we are going to look at fine-tuning our project management skills. There are three stages in managing a project: planning, controlling and evaluating. If we fail to manage these three stages effectively, the project may well end up in the project graveyard. A quick glance through the papers on the desk or gathering dust in the filing system will invariably reveal many projects which we started enthusiastically but which were never completed.

> *Project management*
>
> - planning
> - control
> - evaluation and review

A project is a series of interrelated tasks leading to a definite end. We spend a large proportion of our time juggling projects ranging from writing a report to launching a new product. Smaller projects can be dealt with by writing the individual tasks on our daily to-do lists, while larger projects require a more sophisticated approach. It is these larger projects on which we will concentrate today.

Working through this chapter provides you with the ideal opportunity to plan a project which you are about to take on. After reading the chapter once, you should choose a project and work through it according to the principles outlined. You should also compile a list of all upcoming projects in your time management notebook, and schedule time for planning them properly.

Before going on to look at the three stages of project management, it will benefit us to look at the 10 most common reasons why projects fail.

1 Taking on too much
2 Inadequate planning
3 Project costs outweighing benefits
4 Ineffective delegation of project tasks
5 Procrastination
6 Failure to spot potential problems
7 Focus on more immediate, but lower pay-off, items
8 Lack of overview
9 Lack of a clearly defined objective
10 Poor communication between members of project team

Looking back over the last three unsuccessful projects you took on, you should compile a list of the reasons why they failed. Once that has been completed, you can look at ways of ensuring the success of your future projects.

Planning

The more time you spend planning the project, the easier its implementation will be. With project management, you need to be pro-active rather than re-active. You need to anticipate problems rather than waste time trying to sort them out once they have occurred.

There are five major stages in planning a project. Each stage should be followed as you plan a current project.

1 Identify the objective
The objective provides the focus for all the individual tasks that must be performed as part of the project. It should be stated clearly and concisely because, if the objective is stated ambiguously, then the different members of the project team may end up working towards different ends. The questions below will help you to identify the objective. A project overview page should be set up in your time management notebook for each project we undertake and the answers to these questions written down.

- When the project has been completed I will have achieved . . .?
- What problems will the project help to solve?
- How will the project be completed?
- Who else will be involved in completing the project?
- What is the scope of the project?
- How long will it take to complete the project?

2 Cost-benefit analysis

Many projects are undertaken without proper consideration of the costs involved and then when these costs escalate alarmingly during the project, it has to be abandoned. For the project you are currently planning, you need to examine the costs of undertaking it, as well as the rewards to be gained from completing it. These rewards may be financial in terms of increased revenue or decreased costs. The intangible rewards which cannot be measured in financial terms should also be considered.

- What tangible benefits will result from the project?
- What intangible benefits will result from the project?
- What are the costs involved in completing the project?
- Do the benefits outweigh the costs?

In your time management notebook, you should compile a list of costs on one side of the page and a list of benefits on the other. The project should only proceed when you are satisfied that the benefits outweigh the costs.

3 Break the project down into individual tasks

▄▄▄▄ S A T U R D A Y ▄▄▄▄

Sometimes, when we are faced with a large project it can seem overwhelming. Where do we make a start? Often, we make a start, but not at the beginning, and then leave key tasks until it is too late and we have a crisis on our hands. On one page in your time management notebook, you should break down the project into its individual tasks. Start with the major tasks and break them down into smaller tasks until everything that needs to be done has been identified.

For each individual task, you need to ask, 'What could possibly go wrong?'. The answer to this question will help you to set up contingency plans.

4 Schedule the tasks

Alongside each individual task you should write down an estimate of how long it will take to complete. Next you should decide on an appropriate deadline for each task. Many tasks can be completed at the same time, while others may have to be performed sequentially. You should be realistic here and allow for delays. It might take you 10 minutes to obtain an item of information from a colleague, but it may take you a week to arrange a meeting with them. Once you have completed your scheduling, you can set a deadline for the project. Finally, the deadlines should be transferred to your to-do lists for the relevant day. Key project tasks which, if not completed will cause the project to fail, should be highlighted on your to-do lists.

5 Delegate tasks where appropriate

Many of the projects we undertake will involve us working with others. This means that the project workload will be spread out, and we will also benefit from the input of others at the planning stage. When delegating tasks, you should negotiate a deadline for their completion and write it down on the relevant to-do list.

Delegation is the art of getting things done through others. As you progress through your careers, you will find it necessary to rely more and more on your colleagues to get things done for you. Many managers fear delegation and the loss of control it brings, but it is essential to free up your own time for higher pay-off activities.

Five steps to effective delegation

1 Communicate clearly what needs to be done.
2 Agree a deadline for completion of the task.
3 Let go of the task and trust the delegatee.
4 Reward successful completion of the task.
5 Be considerate and avoid dumping tasks on others.

You should spend five minutes writing down all the activities that should be delegated to others.

Recording a project

Keeping an accurate record of a project is vital to its success. By recording the stages as they are planned and due to be carried out, a check can be kept on how the project is progressing. At the end of the project the record will show which strategies were successful and suggest ways in which the next project could be improved.

Keeping basic records

Project records do not need to be complicated but they should be made regularly and kept up-to-date. If possible, keep them in one bound book or loose leaf folder. The records should include:

1 The project's aim, participants, expected timescale and cost.
2 A plan of the project including a day by day plan.
3 Details of who will be doing what and by when and confirmation of when each action was completed.
4 A running account of costs.
5 Notes of problems and possible solutions.
6 A daily, weekly and monthly summary of results.

The project manager should keep the overall record but individuals should keep their own records so that these can be checked with the main record. In large projects there will be particular record keeping roles for an accountant.

Control

Project control is the process of monitoring projects to ensure they are on track, and taking corrective action where necessary.

The project overview in your time management notebooks will prove invaluable during this stage. When you are dealing with a large number of projects, essential tasks may slip through the cracks. You should constantly refer back to our list of tasks on your project overview page and tick them off as they are completed. If there is a lot of time-sensitive paperwork involved in the project, you will need to use a bring-forward system for keeping track of everything.

One or more project files should be set up and kept in an accessible place. You should purge the file after each major stage of the project has been completed, so that you are not constantly shuffling through piles of unnecessary paper whilst looking for something important. Many people leave all their project paperwork on the desk and say, 'I have people coming into the office all the time to discuss things, so I need to have everything where I can lay my hands on it'. However, this method means that important documents often get buried, and the papers relating to different projects get scattered around and mixed up.

■■■■■ S A T U R D A Y ■■■■

The most important part of project control is to avoid being distracted by the urgent but unimportant items that land on your desk every day. You can easily fall into the trap of getting busy with the quick, easy, fun and comfortable paperwork while the important things hibernate at the bottom of the in-tray. Using a prioritised to-do list, you should constantly monitor yourself to ensure that you are focused on the high pay-off project tasks.

Control checklist
- Monitor scheduled project tasks on a daily basis.
- Always assign an 'A' priority to project tasks.
- Keep track of delegation deadlines using the diary.
- Periodically refer back to the project overview page.
- Use a bring-forward file for time-sensitive paperwork.
- Keep project paperwork together in a project file.

Evaluation and review

Reviewing completed projects is a brief but essential exercise. During the planning stage, the evaluation should be scheduled as the final project task and this will help you to avoid focusing on activity rather than achievement. If the project has not gone according to plan, the review enables you to analyse what went wrong so that you can avoid similar problems in the future. If the project has been successful, the review enables you to identify why things went well, to acknowledge the positive contribution of others, and to congratulate yourselves. Any lessons you learn during the completion of a project should be noted down on a special page in your time-management notebook. This page can then be reviewed during the planning stage of future projects.

When evaluating the project, you should ask yourself the following questions:

Project review checklist
- Was the project objective achieved?
- Was the project completed by the deadline?
- If not, why not?
- Was adequate time assigned to planning?
- Were all the project tasks identified beforehand?
- What avoidable crises occurred during the project?
- What problems could have been avoided by prior action?
- Were the right people involved in the project?
- Was everyone motivated to complete the project?
- Was the project completed within the allocated budget?
- What would I do differently if I could start again?

Finally, you should rate the overall success of the project on a scale of 1-10.

You are now equipped with the right tools for tackling any future projects. Your professional reputation in the long term is dependent upon your ability to manage projects effectively.

Dealing with Difficult People

BRIAN SALTER
NAOMI LANGFORD-WOOD

WEEK FOUR

C O N T E N T S

Week Four

■I N T R O D U C T I O N■

Although it is actually part of life there can be nothing potentially more demoralising than having to deal with difficult people. When you have prepared yourself for the day with positive thoughts about what you have to do and what you'd like to achieve, and have a spring in your step as the day goes by, you can suddenly find the whole day 'ruined' by a brief encounter with a 'difficult person'. It upsets your state of mind and your sense of purpose and prospective achievement. You get to meet these difficult people everywhere – in your business dealings, bus queues and supermarkets, on the motorways and at airports, and in a whole variety of areas where stress can lead quite 'normal' people to behave rudely, impatiently or emotionally; or even a devastating combination of all three.

Sadly, many difficult people do not even realise that they are behaving badly; others, on the other hand, do so systematically because:

- It wrong foots us.
- It makes us feel uncomfortable, anxious, upset or angry.
- It instils a feeling of negativity in us.
- It coerces us into doing things we would rather not do.
- It prevents us from doing what we would like to do.
- It makes us feel guilty if we do not go along with their wishes.
- They chose an arm's-length communications medium which stops us from feeling we have any say.

In short, it makes them feel they have the upper hand in our lives.

In the workplace, perhaps more so than anywhere else, learning to handle difficult people can result in getting the best out of them, and by a natural extension, the best out of us, whether they are fellow workers, aggressive managers, customers or suppliers. 'Charm School' training within the area of customer support is considered essential but really applies to all areas of work.

Learning about what it is that may make these people behave in the way that they do can reduce our stress levels, and allow us to operate much more effectively, whilst at the same time ensuring that we become much more valued as team members amongst our peers – whatever our level within the business and whatever area of work we are in.

This week is a step-by-step guide to encourage managers to stop for a moment, to look for the warning signs in people's behavioural patterns before they get out of hand and disrupt others and the relationships essential to the smooth running of the workplace, and to analyse what it is that makes them tick.

After all, as difficult people rarely see themselves as difficult, they are most unlikely to think that they should read this. Quite a number of people tell themselves they have read it for management purposes rather than confront the fact that they might be difficult too – but not all the time.

Understanding yourself

To start at the beginning, we should perhaps define what we mean by the term 'difficult people'. When you interact with someone, the process is essentially two-way. Just as you will respond to the words and actions of another person, so they will do the same to you. To really understand yourself takes courage because there are always things that we really do not like about ourselves and which we would prefer to hide from our appraisal of our strengths and weaknesses.

Over time from the day we are born, we all get to learn what is expected in our behavioural patterns to elicit the best responses from those with whom we are having a dialogue. At birth, a simple yowl is usually sufficient to get mum to come rushing forward to feed us, clean us and give us a cuddle. Effectively, then, we are taught from birth that when we demand noisily enough, we get what we want or need.

As we get older, however, we learn pretty rapidly that it is a question not just of getting the meaning of the words right, but also of the expressions that go with those words, the epithets that add politeness, respect, or whatever feelings we want to go with them, and the gestures that can also accompany such a dialogue.

The patterns of our personality are set very early on in childhood. Events and other people will have caused us to grow up the way we have, with all the self-doubts and prejudices that we all have. The way in which our mothers and fathers treated us, for example, will have had a

S U N D A Y

SIBLING RIVALRY
WHEN HE WAS A
KID

profound effect on our sense of self-worth. It is all too easy
(and all too sad) for the most well-meaning adult to inflict
all kinds of mental scars on his or her children. Being over-
protective, for example, can lead a child to become over-
reliant on others to fight their battles, leaving little sense of
self-worth. Most parents do only what is best at the time in
their opinion and it is a great shock to them that something
they regarded as insignificant and perhaps have all but
forgotten, was a milestone in the life of the child.

Someone who has an unsettled childhood can also suffer in
later life from being unable to form positive relationships
with others. The effect of this is that they feel inadequate
and inferior to their peers. And so we have a potential ever-
decreasing spiral of self-image in the making, the behaviour
pattern of which is very difficult to jettison in adulthood.

These feelings of inadequacy translate into everyday
behaviour and actions. We are all a product of our
upbringing. When you next encounter the bullying type,
instead of reacting with the inner thoughts 'What have I

done to deserve this?', ask yourself what kind of an upbringing they might have had. Does he or she feel inadequate as a person, and are the bullying tactics perhaps a cover for the way he or she feels about themself? Ask yourself also why you have reacted in that manner – what is it about your inner self and sense of self-worth that makes that your first reaction?

Why are people difficult?

When we talk about dealing with difficult people, what we really mean is dealing with difficult behaviour. By learning to understand what it is that makes someone else behave and talk in a difficult way, we are in a better position not only to take charge of the situation, but also to help the other person resolve the conflicts that made him or her 'difficult' in the first place.

The crazy thing is that the natural way in which many of us react when we meet a difficult person is often more inclined to make that person's behaviour even more difficult. Ask yourself if you have ever reacted to someone by:

- Sharply answering back.
- Becoming defensive rather than dealing with the problematical issue.
- Ignoring the meaning of what they are saying because you are so annoyed with the way they have spoken to you.
- Feeling confused and frightened.
- Becoming speechless with rage.
- Becoming unable to think of anything else at the time.

S U N D A Y

The likelihood is that you will have experienced each of these reactions on numerous occasions. Many of us react in ways that make the problem worse, because we are reacting rather than thinking first. Yet, by stopping and thinking things through from the other person's perspective, by controlling the way we feel and attempting to act calmly and completely rationally, we can benefit in a number of ways:

- We will feel more in control of ourselves and our own destiny, as well as the situation as a whole.
- By reducing our emotional reactions, we will be better able to think clearly and objectively.
- We will feel less hampered by frustration or anger.
- We will feel better about ourselves for not having responded like with like.

So ask yourself – and be honest – do you let others dictate the way you feel about yourself? Turned round the other way, do you think your moods or actions could affect the behaviour and actions of another person? Depending on your current state of mind this may or may not be easy to answer. If you feel considerably discomforted by the potential grasping of the truth, then it might be a good idea to leave this until you have reflected overnight. As honest an appraisal of this now is vital to getting to grips with other people and their difficult behaviour – and how you are going to be able to cope with it better.

Let's face it, turning round a difficult person to become good-natured and easy to deal with is not something that you can achieve instantly – if at all. It may be that in time

you can make them appreciate how unreasonable their behaviour is, and get them to change their ways. Over the short term, if you cannot change them, then maybe the next best thing is to change the way you react. After all, it is invariably the recipient of his behaviour who gets hurt or demoralised, rather than the difficult person themself.

Communication is a two-way process

All communication is a series of reactions and counter-reactions, if you think about it. Your difficult person will react to what you say or write – and to your body language – in the same way as you will react to what he or she says. But if your reaction is different from what he or she is expecting, it is possible to break the cycle – to get him or her to counter-react in a different way from the way he or

S U N D A Y

she was expecting to do – and very often this has the effect of defusing the unpleasant situation and improving communication between the two of you. It can happen very fast.

Everyone reacts to awkwardness in a different way. It's not surprising when you consider that some people might be shy and retiring whilst others are extrovert and apparently over-confident. By making others feel low and bad about themselves, insecure people can give themselves a boost by inwardly telling themselves that they are better than others. By giving in to a bully, for instance, all you are doing is letting him or her win. But by responding in a calm and collected way, you can influence the way he or she counter-reacts to you, and often it is possible to do this without him or her even knowing.

We talked earlier on about the way in which you react to a difficult person. Do you normally answer back sharply to someone who needles you? Although perfectly natural, this response is hardly likely to improve the situation, except that in the short term you might feel better for being able to get your feelings off your chest. But what have you achieved? Difficult people are so used to behaving in a particular way, and leading their victims to react to them in such a way that they can then 'move in for the kill', that by denying them the wherewithal to play their trump card, you have effectively got the better of them. By not responding in a 'natural' way, you can break the cycle that your antagonist has set up for you to fall into. If you neither cower before a bullying manager, nor angrily explode at a subordinate, you effectively deny him or her the inner satisfaction of his or her own personal superiority factor; and when difficult behaviour no longer works, most such antagonists fall back into a more reasonable frame of mind – what else can they do?

Suppose that one of your clients shouts at you and creates a row for something that was clearly not your fault. (Many people manning telephone help desks get this kind of treatment on a regular basis.) You can respond in a number of ways. For instance, you could:

- Defend both yourself and your company.
- Be calm and identify the real problem.
- Concentrate on his problem, rather than on your own feelings, recognising that the client is angry with the present situation – not at you. There is therefore no need to defend yourself.

The first response is likely to satisfy neither you nor your client. So why do it? You are simply allowing yourself to become the punch bag of your frustrated client. But if you concentrate on his or her problem, rather than your own feelings, as in the second alternative, the client is more likely to end up in a positive frame of mind and think better both of you and of your company.

Frankly, the customer is not interested in who made the mistake in the first place. All he or she wants is the problem to be resolved and he or she is frustrated as well as being anxious as to whether the company will take his problem seriously; and you will stay calmer if you don't become all defensive. In short, both sides win.

So by taking a moment to reflect before you react, especially if you know that this person is difficult to deal with anyway, you have a much better chance of coming out on top. Simply having a shouting match brings you down to his or her level and achieves nothing at all – and it potentially creates a stalemate situation, which is even more difficult to resolve.

Similarly, if one of your fellow workers shouts at you, for whatever reason, which of the following scenarios is most likely to be conducive to a healthy outcome?

- You fly into a rage and tell them what you think of him or her.
- You pause and tell them in a calm and controlled manner that you feel angry about what has just been said.

The first scenario is almost guaranteed to get him or her to scream back at you, and in the end neither of you will take the slightest notice of what the other is saying, regardless of whether there is any truth in what one or the other of you is saying. The second scenario, on the other hand, is far more assertive, and by controlling your emotions, you will also have much more likelihood of getting your point of view across.

If this person has a reputation for being difficult generally, it should also help that you know instinctively that it is not really you that is being attacked. Admittedly, it can still be pretty unpleasant being on the receiving end of such behaviour, but at least you can hold your head up knowing that if anyone is inadequate, it is not you. You therefore also need to identify and then come to terms with the impact your behaviour has on others – good or bad.

The classic example ...

How often have you been driving along a road when some inconsiderate motorist overtakes a whole stream of cars on a bend and all but causes an accident to happen in the process? It is, unfortunately, all too common an experience these days. The natural reaction of many is one of fury: to swear at the careless driver and to fume at all inconsiderate motorists. But in the process, your concentration lapses and your driving may suffer as a consequence. And the corollary of this is that other people then sound their horns because they are suffering from the bad driving of someone else. Meanwhile, the original driver who caused all the problems in the first place is miles away, probably upsetting yet more people at this very moment.

In this case, the ones to suffer are the 'victims' of that first bad driver. Anger would have been the perfectly natural reaction, but it has achieved nothing except to allow the actions of someone else to affect their feelings and judgement.

In the same way, if you allow yourself to become stressed at the behaviour of others, don't be surprised if the one to suffer most is you. Not only will you fail to get an adequate response from your protagonists, but you will, more than likely, be the one who is left feeling exhausted and emotionally drained.

Feeling inadequate

But getting angry with difficult people is not the only harmful way of reacting to them. It is just as bad if you don't stand up to them or if you make excuses and become all defensive. Think what you are saying to them with these kinds of responses. 'You're probably right and I'm really the one in the wrong.' Is that what you want to convey?

And what about feelings of negativity? Suppose you are due to go for an interview next Tuesday and you spend the previous week thinking of all the reasons why you may *not* get the job or be put in charge of that project. Think about it: not only may your feelings of negativity cause you to see the worst in every situation, but it will also cause others to see the negative aspects in you. Rest assured, then, that if you go into the interview in this frame of mind, you will certainly not convey the best impression to the interviewer, thus confirming your worst fears to your inner self. And worse still, the entire week may have been ruined by your fear of the unknown.

Now think things through the opposite way round. Begin by making up a list of all the bad things that have happened to you this week. Study it well and ask yourself if any of these things would have happened without you there anyway. Now make a list of all the *good* things that have recently happened to you and of all the *good* characteristics that you can boast of. Doesn't it put it all into perspective?

We know of one married couple, who were going through a difficult patch, who every night wrote out a 'disaster diary' of everything that had gone wrong that day. It didn't matter how small or how annoying the 'disaster' was; everything got entered into that book. The wonderful thing was that when they read a given entry the following day or the next week or whenever, what had at the time appeared to be something dreadful became in time totally insignificant. The effect was that their marriage improved dramatically, and the feelings of negativity which had at one time appeared to hover over them like a black cloud, simply evaporated away.

So what do others think of you?

We have so far talked about the reactions we have to difficult people. But have you ever really stopped to think about how others see *you*? It's all too easy to think that the way we see ourselves is the *same* as the way others see us. In fact, the opposite is much closer to the truth. Perhaps you believe it is important to say what you are thinking, regardless of the consequences. But how would you feel if someone treated you in the same way? In causing others distress by the things that you say, you are then no different from the difficult person that you suffered from before. How will others, then, regard you? The likelihood is that they will turn away from you, and you will end up feeling isolated. And it will be your fault entirely. Don't be surprised, then, if this leads you into more negativity in the way you treat others, and your behaviour gives others cause for concern.

What, then, can we do about it?
Despite our upbringing and effects that parents and other mentors have had on us, the fact is that the way we think

of ourselves is not some immovable concept cast in stone. The great thing to realise is that we can actually choose to change our self-image.

We all have mini-disasters in our lives. Perhaps none are so public as those of professional sportspeople competing in international competitions. Even the best champion ice-skaters fall over; Premier Division footballers miss easy goals; and many a great cricketer has chided himself for being bowled out. But all of them realise that nothing is served by punishing oneself after the event. The ice-skater picks himself up and carries on; the footballer concentrates on lining up another goal; and as for the cricketer – well there is always another day!

It is only worth looking back at one's failures if there is a lesson to be learnt from them. And if you do learn from a mistake, then it can be regarded as something positive – not something to be ashamed of. So leave your failures behind you where they belong: in the past.

In the same way, you should try to build on your successes. Make a mental list of everything that you like about yourself. Even if you feel you are in the depths of depression, there is always something that you can find to add to that list if you think hard enough. People who have a poor image of themselves, for instance, often think that they can think of nothing good to say. The truth is, however, that such people are often highly sensitive and tend to be kind and compassionate. If those characteristics applied to a stranger that you met, you would react positively to them. So react positively about yourself and continue the list in that vein.

Now try listing the good things that have happened to you throughout your life. Everyone has successes, however small. Recall how good you felt when you had achieved those successes.

By learning to improve your self-image, you are more likely to be able to resist the damaging words and actions of difficult people; and by gaining a better insight into yourself you will automatically gain an insight into the way others act and speak; you may even begin to understand why they are acting the way they are; and once you can begin to feel pity for someone, however dreadful a person they are, you will find you no longer feel hurt by the things they say to you.

Later in this week you will learn the techniques of how to deal with all manner of difficult people in a variety of situations. By learning to deal with their moods and their own feelings of inadequacy, you will be more likely to succeed in coping with them and turn a potentially negative situation into one which will prove to be positive for both parties.

S U N D A Y

Summary

Today we have seen how the patterns of our personality are set very early on in childhood. In successfully dealing with difficult people, the key factor is to understand what makes them behave in the way they do. So the things we have to consider are:

- Perception of self-worth is often a main constituent of peoples' personalities.
- Many of us react too quickly in ways that can make a problem worse.
- Everyone reacts differently to awkward situations.
- By becoming stressed in a difficult situation, you are likely to suffer more.
- We can all choose to change our self-image and build on our successes.

So, by learning to improve our self-image we are more likely to be able to resist the words and actions of difficult people.

Different styles of behaviour

When we talk about the different styles of behaviour of individuals, it is very easy to impart an almost limitless number of descriptions. For instance such people could be thought of as ogres, wimps, bullies, lecherous, uncaring, dominating, and so on. Yet, when you think of it, almost every behavioural style can be subsumed into one of three main categories:

1 Passive
2 Aggressive
3 Assertive

When dealing with difficult people it is important to be able to recognise the signs that they are exhibiting and to see these for what they are. That way, you can minimise the effects that they have on you, for it is a truism that you can really only expect to influence others when you can see them as they are, rather than as they would wish to be portrayed, or as you wish they were. Understanding someone's behaviour does not necessarily imply that you approve of it, but it does mean that you can cope with it, at worst, and work with it, at best.

Passive behaviour

Passive behaviour is most typified by people who put other people's needs before their own. Whilst on the one hand this can be an attractive trait in some, it can also show that they have little respect for themselves, especially when they are reluctant to stand up for their rights. The result is that

M O N D A Y

they are often put upon by others, even by those who are not normally aggressive.

The passive person is usually pretty insecure and will often show signs of an inferiority complex. Just as they have little respect for their own abilities and will often talk down their gifts, their own feelings of inadequacy are reinforced every time they meet an aggressive type, and are more likely to take criticism as justified without stopping to consider if that is in fact the case. They will often accept the criticism, and only at a later date will they question its validity. So, the passive person is often frustrated by their own inability to be assertive.

This hapless individual is also likely to be angry with themselves since they can see how others take advantage; yet is unlikely to do anything to improve the situation as they sincerely believe that others will not take them seriously. This in turn causes them to experience even greater feelings of inadequacy, and the whole situation becomes a vicious circle.

M O N D A Y

In summary, a passive person is likely to feel:

- Angry, because they know only too well that others are all too ready to take advantage and they find it difficult not to let them.
- Anxious, because they feel out of control of their own destiny.
- Negative, because he or she feels that whatever he or she does, he or she is unlikely to get his or her way.
- Insecure, because he or she lacks self-confidence and is afraid of trying out anything new since he or she 'knows' instinctively that he or she will fail anyway.
- Frustrated, because he or she believes he cannot get his or her own way.
- Withdrawn, because no-one 'wants to listen to him or her'.
- Lacking in energy, because everything he or she does is to satisfy someone else's desires, rather than his or her own.

The descriptions of passive behaviour above may appear at first reading to be extreme, and to an extent this is indeed the case; however, although the degree of passivity may vary, such people are all around us.

Now, wouldn't your first reaction in meeting such a person be one of sympathy for him or her and to want to help him or her boost their confidence? Well, unless you were a natural aggressor, you might well feel that. However, it is remarkable that after a very short time, the majority of those trying to help can end up feeling annoyed with the person for not trying to stand up for themself. This in turn can lead to an aggressive attitude towards that person because they have all but invited others to lose any kind of respect, and so they end up treating them the way they come to expect to be treated!

When you try to compliment a passive person, they will often reject what you say. It can, indeed, be quite tiring coping with someone who is so negative in everything they do and say, and it can also cause guilt feelings in oneself because you can feel responsible for that person being taken advantage of. Because of this, many will avoid passive, negative people, and this only acts to shore up their own feelings of inadequacy.

So just as passive people feel bad about themselves, others dealing with passive people can feel:

- Annoyed, because they wish they would just stand up for themselves occasionally.
- Worn out, because they feel they are wasting valuable energy dealing with their own negative reactions to such behaviour.
- Superior, because they have lost respect for someone who is unwilling to stand up for themself.
- Withdrawn, because such a negative attitude undermines their own positive attitude.
- Negative because of the amount of time needed to boost the passive person's ego before beginning to do the work or task in hand.

Aggressive behaviour

Aggressive behaviour can best be summed up as satisfying one's own needs at the expense of others. Such a person is often a verbal bully who enjoys a feeling of power over other people. But just as physical bullying is often the outward manifestation of someone who is cowardly by nature, oddly enough, aggressive behaviour is often the result of feelings of inadequacy and lack of self-worth. In that respect, aggressive behaviour is the classic bedfellow of the passive-behaviour person.

Aggressive people are also, as often as not, lonely. Their behaviour results in others shunning them, both in their personal lives and at work. They are so busy reassuring themselves that they are the best, that they end up being overly critical of others. Nothing is ever *their* fault, and by extension, anything that goes wrong is due to someone else. Their lack of self-esteem does not allow them to admit faults.

People who exhibit aggressive tendencies often feel:

- Energetic, except that their energy is often destructive rather than constructive.
- Powerful, because they enjoy having others rush around carrying out their orders.
- Somewhat guilty, since they know they take advantage of others.
- Lonely, because their aggression alienates them from other people.
- That they are always right, and that they have a monopoly of good ideas.
- Threatened, in case others might see through the veneer of outward confidence.
- Exasperated by the passive people who don't share their energy and speed.

M O N D A Y

Some people are inclined to mistake aggression for strength and act accordingly, in the belief that if they show others a 'soft underbelly', they will be regarded as weak. But such behaviour is more inclined to have the reverse effect on others, who may feel angry or frustrated because they might be powerless to do anything about it. For instance, if a manager behaves in such a way to a subordinate, the latter may be fearful of losing their job if they tell their boss exactly what they think of him or her. The 'victim' will therefore be resentful of the way in which they have been treated, but the aggressor may not even realise that they have caused such feelings in the subordinate. The end result is one of a breakdown in communication, with a resulting lack of efficiency and with neither party understanding where 'things have gone wrong'. In these cases it can be a very uphill job to rescue the situation once the patterns of behaviour have been established.

So, people who exhibit aggressive behaviour can cause *others* to feel:

- Defensive, because they feel that anything they do will be attacked unfairly.
- Resentful, because the aggressor appears to wield power unfairly.
- Threatened, because they resent such tactics.
- Humiliated, because no-one likes to be made a fool of.
- Frustrated, because they are always having to be on the defensive.
- Withdrawn, because they try to avoid possible confrontations with the aggressor.

M O N D A Y

Those who deal regularly with an aggressive person are inclined to suffer high levels of stress, and this can have a damaging effect on their well-being. The aggressor, on the other hand, enjoys his apparent feelings of power since it appears to boost their authority. The result is that people tend to avoid aggressors if they possibly can, which in turn leads the latter to believe they are somehow special. And this makes them act even more aggressively, and once again we have a vicious circle.

Assertive behaviour

The third category of person that we mentioned at the start of this chapter is the *assertive person*. This person is concerned not only for their own rights and opinions, but also for the rights and opinions of others. In trying to obtain a win–win situation with others, the assertive person is willing to make compromises in a positive way, at the same time arguing their corner for what they passionately believe in.

Because respect plays an important part in the assertive

M O N D A Y

person's attitude, it engenders respect in the attitudes of others with whom they are in daily contact, encouraging them to co-operate as fully as possible with that person. This in itself produces a healthy atmosphere in which creative work can be carried out and in which people know their work will be appreciated by others. All in all, this then leads those others to do their level best to perform even better, whatever the job in hand.

An assertive person is also one who is able to understand their own feelings and can impart how they feel to others. The trick is to be able to explain what you feel in such a way that you will not cause others to resent what you say. The reality is that people are much more comfortable knowing where they stand, even if there is implied criticism of their position, rather than having to guess at the real meaning behind the words.

Being assertive means you can be proud of your successes; but equally it means that you are not conceited about your achievements. It also means that you can learn from your mistakes, that no-one has a monopoly on good ideas and that others can catch the enthusiasm that is such a characteristic of the assertive person.

People who can best be described as assertive often exhibit the following tendencies:

- They approach new tasks in a positive frame of mind.
- They are enthusiastic in their approach.
- They are honest in dealing with others.
- They are energetic, and direct that energy into reaching their goals.
- They have good communication skills with others.

- They are willing to take risks, but at the same time they know their own limitations.
- They understand that other people have needs and feelings just as they do.

Assertive people are generally the ones other people most like to be associated with. Because they are not seen as manipulative, people work easily with them. Because their behaviour is consistent, communication by whatever medium is open and trusted. Regular communication lets others know what is expected of them, and so the whole team is able to turn its energies to achieving goals, rather than infighting and self-recrimination.

When dealing with assertive people, others are most likely to feel positive because:

- They sense that their success is a shared success.
- They know where they stand.
- They can reciprocate feelings of respect.
- They can direct their energies into constructive areas.
- They feel they can trust you and respond to your positive influence by helping you.
- They will find the enthusiasm contagious.

Now, from the above, it must be perfectly clear that the most desirable camp to be in is the assertive group. Most of us, however, exhibit a mixture of different styles, and so to succeed in minimising the negative effects of difficult behavioural patterns in others, it is necessary to move oneself as far as possible into the assertive area.

M O N D A Y

Who wins, after all?

Passive people rarely achieve their own goals because they seldom identify their own goals in the first place, relying on others to give them a lead.

Aggressive people often achieve their goals in the short term, but often this is at the expense of others and this fact can then backfire on them at a later date when they come face to face with antagonism and retaliation from those whom they have put down in the past. Worse still, there is no loyalty engendered in others during the process of 'winning', and so there is no pool of loyalty on which they can draw when times get tough.

It is assertive people who usually achieve their goals because in their view everyone can win. They are willing to negotiate for what is right rather than for short-term expediency, and they gain the respect of others whilst doing so. Enlightened self-awareness can enable us to get into the right attitude to make the most of our own assertiveness, but we will deal with this later.

On Wednesday and Thursday we will see how putting ourselves into the balanced assertiveness camp can help us

in handling conflict as well as with our basic
communication skills.

Summary

Most styles of behaviour can be categorised in three basic
ways:

1 Passive
2 Aggressive
3 Assertive

and in order to be able to deal with difficult people
successfully, you need to recognise them for what they are.

- What would you say are the main characteristics of
  each?
- Which would you rather be yourself?
- Can you identify the most difficult person in your life
  at the moment? In what style of behaviour would
  you categorise him or her?

Coping with different problem people

What do we mean by problem people? They come in all shapes and sizes, but the one common trait that they all exhibit is a type of behaviour that gives someone else a problem.

If you put your mind to it, you would probably be able to come up with at least 50 different types of behaviour that can cause problems for others. Being able to distinguish and categorise a particular type of behaviour will put you in a much better position to be able to do something about it. Of course, you could always ignore the problem, but that isn't very constructive and could even make the problem worse for others as well as for yourself. If you cannot even recognise what it is that someone does or says that causes problems for others, how on earth are you going to be able to improve that person's behaviour for the future – or, more to the point, your reaction to it?

Not all people problems are necessarily daunting. Some types of behaviour might be a trifle irritating, but are easy enough to shrug off without anything further needing to be done. Others, on the other hand, seem to have a never-ending impact and they can leave you feeling totally at a loss to work out how best to cope.

Very often, the person whose behaviour causes problems is totally unaware of the conflict he or she causes for others. That being the case, it works out that the person who has to deal with the problem is actually you. You have to 'own' the problem, just as if you were 'owning' a problem of late delivery or poor quality production in a factory.

Yet, however inconsiderate or boorish someone else's behaviour, it is equally true that we all react to one another, and the way someone else reacts to you has a feedback effect on the way you behave in the first place. Sometimes we are therefore actually responsible for the problematic behaviour in others. Whilst one could regard this as part and parcel of life's rich tapestry, it does matter, not least because:

- It creates unnecessary stress, leading to low morale.
- It wastes time, because effort is being expended on griping instead of on productive work and relationships.
- It distorts the decision-making process, since those who display difficult behaviour are often circumvented in order to ease the burden on others.
- It can encourage a selective emigration of the best employees to more conducive working environments.
- It stops work being in any way fun.

When encountering a difficult person for the first time, it is all too easy to hate them or to label them as deficient in some way without properly understanding what it is that they are going through. Yet if you are serious about wanting to change his or her behaviour, you will only be able to do so if you learn to understand them from their point of view. Pigeonholing people on sight is one of the most destructive things you can do within a workplace or community.

Within a work environment, it might appear that those with behavioural problems can be broken down into three main categories:

1 your supervisors
2 your subordinates
3 your fellow co-workers

The supervisors might be poor motivators, aggressive, or have poor supervisory skills; the subordinates might be error-prone, daydreamers, time wasters, or dishonest; whilst the co-workers might exhibit unprofessional behaviour such as putting things off, 'passing the buck', being overly critical or shirking.

Whilst the way in which you might deal with the person will vary, depending on where they are in the hierarchical structure relative to you, each of these categories of worker can display common behavioural problems. So let's look at some of the more common types of behaviour and consider how we might deal with them.

Although there are very many types of personality display, we have chosen to break down the different behavioural patterns into four main categories:

1 *insecure* – one of the most basic reasons for people displaying problematic behaviour;
2 *negative* – it can be very wearing to deal with this when exposed to such behaviour for long periods;
3 *selfish* – whether they are consciously so or oblivious to the fact that they are what they are, these types are easier to diagnose and to 'turn around';

> **4** *pleasant* – this is sometimes the most difficult type of behaviour to deal with as you do not want to hurt their feelings.

Insecure people

Insecurity in people can take a number of forms. In its most basic, the insecure person needs to boost their own self-image, but the problem is that they do this by criticising others. The eternal put-down can be very wearing, and if this then turns into your being hurt or even becoming openly hostile in return, it can have a bad effect on any kind of working relationship.

Perhaps worse still is the type who is, on the surface, perfectly pleasant to begin with, until something that most would regard as quite innocuous causes him or her to lose control and let fly with insults. Basically, this type of person has never quite got over the habit of childhood tantrums and is turning on a defence mechanism; perhaps they feel personally threatened, or under pressure. Their immediate reaction, therefore, is to react before anyone has even launched an attack.

Insecurity also makes itself felt by the ponderous types who either cannot make up their minds, or will always find some reason for putting off any kind of action. It may be that this kind of person has such low self-esteem that they are afraid that anything they do will be wrong, even though they genuinely want to help. Equally, however, it may be that they simply do not feel that anyone else's efforts are good enough, and having asked someone to do something for them, they will then set about doing exactly the same task alone just to 'make sure' that the information, or whatever, is adequate. This can be taken to extremes by their forever trumpeting their triumphs and focusing everything on themselves, rather than focusing on the job in hand or other people.

On a bad day, dealing with insecure people can leave you wondering whether the effort is worthwhile. Yet all such responses need to attempt to build up that person's self-esteem by not knocking them down – perhaps subconsciously – expecting that very reaction. Reassurance is all, but in addition you should attempt:

- Never to snap back, since this is what he or she may expect, and so by refraining from doing so you are breaking a vicious circle.
- To be assertive in attempting to find out what the problem is from their point of view and to understand what is troubling them.
- To remain absolutely silent if he or she is throwing a temper tantrum, and only then to ask him or her to explain.
- To set deadlines for those normally incapable of setting timescales for themselves. This gives them confidence that it is not just they who are having to take responsibility for meeting deadlines.

You can also use humour to get you through difficult times with problem people. Some even recommend conjuring up a mental image of the difficult person to relieve the stress of having to be on the receiving end of some of his tirades.

For instance, if your boss throws a temper tantrum, try picturing him or her still wearing a nappy and throwing his or her toy out of his pram. Such an image can do wonders to keep oneself calm whilst others around are losing their cool.

Negative people

Negativity in a person is also very tiring to deal with and can be extremely depressing because if one is not careful it can almost infect you – in the same way that one person yawning in a room can often 'infect' others with the same action.

Such people may well be trying to protect themselves from future failure, but in so doing their immediate reaction is to ask 'What's the point ... ?' Rarely will they come up with any better suggestions for carrying out a task. Worse, if you attempt to offer an alternative solution you are likely to get a similar negative response.

Another type of negative person is the aggressive, verbal bully – the type who believes they know better than anyone

T U E S D A Y

else how something should be done and doesn't waste a moment in telling everyone of their infallibility. They will often tell you that you are wasting your time because you are not doing things their way. As often as not they are very thorough and highly efficient, but that does not stop others from feeling resentment and ignoring them on principle.

The first thing when dealing with such people is not to let their negativity invade you. In addition you could:

- Try to get them to explain why they feel that way.
- Tell him that as you are convinced in your own mind as to the right course of action, you will do so anyway, regardless of whether they are 'with' you or not.
- Resist wasting time arguing.
- Make sure you have done your homework before tackling the negative, assertive bully.
- Ask yourself whether at the end of the day it is worth dealing with such a person anyway – assuming that's possible – since they are unlikely to change their behaviour and will continue to give you grief for some time to come!

Selfish people

Selfish people often act the way they do without pausing to consider for one moment that what they are doing is destructive or hurtful to others. Sometimes they are as they are because in childhood their parents had never trained them out of their natural selfish state that we are all born with. (Consider a baby crying, for instance. As far as it is concerned, its comforts are all that matters, and naturally, it has not yet learned that others have needs too.)

Selfish people will often be so busy telling others of their thoughts and needs, that they may be oblivious to the fact that others might have something to say, or an opinion to share. Those who bulldoze their way through life can be extremely disruptive in a work environment. Since they are so busy trying to get their own way, their co-workers may put up with this for a while, but soon they start to build up resentment which leads them to ostracise that person, or worse still, they may lose their temper with them. However, that is the last thing one should do since the selfish person will invariably win this type of 'argument'.

Another type of selfish behaviour is displayed by a fundamentally aggressive person who is covert in his or her attacks on others. The end result of this person's making jokes at others' expense, normally behind their backs, can be that the victim is much more hurt than he or she would be if the 'joke' had been made out in the open. If the victim then takes offence, the aggravator can accuse the victim of being a bad sport, or of not being able to 'take a joke'.

This type of person thrives in front of an audience but will rarely continue such behaviour in private. So, to attempt to change his or her behaviour, you should:

- Get them on their own, explain what they are doing and ask if they are genuinely trying to hurt you.
- Avoid getting into an argument with them, but do stand up to them and keep your body language assertive.
- Not sound either angry or submissive as this will feed their feelings of superiority.
- If they are making derogatory remarks about you behind your back, suggest that in future they make them directly to you. They won't!

Pleasant people

Perhaps the most difficult people to deal with are those who are on the surface pleasant in their ways. This is because it makes us feel guilty to confront them with their problematic behaviour, especially if they react in a manner that shows that they are hurt that anyone could have found something wrong with them.

Not all pleasant, problematic people are wimps, of course. Whilst some might keep a low profile because they are genuinely confused, others may be perfectly nice but just unreliable. Yet again, someone might be anxious to gain respect and friendship, but be unwilling to make any efforts to achieve this.

Some unreliable people need so much to feel liked by everyone, that they will promise to do all kinds of things, and only subsequently realise that they cannot deliver their promises. They then feel obliged to make even more promises to make up for their earlier shortcomings, and a vicious circle sets in.

Although it can be embarrassing to deal with such people, they are probably the most worthwhile in the end to have to deal with since there is a good chance that you can turn them around to face the realities of a situation and they can then become valued players in a team. The trick here is to offer reassurance that they are likeable and that their views are valued, just so long as they are willing to say what they think, rather than agree with everyone simply to make the peace.

In addition, you should:

- Keep your body language open and friendly.
- Reassure them that you value their opinions.
- Pay them compliments, so long as these are genuine, in order to demonstrate that they really are valued members of the team.
- Encourage them to come up with suggestions and solutions to problems.
- Help them save face by stating the facts, rather than your opinions, and then getting them to suggest ideas of their own.

We said at the beginning of this chapter that it should be easy enough to think of at least 50 different types of problematic behaviour. The four main categories that we have just looked at will not necessarily encompass every one, just as many problem people will exhibit characteristics of more than one of them. But by reaching

T U E S D A Y

out and attempting to understand what it is that drives people to behave in the way that they do, you will have a better chance of being able to turn them around from being a difficult person to a valued member of your team.

Summary

We have spent Tuesday looking at behavioural problems exhibited by difficult people. If you really want to change their behaviour, the best way forward is to try to see how the world looks through their eyes.

- Is your difficult person basically insecure, negative, selfish or pleasant?
- How do you think you should approach dealing with them now?
- How do you think you should modify your behaviour when dealing with them?
- Is this achievable?

Managing conflict situations

Unfortunately, there is nothing unusual about conflict. It is an integral part of life, and without the differences between us we would all be the poorer. Just imagine how boring things would become if we all thought and reacted in the same way!

But just as, paradoxically, we need conflict to brighten up our lives, we also need to be able to manage it so that it does not get out of hand and start to dominate a situation, for in that case it can lead to highly stressful times.

Conflicts invariably stem from one root cause: in essence both sides want to have their own way, and unless a compromise is achieved, conflict is inevitable. Throughout our lives, we have to come to terms with the conflicting forces of logic and emotion. Sometimes it is all too easy to react emotionally, but inevitably it is when our reactions are based on logic that we are better able to handle difficult circumstances. We must also not forget that the emotional content of our relationships gives them their raison d'être and comfort zones – as well as the potential for conflict. Emotion must be valued too.

To many people, it is much more difficult to get into gear with a logical approach, but it is, nonetheless, perfectly possible to develop the ability to use logic by first analysing the situation and then applying techniques to control your feelings and reactions instead of allowing your emotions to rule the day.

It is really down to a question of:

- Let's step back and look at the situation a bit more clearly.
- Let's get the emotion out of this.
- How can we move this situation forward toward achieving the common objectives?

Only then can individual problems and sensitivities be accommodated rather than their dominating and waylaying progress within the relationships.

There are, of course, many reasons for conflict between two parties. For instance:

- each may wish to achieve different goals
- there is a difference in the perception of the problems involved
- there is a clash of personality which stifles communication
- each party may be in competition with one another
- either party might not want the responsibility imposed by a certain course of action
- there is poor communication

Although such conflict can cause depression or apathy, it is equally true that many stressful situations can lead to positive results, such as the generation of enthusiasm or the finding of a solution to a problem that had remained stubbornly impenetrable. So the problem is not actually a situation where there is conflict, but more one where the conflict is negative – where stress turns itself into distress.

The real danger of stressful conflict is that it can be so damaging. For instance:

- it can divert attention away from the real issues behind the conflict, and the objectives can be lost
- one or both parties to the conflict can become so frustrated that it impedes a settlement, and ultimately one or both sides become unco-operative

Many conflict situations arise because one of the parties feels that someone is attempting to take advantage of them, or because they feel they have to defend themself against an aggressive person. Basically, when any conflict situation arises there are three possible outcomes:

1 both sides can pretend there is really no problem. If the matter is not particularly important, then this can often be the best outcome;

2 one person wins, whilst the other loses. This may solve the present conflict, but it can cause an imbalance that can lead to a build-up of resentment and make it more difficult to resolve the next crisis point;

3 each person understands that the final solution has to take account of both parties' wishes. By working to a common goal, both sides have to make compromises, but the final solution is stronger because of this.

W E D N E S D A Y

In understanding what situations lead to conflict, a person will more easily be able to avoid it. There are, of course, no hard and fast rules about reducing potential conflicts, but the following list demonstrates some of the areas which are ripe for examination:

- By attempting to see things from other people's points of view, you are better able to accept that no one person is ever always right or wrong.
- It is equally not possible for everyone always to agree on everything. By accepting the fact that compromise is better than conflict, you are better able to find a way forward, rather than wallowing in an impasse.
- Many of us are all too prone to make snap judgements. It follows from the above that if we can hear out the other person without jumping to conclusions, we will be better able to find a way forward.

When it comes to recognising the early stages of a conflict in the making, very often the cause has more to do with the characters involved, rather than the situation itself. For, if logic is the most positive way of resolving a conflict, then it follows that wherever emotion gets a stranglehold, then a resolution can become more difficult.

When it comes to determining different personality types with regard to handling conflict, most people can be diagnosed as being in one of four basic categories: *dictatorial, enthusiastic, empathetic* and a *processor*.

Dictators

Perhaps the most difficult type of personality to come to terms with, dictatorial people tend to be egoists in the extreme. They always want to have their own way and will often bulldoze people into submission. Often they can be extremely hurtful because they say what they think regardless of how others will react. They are totally results-oriented and have little time for individuals.

The problem in dealing with such people is that being aggressive in return is generally counter-productive. Similarly, acting submissively will only reinforce their feelings of superiority. The only sure way of interacting with a dictator is to deal in facts, for to them, facts are an extension of logic. This will also enable you to get to the heart of the matter at the earliest opportunity, and to reach a solution. They may well have alienated you in the process, but ultimately that will be their problem. The main thing to ensure is that it should not be yours!

Enthusiastic people

Enthusiasts are normally energetic and have a strong ability to motivate others. They can often be described as charismatic and are often popular. Enthusiasts are sometimes want to talk rapidly and loudly, but ultimately if they do not get the necessary feedback they are more likely to drop out of a project before seeing it through to completion.

Dealing with enthusiasts requires you to be almost as energetic as they are. Offering support and encouragement are the most likely ways to get the best out of them and to work with them – and to get any project happily completed.

Empathisers

Into this camp fall what are sometimes referred to as 'people persons'. They are typically genuinely caring but are not the best at getting things done in a hurry, and can be frustratingly indecisive.

Accordingly, if you want to get the best from empathisers it is wise not to hurry them, and to listen attentively to what they have to say.

Processors

Such people, who may appear somewhat tedious or boring on the outside, nevertheless exhibit analytical skills that involve paying great attention to detail. They are usually efficient, if a little on the unimaginative side, and organised in the extreme. Processor types often end up in professions such as accountancy where accuracy and detail are paramount; but it is not for nothing that comedians tend to use them for the butt of their jokes (e.g.: Monty Python's 'Ich bin ein Chartered Accountant' sketch).

Dealing with processor types invariably works well when presenting them with logic and facts. They are not always the fastest thinkers as they like to assimilate new information, building on, and assessing it with, what they already know. In addition they invariably lack vision and, as a result, take longer to buy in to a new concept.

As we have said, not everyone falls precisely into one category or another. But it soon becomes clear, when taking these four basic types, that conflict can easily arise if, for instance, a processor comes into discussion with a

dictatorial person, or an enthusiast has to deal with an empathiser.

Just as it can be quite exasperating to deal with colleagues at work, it is often even more problematic dealing with difficult clients or customers. The old axiom that 'the client is always right' may well form the backbone of customer service, but it can leave employees feeling frustrated and stressed.

Those at the receiving end of a customer's anger – be they at the end of a phone, or in a meeting face to face, or increasingly by electronic communication – are often the main point of contact between a client and a company, and so they become the butt of the client's anger. Yet, reacting in an impatient or insensitive manner is not the way to get the customer to move over to your point of view, and certainly not the stuff of professional customer relationships and service.

■■■■ W E D N E S D A Y ■■■■

Nowadays, especially, where customer service is what differentiates one company from another in an increasingly global marketplace, any form of negative behaviour or reaction from a company employee could result in a customer staying away and taking their business elsewhere, which is considerably easier since the arrival of the World Wide Web. Worse still, the customer may tell friends and they could stay away too. Trying to win customers back is twice as difficult as getting them in the first place – as if that wasn't hard enough! So, the way in which an employee acts with, and reacts to, a customer can be far more important than the advertising or PR that a company puts together to build up its image.

Successfully dealing with difficult clients necessitates putting yourself in the client's shoes and understanding what it is that makes them annoyed, or even more basically, what they wanted in the first place. There are at least two sides from which to look at every situation, and people don't generally complain unless they have something specific to 'beef' about.

In general, a customer can get annoyed with a company for one of five main reasons:

1 they feel no-one will listen to them;
2 something went wrong, and they feel no-one is willing to accept responsibility or make redress;
3 they need help or guidance, but can find no-one to give it;
4 the product does not work, or the service provided is inadequate;

5 they thought through and planned everything to do with the purchase or installation, and yet it still went wrong.

By finding out what it is that the client is unhappy about, you can then concentrate on solving the problem. Remember, the customer is not necessarily interested in a third party finding a solution. As far as they are concerned, you are the company representative and so it is up to you to find a solution. Your blaming another part of the organisation will only inflame the situation further.

It may not, of course, be possible for you to be the solution provider. So what should you do? The first thing is to attempt to find a position of empathy with the customer's plight. Nothing is more frustrating than feeling that no-one understands your problem. So, by showing understanding and getting over to the customer's side, you are immediately getting rid of their first frustration. Only then should you start to help deal with the problem.

Sometimes, customers are not really sure what they do want apart from tearing someone off a strip for the wrongs they feel they have suffered. So a good technique is, having empathised with their situation, to ask what they would like you to do to help out. It may well be that you personally can't help them in this case; so state what you can do, offering one or two alternatives. You have effectively returned control of the situation to the customer. Sometimes there will be nothing at all that you can do – in which case you will need to explain the company's policies and try to find a common solution. By spending time showing sympathy and understanding, you might not have put

things totally to rights, but your client will know that they are not likely to get the brush-off – which is what angers people the most.

Dealing with someone face to face is often easier than doing so over the telephone, email or fax because you can use body language to convey your feelings. However, there are some standard dos and don'ts when dealing with difficult clients over the phone:

- You should always follow the '3 Ps' code: come across as professional, polite and pleasant.
- The caller must be made to feel important.
- You should try to avoid wasting not just the caller's time, but the company's time as well.
- You want to help the caller achieve their desired objectives.

Email has its own dos and don'ts.

- Address the customer with respect.
- Deal with the problems succinctly.
- Be aware that the immediate nature of the medium can exacerbate misunderstandings.

- Ensure you build a personal relationship rather than remain anonymous.

Whether the conflict situation is over the email or phone or face to face, you should always remain cool and calm and do your best to appear concerned but impartial at all times. There is nothing wrong with expressing contradictory ideas, but the secret is in knowing how to put them across without it escalating into a heated debate.

At the end of the day, it is not the fact that you have a contradictory idea that causes problems; more, it is the fact that two personality traits come into opposition. The first should not be smothered; the latter should be circumvented if at all possible.

Summary

On Wednesday we looked at the likely causes of conflict and why they can lead to such damaging and stressful situations. When you look logically at the people involved, bearing in mind the emotional content:

- Can you identify the goals that each has?
- Does each see the problem the same way?
- Is there a problem of 'personal chemistry'?
- Are they all working to the same objectives?
- Are any of them reluctant to stand up and be counted?
- Are there any communications problems?
- What are the *real* issues anyway?

If you have a situation of real conflict now, or can see one
arising, can you identify which personality type best
describes the difficult person with whom you have to deal?

Basic communication skills and body language

Communication is at the heart of any relationship between two people; and very often a lack of good communication is the single most important barrier to getting on with a so-called 'difficult person'.

Anyone who feels they are consistently misunderstood is often guilty of nothing more than their own propensity to make assumptions. What you think you say and what someone else understands you to say are very often not the same. The lack of care in writing emails often exacerbates the problem. Re-read them before you send them off!

For instance, you might *think* you say something, but *actually* say something else. Someone else might *think* you said something but *actually* hear something else. He or she might then *think* he or she has responded to you in a certain way, but *actually* respond differently, and you might *think* he or she has responded in a certain way even though you *actually* heard him or her say something else.

Confused? So you should be. It was all wrapped up rather nicely when Humpty Dumpty said, 'Words mean what you want them to mean.'

Luckily, good communication is not just about speaking and listening. Although they are obviously very important, the words only account for a small proportion of any useful amount of comprehension between two people. The intonation and expressions inherent in the voice are also key factors, as are the messages contained in what we call 'body language'.

Even though a speaker may actually be perfectly coherent, they may still be misunderstood. This is often as much to do with the listener as the speaker. Consider, for instance, if the listener:

- has a low level of concentration – he or she may not actually be taking in what you are saying
- is prejudiced in some way – in which case he or she will automatically be colouring the meaning of what you are saying
- has no background experience of what you are saying – in which case, how will he or she assimilate new material when there is no 'peg' in his or her mind on which to hang it?
- is stressed in some way – he or she is unlikely to be able to concentrate
- feels that he or she is out of depth in the subject matter and therefore *expects* not to understand

There are numerous other reasons why someone might not take on board all your instructions. Often the use of paraphrasing what you are saying is a good way around this problem as what it does is to reach the listener from a number of different viewpoints, thereby offering a better chance for the message to get through. It also shows that the message is getting through in the way that the speaker intended. In this way misunderstandings can be avoided – and that has to be a good thing in any communication situation.

Feedback is another important part of the communication process. This can not only show how you react to something someone is saying, but can also help the speaker clarify his or her message if this is not getting through. The best sales people always ensure they have the necessary feedback – and a lot can be learned from them.

To amplify, it is entirely appropriate to offer feedback in order to let others know when:

- you have understood what they are saying
- you have *not* understood what they are saying
- you are upset or embarrassed about what they have said
- you disagree with what they are saying
- you approve of what they are saying
- you are amused by what they have said

Gossip plays an essential part in communication processes. It can reinforce the interest, understanding and comfort in one another and thereby it can put you on a common plain when communicating one with another. A little social intercourse can often identify potential problems before they turn into a conflict.

So that there are no misunderstandings in email, for instance, writing the reply in a different colour throughout the received email can ensure each point is dealt with thereby more easily diffusing a difficult situation.

In giving feedback, you should:

- Make sure that the speaker is ready to receive your contra-messages.
- Be specific, rather than give 'woolly' examples.
- Do so as soon as possible after the event so that the subject is still 'warm' in the speaker's mind.
- Do so in private if at all possible, if it is a sensitive situation, since it can be quite damaging if done in front of others.
- Be positive in order to lead the situation forward.
- Encourage the recipient to give feedback in a like manner in order that no-one is seen to be scoring points at the other's expense.

Of course, some people are much more difficult to deal with than others, and there is always a danger, when giving feedback to a difficult person, that your attempt could backfire, especially if he or she is higher up than you in the management hierarchy. In such cases, advance preparation is absolutely essential:

- You must begin by identifying the problem and concentrating on what can be improved by the person in question.
- If possible, you should try to determine why the person is behaving in such a manner.
- You should always be prepared for a confrontation if giving a difficult person feedback about his or her general or specific behaviour. How will you handle his or her reactions? Try to imagine what defence he or she will come up with.
- Rehearse both your arguments and counter-reactions thoroughly so that you know instinctively what you are going to do or say at the right time.
- Be positive in what you are saying to the difficult person. Explain simply why what he or she does or says upsets you, and express your willingness to help adapt their ways.
- Try to work out and agree a plan of action on both sides.
- Comment positively on progress that you observe in his or her behaviour in order to encourage.

We mentioned earlier on that in face to face meetings speech and listening are only two parts of any communication process. But being able to interpret non-verbal signals is also an extremely important adjunct in ensuring understanding.

▬▬▬ T H U R S D A Y ▬▬▬

All of us have a propensity to 'hear' other people by observing their physical reactions. Indeed, it is said that you can sometimes tell much more from watching someone than from listening to what they are saying. Usually this feedback is positive in that it reinforces what someone is saying, at the same time demonstrating what we feel inside. But equally, body language can give false signals which can override the verbal message that is being given out, and thereby harm the communication process.

There are very many types of body language, just a few of which are shown below. What do you read into the situation when you see people:

- frowning? Usually this indicates that they either disagreed with what is being said or simply don't understand
- avoiding eye contact? This is a sure sign that they are bored or lack confidence, or perhaps have something to hide
- scratching their nose? They may be puzzled or may dislike something, but equally they may just have an itchy nose!
- speaking rapidly? Perhaps they are anxious or worried
- raising their voice? It is likely that they are angry or worried
- shifting from one foot to the other? They might be impatient, but equally might have been standing for too long!

People who lie often give themselves away by their body language, whilst those who are genuine are usually easy to spot. Liars will often avoid looking directly at you whilst

blinking or swallowing rapidly, clearing the throat or covering their mouths whilst speaking.

It is not for nothing that the expression 'having a poker face' is used to convey the picture of someone who has so mastered the control over his or her involuntary body movements that it is well nigh impossible to guess what they are thinking. But would you trust someone with a poker face? Whatever it was that they said, the chances are that you would instinctively mistrust them.

Variations in the amount of eye contact can also tell you a great deal about the person with whom you are conversing. Think back to when you were last angry with someone. Did you look him or her right in the eye as you spoke to him or her? As a rule of thumb, most people are comfortable with eye contact for up to around five seconds. Anything more than that and it can make the recipient feel uncomfortable – which is exactly why aggressive people stare out those whom they feel to be their inferiors.

Fixing someone with a stare is not the same action, of course, that people in love appear to enjoy. If you look at the latter, their eyes dart backwards and forwards between the eyes and across the face – very different from a single fixed stare.

T H U R S D A Y

When people blink a lot, this can also be a sign that they are nervous, which itself may be an indication that they are not being entirely truthful with you – but they might also be contact-lens wearers and therefore need to blink a lot! On the other hand, if someone hardly blinks at all, this could be an indication that they are either listening intently to what you are saying or watching for your reactions. As always, there is no hard and fast rule about what to look out for, but rather it is a combination of different signs.

So, summing up, what should we look out for when trying to sum up someone's body language? Getting back to our three types of behaviour – aggressive, passive and assertive – there are certain behavioural patterns that become all too obvious.

For instance, someone who is assertive will usually maintain good eye contact, be relaxed and will smile or nod to encourage the other person as they speak. A submissive person, on the other hand, will often lower their eyes in a downcast position so as to avoid eye contact; they might have a poor posture such as slouching or drooping their shoulders, and they might cover their mouth with their hand in a defensive posture. Someone who is aggressive, however, will often maintain unwavering eye contact whilst standing with their feet apart and placing their hands on their hips in an impatient manner.

These same three behavioural types can also be identified from such a simple thing as shaking hands. For instance, an aggressor will often tend to grasp your hand with their own uppermost with palm facing downwards. A passive person will offer their palm face up, whilst the assertive

▰▰▰ T H U R S D A Y ▰▰▰

type tends to shake your hand at the same angle as yours – i.e. at right angles to the floor.

But you can take it even further than this. How often have you been to a party and experienced all manner of hand-shakes? There's the traditional limp shake whereby a floppy hand suggests that here is a weak and indecisive person. On the other hand, someone who grasps your hand tightly may well be the type of person who wants to show they are both tough and in complete control. People who proffer just their fingers and thumb rather than their whole hand are as often as not insecure, whilst someone who holds their arm out stiffly might covertly be suggesting to you that they intend to be in control of the entire situation. However, you still have to bear in mind any physical disabilities in this too. The person who does not notice rheumatoid arthritis in a hand that they shake may cause anxiety and pain when shaking hands firmly instead of the friendly gesture that was intended.

Non-verbal language can therefore be very useful in summing up a particular type of person. Body language often reflects a person's mental approach to life, and difficult people, in particular, will often give themselves away by their actions – both voluntary and involuntary. By learning to read the signs, you will be in a much better position to adjust your own responses and to be in better control of the situation.

Summary

Today we have been examining the necessity for offering feedback in a two-way communication process and the need to think through different ways of offering feedback that will be positive to the situation. These are:

- paraphrasing
- clearly stating specific examples of the point in question
- being sensitive to the feelings of others
- body language – in all its forms

F R I D A Y

How to say 'no' and deal with difficult clients

Most people find it difficult to say 'no'. It is in our nature not to do so for a number of reasons, not least because we want to avoid confrontation and we all feel the need to be liked and to be appreciated, and refusing a request can make us appear selfish to others.

The problem is that by not being able to say what we really feel on such occasions, there is not just a possibility, but a distinct likelihood that we will become over-burdened, and this can lead to stress and worry. This is particularly true in the workplace where by agreeing to do everything that is asked of you, you could end up with an in-tray a mile high, whilst others appear to cope much more easily.

Nobody likes to feel they are being taken advantage of, yet people who have difficulty saying 'no' are the very type to feel put upon by their work colleagues. If they refuse to do what is asked, they may well feel that they will no longer be liked or appreciated by the person doing the asking. They might even be fearful of an aggressive reaction if they say 'no' and therefore cave in since they may feel it is the better of the two options to cope with.

The point is, though, that by failing to make a stand you are more likely to store up problems for the future. For instance, if you were really too busy to take on some extra work, no-one will thank you for handing in something that has been rushed and is of low quality. By avoiding causing displeasure in the first place by not refusing to take something on, you are much more likely to compound the problem at a later date.

F R I D A Y

Such a scenario is especially true where a boss hands a member of staff vast amounts of work, knowing that that person is normally efficient and trustworthy. In reality, the member of staff might be unwilling to say 'no' because:

- He or she does not wish to appear inefficient or incapable of completing the task.
- He or she is afraid that his/her boss will get angry and that ultimately this could put his/her job 'on the line'.
- He or she wants to be liked and appreciated by all his/her work colleagues.
- He or she wants greater prospects for promotion.
- He or she has low self-esteem and wants to build up the esteem of others.

However, you are much more likely to be appreciated by others if you are open and honest with your work colleagues, rather than struggling on alone, trying to keep up and ultimately not producing work of the required standard. It is quite possible, for instance, that the people asking you to do something might not have appreciated how much you already have on your plate; and how can they plan their own workload properly if they get no feedback from you on whether what they are asking is reasonable or not?

By struggling on and then not managing to cope, you are much more likely to cause others to get angry with you – so the whole point of caving in to the original request backfires dramatically. So by not saying 'no', you can easily shoot yourself in the foot and actually become inefficient and late in your work – and ultimately overtired and unable to cope at all.

Now think of it the other way around. By being assertive and explaining that you cannot take on yet another piece of work, you are more likely to gain the respect of others and also to allow them to understand that there is a physical limitation that everyone comes up against in being able to cope with all that is thrown at them.

There is also the question of self-respect. Those who fail to produce quality work – regardless of whether it is 'their fault' or not – often end up with a low estimation of themselves. If, on top of that, they realise that by having the courage to stand up for themselves they could have avoided the situation in the first place, they are likely to feel doubly dejected.

Of course, if others perceive you to be someone who has little self-respect, they will begin to start treating you in that way, and any negative feelings towards you could intensify. At the opposite end of the scale, if others see you as being a positive person, then that is how they will react to you.

F R I D A Y

The problem that many find extremely difficult is just how to say 'no' – especially to a superior member of staff. Doing so by making excuses is quite definitely not the way to go about it. Apart from the fact that these excuses can either sound very lame, or be seen for what they are – telling downright lies – they are also highly likely to make the apologist feel nothing short of cowardly, which again is hardly likely to make them feel good about themself.

No, the only way you can say 'no' in this context is to be assertive. That does not mean that you have to be aggressive in your response; but by explaining why you cannot or will not do something someone that has been asked of you, you may well find that it actually clears the air, rather than making the situation more difficult.

Of course, you will want to have convinced yourself first of all that what is being requested of you is something that you do not want to do. It may even be that you will need to ask for further details before you make up your mind. But it is much better to refuse at the outset once your mind is made up, rather than let it fester in the background.

It often helps to give a good reason why you do not wish to carry out a particular request. This does not mean that you should hand out a string of excuses. The person whose request you are refusing will respect you much more if you quietly, but firmly, explain your reasons for refusal, keeping your emotions firmly under control.

Finally, if you really do want to help the other person, but are unable to do so for whatever reason, it can do no harm to ask him if there is any way you can help him or her to find another solution to his or her problem.

F R I D A Y

Saying 'no' to one's boss or work colleagues is one thing. Saying 'no' to a customer or client is quite a different matter. Being on the front line, representing the company can often be quite a stressful experience. We all know the expression 'The customer is always right', but in reality it can be quite galling having to deal with difficult clients.

All of us are clients or customers, and we all appreciate being shown courtesy and consideration. It follows that many clients who may appear angry or aggressive often do so as a result of what they regard as poor service, or of being treated badly by the company in question.

Yet good customer service is important in dealing with the clients of any company, regardless of whether you work in a service industry or in manufacturing. Put yourself in your clients' shoes and ask yourself how you would respond in their situation. If they have encountered bad or inefficient service, don't they have a right to complain? And if they do feel that way about the company, then to whom are they going to make their feelings known? Why, to you, the front-line staff of course. So there really is no point in taking their abuse personally.

Often, it is extremely stressful to be harangued by an angry client. Keeping calm really is the only way to deal with such people because if you become irate as a result of how you are spoken to, then absolutely nothing will be achieved, and the customer's current perceptions of you and your company will only be reinforced. The logical consequence of this is that the customer may never come back for a second time, and worse still, may bad-mouth your company to all their friends, thus ensuring that they never use your services either.

F R I D A Y

People don't get angry for no reason, and dissatisfied clients are usually angry for only a small number of possible reasons. Perhaps they feel:

- no-one appears to want to listen to them, or to take their complaints seriously
- the product they purchased does not work in the way it should
- they are not getting the help they require
- their expectations have not been met
- their complaint does not appear to be taken as seriously by the company as it is by them

In all of these cases, it is necessary to show them that you take what they are saying seriously. And that means listening, and showing them that you are not only listening but also taking notice. Take time to take in a few deep breaths, and try to relax your posture. If you are tensed up, you can never hide that fact from the other person.

Body language is very useful in this situation, as is paraphrasing what they have said to show that you have absorbed the essence of their concerns. By asking questions to learn more about their complaint, you would get to the heart of the problem more quickly.

In dealing with angry clients, you should also attempt to empathise with them. At the start of your conversation, you are unlikely to know if they have good cause to be upset. Try putting yourself in their position, listening carefully, maintaining eye contact and generally getting on the same wavelength so that you can demonstrate to them that there really is no question of it being a situation of them against your company, but rather that you are on their side to try to get things sorted out.

Once you have dealt with getting their feelings back on an even keel, you should set about dealing with the problem itself. One of the most powerful things anyone can do in such a situation is to ask directly 'What can I do to help?' However, it is no good then turning around and saying you cannot solve the problem. At the very least you will need to offer some alternatives so that at least you are seen to be making the effort to get somewhere close to resolving their problem.

Give your clients at least two alternative solutions so that in effect you are giving them the option of taking control of the solution once again. Sometimes there may be no options for you even to offer, in which case you should explain why it is impossible to accede to their wishes. However, you should still do all you can to come up with some acceptable solution so that they can see that you are genuinely trying to help, and not to give them the brush-off.

The last thing you should do is to offer excuses as to why something has not been done. Frankly, customers do not wish to know whose fault it was. As far as they are concerned, you are the public face of the company and it is the company that is at fault; therefore, by a logical extension, you are at fault. The most important thing is to get whatever was wrong put right. Once you have decided what must be done, explain what you intend to them and then make sure that you actually do it.

In summary, then:

- As soon as it becomes obvious that you will have to deal with a client who has a complaint, take a few deep breaths and try to relax yourself as much as possible.
- Remain calm at all times and take an assertive stance, showing the client that you are unfazed by his or her temper.
- Try to see the situation from their point of view and empathise wherever possible with their predicament.
- Listen, question and paraphrase wherever possible in order to demonstrate that you really do understand what their problems are.
- Find out what, if any, the client's solution would be to the problem.
- Offer a solution – if at all possible, incorporate the client's suggestions; but if not, attempt to create a solution acceptable to both parties.

F R I D A Y

Complaints over the telephone, email and other electronic media can add further complications to finding a solution, for it is an unfortunate fact that many people, who would not dream of being rude to anyone directly, become much more aggressive where no facial contact is taking place. And because there is no non-verbal feedback going on – i.e. the facial expressions and the hand movements that we all take for granted in normal conversation – some people are altogether less coherent when talking over a phone.

How many times, also, have you been put on hold for an eternity by a not-very-bright receptionist and then put through to someone who is unable to help you anyway? It happens to all of us, and the worst part about it is not knowing what is happening at the other end of the line. Have they forgotten us? Do they care? Does anyone want to help us solve the problem? Would we be better off taking our business elsewhere?

So dealing with complainants over the telephone can often become even more stressful than facing the wrath of a difficult customer eyeball to eyeball. But equally, it is even more essential that you remain cool, calm and collected when dealing with such a person over the wires. Without the feedback inherent in body language, it is very important to give verbal feedback to the complainant that you are not only still listening, but also understand the problem and wish to help find a solution for them.

When dealing with a difficult person over the telephone, you should:

F R I D A Y

- Always ensure you have a notepad or screen beside you so that you can note down all complaints; there could be more than one, after all!
- Make sure that if you cannot help find a solution there and then, you will tell the client that you will get back to him or her at a later time – and make sure you do!
- Explain fully if you are unable to resolve the client's problem yourself, and that you will ask the relevant person to ring him or her back.
- Make sure that you have all relevant details – the client's name, telephone number and address, and the reason why he or she called you in the first place.

Unfortunately, there are sometimes occasions when the level of frustration or anger of the client reaches boiling point and he or she starts to swear or exhibit threatening behaviour. What should you do in such circumstances? There is a school of thought that says that no-one should have to put up with threatening or abusive language, and that in such a situation you should either put the phone down on the complainant or, in a person-to-person situation, simply walk away. Unfortunately, life is not that easy. There are quite a few scenarios, such as dealing with patients and their relatives in hospitals, where it would obviously be quite inappropriate to absolve oneself of their problems when they are emotionally charged up. Equally, however, no-one should normally have to be on the receiving end of such behaviour, and it is best if you are likely to find yourself in such a position that you discuss what is the company's policy on such matters before it actually happens.

It could also be a very good idea to see what it is that is making the clients unhappy with your service. Have you, for instance, given them expectations that cannot be met? Do you know what promises your sales people are making? Is the competition giving better service or better-quality products for the same price? If so, a proper review of your place in the market may well reduce the number of 'difficult people' you have to deal with altogether.

Summary

This Friday we have discussed the difficulties faced by many in having to say 'no' to a request, and to fend off unwarranted abuse from a difficult client.

- Do you have difficulty in saying 'no' to someone in authority?
- What is it that 'gets in the way' of your standing up for yourself?
- How do you intend to tackle this in the future if you find yourself in such a situation once again?

FRIDAY

At the end of the day, dealing with such people is part of the job itself, and if you are easily offended or intimidated and feel you are unable to handle it, then maybe you should be doing something else for a living!

You're in control now

In going on this journey through the past week, it will have become clear to you that truly assertive behaviour is the most positive and productive way forward – the most likely to succeed, both for you and for the people around you. It is also the least likely to turn *you* into a difficult person.

If we look back to Monday, and the general definitions of the three basic character types, we see that assertiveness means being able to act without anxiety or fear, whilst expressing your needs and preferences without behaving in a threatening manner to others. It is the positive attitude toward the whole of the work and human relationships that can make the world go round, rather than punctuating life with a series of Mexican stand-offs or even a complete stalemate and abandonment of the plans and relationships involved.

S A T U R D A Y

As part of understanding that attitude, you have first to get to grips with understanding yourself and learning how to amend your behaviour and reactions to enable you to interact and work more effectively with others. Whatever your role in life, your understanding of where other people are coming from and why they are taking the stance they are, takes you more than halfway to being able to dynamise your relationship with them and improve it in so many ways. If you apply this philosophy in your workplace as well, you will enable your colleagues to work with you much more effectively.

The first step, then, is to understand yourself, however uncomfortable that may make you feel. After all, coming face to face with yourself is not always a pleasure; stick at it and make sure that you are not deluding yourself about any aspect of your own behaviour. You'll probably like yourself better afterwards too!

We have all seen friends and acquaintances deluding
themselves on a daily basis, such as when:

- they only tell 'white' lies when they amend their CVs in
  order to change the substance of their recorded personal
  history
- they think that they are quiet, shy and retiring, when they
  are truly gregarious and tend to show off!
- they say they are 'on a diet' when, in reality, they snack
  all day

We are usually our own worst enemies in life anyway, and
we are always sad to see friends who labour away under a
damaging false premise - but how many of us are actually
brave enough to grasp the nettle and tell them? Indeed,
should we tell them at all?

It is a truism that many of us are the products of our own
upbringing. We saw on Tuesday that although there are
many different types of personality trait, the four main
categories can be broken down into *insecure*, *negative*, *selfish*
and *pleasant*. We would all like to see ourselves in the
fourth camp, but in reality:

- how do others see us?
- how can we find out truthfully how others see us?
- has the experience of childhood left its scar on us for life?
- how much of that scar can we overcome in its negativity?
- have we really learned that others have needs too?
- do we take these into account when we are planning and
  speaking to others?
- can we better ourselves and help others with similar
  problems?
- how can we best develop ourselves to do that?

S A T U R D A Y

Then the knottiest problem of all – why are particular people a problem to us anyway? What is it that they do or say that really gets our goat? Am *I* the real problem here after all?

You need to ask these questions – or slightly milder versions of them – whenever a new situation arises or a potential conflict scenario appears to be looming up to overshadow your relationships and work.

Conflict is the spice of life and arises in all kinds of everyday situations, but it has to be stressed that not all conflict is bad. Your managing the conflict in your life is the key to avoiding stress, and so the perception of what it is that is causing the conflict in the first place is well worth achieving. Put succinctly, conflict can be either positive or negative. By positive conflict, we are referring to a situation in which the generation of enthusiasm can be the catalyst to solving a problem that up till now has remained stubbornly impenetrable. Negative conflict, on the other hand, can lead both to stress and to the failure of the two parties to come to any kind of agreement.

The key is to find common ground and attempt to see things from the other person's point of view. That doesn't necessarily mean they are right; only that the other person's opinion should not be dismissed out of hand: for it is perfectly possible to see things from a number of different angles, each one of which may well be valid. We all know the story of the three blind men stumbling across an elephant. One came across its trunk, whilst the second was fanned by one of its ears. The third walked into one of its massive legs. Who gave the best description of this animal?

S A T U R D A Y

Would the blind man who described a snake-like creature be any more wrong – or right – than one of his colleagues who had experienced a downdraught from a giant fan, or the other who thought he had discovered a giant tree trunk?

Being negative and putting a dampener on things is all too easy. Everyone gets depressed at times, but inevitably it is the positive people in society who get things moving and who win in the end. So if in addition to being positive in your own right, you get others to behave positively to you too, then it follows that you are much more likely to find a way forward in all aspects of your life.

But what do we mean by being positive? It certainly is not the same as being a 'yes' person. Being positive means looking for a way forward through a difficult situation, looking for the good things and working out how to improve the bad. Sometimes that is simply a matter of improving your communications skills in order to give

■■■■■ S A T U R D A Y ■■■■■

feedback to your opposite number. Being able to interpret non-verbal signals and to back up your own conversation with body language are also skills that are well worth developing in order to avoid misunderstandings.

Equally, many people experience great difficulty when finding themselves in a situation where they have to say 'no' to someone. We none of us like doing it, because it is against basic human nature. But being able to say 'no' is an important weapon in our armoury of techniques for being more open and honest with our colleagues. It isn't easy; no-one ever said it was. But by tackling the difficult situation head-on, you are less likely to store up further problems in the future, and equally you will end up better respected by your colleagues who will see you as a straight-dealing type of person to be working with!

At the end of the day, good communication is at the very heart of dealing with difficult people. Many people can be exasperating, and there are times when we all wonder if there is any point in putting up with their general behaviour and attitudes. Yet, give in to the temptation of treating like with like and who wins in the end? You don't, because you will soon see that by behaving like your opposite number you have actually sunk to his or her level. He/she doesn't either, because for a start your respect has been lost and most likely the respect of others around you. It is worth remembering there is an old adage which goes something along the lines of 'When you point an accusing finger at somebody you should watch out as there are always three fingers that are pointing back at you'! Without sounding awfully 'goody goody', assertive behaviour and setting a good example can be an inspiration to others. On the other hand, following their lead and behaving badly, giving others a difficult time, can never lead to a positive outcome. Perhaps Charles Kingsley, in his famous tome *The Water Babies*, summed up the situation perfectly with his two characters Mrs 'Do-as-you-would-be-done-by' and Mrs 'Be-done-by-as-you-did'.

So get positive, try to see the other person's point of view and, above all, communicate, and hopefully other people will soon stop being difficult in your company and will perhaps surprise even themselves. Surely that has to be a good thing?

Summary

The keys to dealing with difficult people can be found within ourselves. Over the past week, we have found ourselves turning full circle until we see a mirror image of ourselves in others. It is only when we can control our own behaviour and see the potential reactions of others more clearly that we can even hope to begin the process of enabling them to react differently. This way we can all learn to deal with difficult people – who may then suddenly start to become less difficult!

Presentation

MALCOLM PEEL
Revised by Jon Lamb

WEEK FIVE

C O N T E N T S

Week Five

■ I N T R O D U C T I O N ■

Speaking in public worries almost everyone, even those who must do it regularly as part of their job or leisure activities.

People worry about such things as 'making a fool of myself', 'drying up', 'not finding the right word', 'not knowing what to do with my hands'. But the real problem is the worry itself, not the form it takes.

By following a few simple steps, we can improve our performance as public speakers, reduce our anxieties and discover that public presentation can be not only deeply satisfying, but even great fun.

If you are committed to a presentation in the immediate future (maybe the very day you buy this book!) then turn first to Thursday's chapter.

S U N D A Y

Basic preparation

The key to successful presentation is good preparation.
Today, we will look at the basics:

> *Basic preparation*
>
> - analysing the occasion
> - profiling the audience
> - learning about the location
> - defining our aim and objectives

Occasionally, we may be called on to speak with little or no
notice – perhaps to reply to a welcome or give a vote of
thanks, perhaps to step in when the intended speaker has
failed to arrive, or perhaps to state our viewpoint at a
critical stage of a meeting. Thankfully, for most of us, this is
rare.

Usually we know that we must speak some time – from days to months – in advance. This period is precious, for it enables us to prepare, and preparation is a main key to success. The problems most of us feel when called upon to speak can be eliminated, or at least reduced, by thorough preparation.

However much (or little) time we have, preparation must begin with analysis of:

- the occasion on which we will be a speaker
- the audience that is expected
- the location at which it is to take place

This analysis may not necessarily be time-consuming – sometimes it may only take a minute or two – but it is the foundation for success.

Analysing the occasion

'Public speaking' and 'oral presentation' are descriptions
which cover an enormous range of activities. At one end of
the scale, we may be presenting the monthly accounts of
our club to a committee of four or five people gathered in a
sitting room. At the other end, we may be making a speech
to a major conference in front of an audience of thousands,
complete with TV cameras and the press.

For most of us, the occasion will fall somewhere in between.
We may be making sales presentations, giving talks to clubs
or societies, addressing meetings or perhaps giving training
sessions.

The basic approach to oral presentation and public speaking
is the same, whichever sort of occasion it is. However, the
type and quantity of material, the aids and methods we
choose and the level at which we present it will depend on
the nature of the occasion; we must learn as much as we can
about this in advance.

Our success will depend on how closely we match the
expectations of the organiser and the audience. We must
know what ground we are expected to cover, how long we
should speak, and how we will fit in with other speakers
and elements in the event.

The starting point for our analysis will be to ask whoever
invited us to speak unless, of course, we are planning the
event ourselves. If the event is a regular one, we may be
able to get information from people who have attended
previously.

S U N D A Y

Here is a checklist for analysing the occasion:

Analysing the occasion

- Which organisation is holding the event?
- What are the objectives of this organisation?
- What is the nature of the occasion?
- How formal is it to be?
- Why have I been asked? What is expected of me?
- Are there to be other speakers? If so, who? What are their subjects? Will they speak before or after me? Is it to be a team presentation?
- How long have I got? When will I start?
- Will there be questions? Discussion? A panel?
- Will there be a Chair for my session?
- What clothes are appropriate? How should I dress?

■■■■■■■■ S U N D A Y ■■■■■■■■

Profiling the audience

The key to success in any presentation is to please and satisfy our audience. It is they, not us, who must be the centre of the event. To analyse an audience which has not yet assembled is not easy, but we must try.

Few things are worse for a speaker than to arrive expecting a small group of friends and colleagues and to be confronted with an audience of hundreds, or to believe he is to address a packed audience of distinguished academics and find he is faced with half a dozen first-year students.

We must make the best estimate we can of the number of people who will be present. This will affect the kind of aids that are appropriate and the style we adopt. Major surprises on the day (whether too many or too few) are also bad for the morale.

The level of expertise of the audience is very important. Presentations which are pitched at the wrong level – either too high or too low – are sure to fail.

It will help if we can find out whether our audience is likely to hold any strong opinions about our subject; whether they have any biasses or preconceptions. Audiences usually feel neutral towards a speaker at the start of a presentation; but if there is any reason why they might be specially hostile or friendly we would do well to be warned.

The more we know about any inter-personal or inter-group tensions within the audience the better. Some people will be influential, others not. To appear to side with one faction may do little good if we thoroughly upset another.

As with the occasion, finding out about the expected audience usually requires us to speak to the organiser of the event (if it is not us), and if it is a regular one, to people who have been before.

Here is a checklist for audience analysis:

Profiling the audience

- How many are expected?
- Why will they be there?
- How knowledgeable will they be in the subject area?
- Will they have strong preconceptions or biasses about the subject? Might they be particularly friendly or hostile to me or to what I want to say?
- Will they be there in their own right, or representing others?
- Might there be tensions or conflicts within the audience? If so, what, and between whom?
- Who will be the key figures?

... ON ANIMAL LIBERATION

Learning about the location

The place in which a presentation is given can have a big effect on its success.

Size may be critical. Nothing will kill an event more quickly than for it to be held in a room which is much too big. Distractions can also be very damaging.

If we do not know what facilities are available or how to use them, we may lose an opportunity to impress, or, even worse, get tangled in embarrassing problems. The equipment available to help a speaker varies enormously. We cannot leave this to chance. To arrive with a set of magnificent 35mm slides, for example, and find there is no projector would probably destroy our presentation.

S U N D A Y

It is always helpful to visit the facility in which the presentation is to be made at an early stage if we can. If we are really lucky, we may be able to rehearse there.

Here is a checklist for learning about the location:

The location

- How do I get there?
- How long will it take? Are there any possible causes of delay? Is there convenient car-parking or public transport?
- Is the setting formal or informal?
- Will I be expected to speak from a platform?
- Is there a podium, rostrum or table?
- How is the audience seating arranged?
- What are the acoustics like?
- Is there public address equipment? If so, what kind of microphone? Who controls the volume? Does it work well?
- What are the visual aid facilities? If there is a 35mm projector, how are slides changed and will it take the same kind of magazine as mine?
- If mine is an electronic presentation will a laptop computer be supplied? If so, does it have a remote mouse to assist in the changing of slides?
- What format is the video? Where are the power points? Is there a flipchart, stand and markers?
- How are the visual aids placed relative to the audience? Where will I need to stand, and where can my aids be put before and after use?

Defining your aim and objectives

The more clearly you perceive what you want to achieve in
a speech or presentation, the more likely you are to succeed.
You must think hard and carefully in advance, and define
your aim and objectives as accurately as you can. It is useful
to write them down – this helps you to think clearly, creates
a record to which you can refer and enables you, if you
wish, to share them with the audience before you begin.

Your audience will have objectives too. They may have
assembled specially in order to hear what you have to tell
them, but even so, they will only be prepared to give their
time and attention to you as long as they believe that you
know what you are doing, why you are doing it, and what
response you would like from it.

The aim
Your aim is the overall target you wish to reach with your
presentation – the reason why you are planning to stand
there and hold forth.

S U N D A Y

In some cases, the aim may be clear and self-explanatory. However, surprisingly often, there may be doubt. You may have been asked, for example, to speak at a conference on a subject in which you are an expert – but why? Are you there to give a general introduction to laypeople, to describe the findings of your latest research to experts, or to engage in a dialogue in a controversial area?

Your aim

You might, for example, decide that your aim was:

- 'To persuade the directors of the XYZ company to use the services of your organisation'

or

- 'To ensure that all members of the golf club understand why the subscription must rise by 50%'

or

- 'To entertain and amuse the dining club and help them to feel the annual dinner was a successful and enjoyable occasion'

or

- 'To improve the cold-calling performance of the sales representatives in your team'

and so on.

The objectives

Your objectives are the more detailed and precise steps you plan to take to reach your aim; not the methods you will use – those will come later – but the components included within the overall aim. Apart from conveying certain information, are you intending to convince, amuse, sell a product or yourselves, obtain immediate action, or what?

Negative objectives
Occasionally you may feel the need to include negative objectives – aspects you intend to avoid. You may wish to hide facets of your subject which are commercially secret. You may wish to avoid areas of controversy, or perhaps angles which might divert the attention of the audience from your main message. There may be parts of your case or members of your team you feel are weak. You may wish to avoid upsetting or offending some or all of your audience in a particular way.

SORRY, OUR MARKETING DIRECTOR IS RATHER SHY...

Your objectives
For example, if your aim was: 'To persuade the directors of the XYZ company to use the services of your organisation',

you might decide that your objectives were:

- To convince them that each individual in your team is a qualified and experienced professional.
- To demonstrate that your organisation has had relevant experience and satisfied other clients.
- To show that you have the capacity to undertake the work they require within the timescale.
- To establish good personal relationships between their senior management and your team.
- To explain your fee structure and establish a basis for negotiation.

The negative objectives might include:

- To hide as far as possible the failure of the contract with the ABC company.
- To avoid a clear statement on price until your next wage negotiations have been completed.

Personal or 'hidden' objectives

There may also be strictly personal objectives, such as:

Personal objectives

- To demonstrate to the new marketing director that I am a highly efficient member of staff.
- To gain the commission which these sales would entitle me to and win the monthly sales award.

There is nothing wrong with such objectives, although we are less likely to want to commit them to paper. They will usually remain hidden and you must beware that you are not misled by such objectives into giving a presentation that is unhelpful or uninteresting to most of the audience.

Behavioural objectives
Throughout your preparation, you should try to put yourself in the audience's place. You should ask not 'What do I want to say?', but 'What do I want them to hear and believe?'. For this reason, it can be helpful to write down objectives in a form which expresses what you intend from the angle of the audience. These are sometimes called 'behavioural objectives' as they are based on the behaviour we would like to see from our audience after the presentation. Such an approach is particularly helpful for training presentations.

Thus, if your aim was 'To improve the cold-calling of the sales reps in my team' you could set objectives in the form:

Behavioural objectives

By the end of the presentation, the representatives will:

- Accept the need for substantial improvement in cold-calling performance.
- Know the steps to achieve cold-calling success.
- Have insight into their own cold-calling effectiveness and the areas in which they need to improve.
- Have set improvement targets and be motivated to achieve them.

MONDAY

Content

Following Sunday's work, you know what you are aiming at. The next steps are to fill out the content of your presentation, to gather (or select) your material and to give it structure.

Content and structure

- gathering material
- selecting material
- structuring the presentation

Gathering material

Do you need to gather?
You may not need to gather material. If you have:

- given the same, or a similar presentation before
- written an article, report (or book!) on the subject
- recently completed research or a detailed study of the subject
- access to and permission to use your organisation's or someone else's material

then we may have quite enough. In this case, your need will be to select and check what you have. This is discussed in the next section.

When should you gather?
You should begin gathering as soon as possible. Material gathered three months in advance of the presentation is far more valuable than the same material gathered three days before. The extra time gives you the opportunity to digest the material and make it part of your thought processes. You can reject it, question it or support it by further research and additional material. If you work at the last minute, all this is impossible – you will have to take it or leave it as you find it.

The key source
If you are not a subject expert, your first aim should be to locate a *key source*. This will be a book, article, report or person that can give you the framework for the remainder of your research. This is not to suggest ruthless plagiarism. Apart from any legal or moral considerations, you shall want to put your own stamp on anything you use; if you do

M O N D A Y

not, you might as well invite your audience to read the source and save everyone, including you, much time and effort. Encyclopedias are a natural key source for many subjects; even if you know a subject well, it is always worth looking it up.

Where to look
There are many sources of material. They include:

Sources of material

- your own experience
- colleagues, family and friends
- books
- journals, magazines and newspapers
- the Web
- original research

M O N D A Y

Your own experience

Far-and-away the richest source of material for any presentation is your own first-hand experience and personality. Audiences warm to this in a way they never will to reported knowledge or facts. However sophisticated or expert the audience, something that actually happened to us will have more interest and carry more authority than a dozen quotations from international experts. This is the advantage of the oral presentation – the audience can read the established wisdom in any library, but a face-to-face meeting allows them to grasp and evaluate the speaker's unique personality and experience.

Colleagues, family and friends

Provided they are not deadly rivals, or planning to attend our presentation to learn from you, working colleagues will often prove an excellent source of material. Most people are quite flattered to be asked to help in this way. If they do help, you should always acknowledge such help in the presentation.

You should never ignore the help partners, children, aunts, uncles and cousins may be able to offer. From secondary school onwards, children can prove goldmines of knowledge, if we are humble enough to ask them.

Books

Books are an obvious source of material, but you need to check that they are reasonably up-to-date. A few books have been written specifically to offer material for public speakers – funny stories, jokes, witticisms, quotations, and little-known facts. Most library staff are extremely helpful and pleased to point you in the right direction.

M O N D A Y

Journals, magazines and newspapers
Recent journal articles will be more up-to-date than most
books, and besides giving you additional material will
indicate what the latest thinking is and what people are
interested in at the present time. There is also more chance
of finding the off-beat idea or the little-known fact in a
journal article than a book.

If you are likely to speak (or write) on a subject on a number
of occasions, a scrapbook can be a tremendous help. Much
is written and happens day-by-day that gets lost, even to
the expert. A scrapbook and a stick of adhesive can preserve
it for us.

M O N D A Y

The Web
The Internet is a source of information for almost any subject on which you might have to present. The majority of its resources are still free, although access is increasingly conditional on you divulging some personal details. Other websites will charge either a one-off access or subscription fee for the information we seek.

If you are not yet linked to the Internet via a personal computer you can alternatively log on at your place of work, at a local library, or at one of a growing number of retail outlets.

Original research
It may be part of your job or you may have the facilities to carry out original research to provide material for a presentation. Usually, however, you shall have been asked to give the presentation – perhaps in the form of a paper to a learned body – because you are known to have already carried out research. If this is the case, you are more likely to need to *select* material than to gather it. This is discussed in the second part of this chapter.

Organising the material
A good method of organising your material is to write the headings of each of your main sections on the top of separate sheets of paper. You can then either jot notes of your other material on the appropriate sheets or, if you have a great deal of material, endorse already-written notes with the section numbers and place them in order in a folder or file.

M O N D A Y

Selecting material

Sooner or later, your task will be to stop gathering material and to select from what we have.

How much material?
The amount of material needed can be difficult to judge, especially if you are not a practised speaker. How much will become clearer as your work proceeds, both in the actual gathering and in the next step – structuring. Having established a structure, you may realise that you need to add more material to fill in a section or support an argument and there will always be some to-ing and fro-ing between these two steps. Occasionally your research may even indicate that your objectives were too ambitious or too limited, and you may need to go back and revise them.

M O N D A Y

Don't prepare too much
Because they are afraid of drying up, inexperienced speakers almost always prepare more material than they have time to use, however much time they have.

If you have any doubt on how long your material will last, you must check by careful rehearsal.

Flexibility
Some speakers – especially when giving training sessions – give themselves greater flexibility by classifying their material in three ways:

- *core material* which is essential to the presentation
- *disposable material* (e.g. extra examples) which can be passed over without harming the message if time is short
- *supplementary material* which can be used if there is time to spare, or in answering questions

Old material
It is comforting to have already existing material when you are preparing for a presentation; you or a colleague may have given a similar presentation before, and the notes and visual aids may have been kept.

But the temptation to pick the material up and use it without further examination must be resisted.

The dangers in using old material, whether your own or someone else's, include:

The dangers of old material

- It was prepared for a different audience.
- The occasion and the speaker's objectives may have been different.
- It may not have worked well last time.
- It may not take account of lessons learnt during previous presentations.
- It may not now be up-to-date.

Structuring the presentation

Any form of communication – a report, an article, a letter, a book – needs a structure, but for an oral presentation, good structure is absolutely essential.

The benefits of a good structure
The audience has only one chance to understand what you are saying. If they lose the thread, they may never pick it up and even if they do, they may have missed vital points. A clear, simple structure is the best way of preventing this happening. With it, you can set up checkpoints and signposts which will help to keep the audience with you. If they do lose you, they can rejoin you comparatively easily at the next junction.

The benefits of structure

A good structure will:

- attract attention
- hold interest
- help understanding
- make your message more memorable

M O N D A Y

Types of structure
Three common types of structure are suitable for an oral presentation:

> **Structures for a presentation**
>
> - logical argument
> - narrative
> - formal

Logical argument
All that you say should be logical. If it is not, you are in trouble. However, this does not mean that to follow one logical argument step by step from start to finish will necessarily provide a good structure for your presentation; this can be extremely tedious for the audience and may be inappropriate for your objectives.

A logical argument will be suitable as your structure if you are presenting a case to a court or tribunal, speaking in a formal debate or seeking to convince an audience of the truth of your opinion. In other situations, other structures are likely to be more effective.

Narrative structure
Everyone loves a good story. The narrative structure or storyline is the one most likely to grab and hold the attention of the audience and make what you say memorable. If you can structure what you want to say as a story, you are on to a winner. But to work, the story must meet three conditions:

A story must be

- good
- well-told
- relevant to your objectives

Unfortunately, few business presentations can be structured in this way as a whole. However, it is often possible to use stories as part of the overall structure, as a separate section or to make a particular point.

Formal structure
If neither the logical argument nor the storyline are suitable for your presentation, you shall need to use a more formal structure. Probably the oldest advice about structure is:

1 Tell them what you are going to tell them.
2 Tell them.
3 Tell them what you have told them.

This structure provides the essential elements of introduction, main section and conclusion. The repetition, if skilfully done, will help understanding and retention. The introduction ('Tell them what you are going to tell them') and the conclusion ('Tell them what you have told them') will be prepared last. Both should be prepared with great care, as they are the most important sections.

The introduction

If you are to command attention, especially in a large gathering, you need to be larger than life – most openings benefit from a touch of drama. Before the introductory summary, the introduction should include something designed to attract the attention, whet the appetite and focus the audience's thinking. You need not go over the top, but you should not be self-conscious. You should avoid spoiling the effect by explanation or too many words. Having grabbed attention, you should maintain the suspense and only release it when you are ready to do so, ideally not before the conclusion.

Methods of grabbing attention include:

Attention-grabbing starts with

- making a joke
- telling an anecdote
- making a controversial statement
- displaying a key visual aid
- performing an arresting action

attention - grabbing

Making a joke
A good joke will gain attention, establish empathy and focus the audience's thinking.

However, the joke must be funny, not too well known, relevant to your subject and well-told. To tell a joke which does not succeed will set you back; it is much better not to try. To tell one which has little or no connection with your subject will not get you further forward; you shall have to start all over again once the laughter has died down.

Unless you are an expert humorist, it is better to stick to good one-line jokes than risk a story of any length. If you have doubts, it is better to choose another method of starting.

Telling an anecdote
You may have a story which, whilst not being funny, grabs attention in other ways. It may be a story of deep human interest, preferably true and ideally which happened to you. Having engaged the audience's interest in this way, you can sometimes hold back the conclusion until the end of the presentation, thus holding their attention right through.

Making a controversial statement
Startling or provocative statements will attract and focus attention and whet the appetite of your audience in the same way as a headline in a newspaper.

For success, you must pick out something that you can explain and justify as you go on – an intriguing aspect, unexpected statistic or main conclusion from your message encapsulated in a pithy way. You must not blunt its edge by immediate explanation; your audience must wait for this, possibly until the end.

Displaying a key visual aid
To display a key visual aid, possibly in silence, can make an excellent start; a slide, foil or pre-prepared flipchart which summarises or focuses on a key aspect of your message. It

should be pictorial, preferably without words, bright, intriguing and simple. You may be able to add animation if your aids are electronic. Producing an object such as a piece of machinery, equipment or clothing relevant to your subject will also focus attention in the same way.

As with the controversial statement, you should not explain it right away, explanation (or spontaneous enlightenment) will come as you proceed. An especially useful device is to produce an ohp foil to which you can add one or more explanatory overlays.

Performing an arresting action
You may start by performing some action relevant to your subject in mime or dumb show – a demonstration (particularly if there is an element of manual skill) or the manipulation of some machinery or equipment.

The opening summary
Having engaged the audience's attention, your next task is to 'Tell them what you are going to tell them': to lay out in summary form the structure of the presentation. This is best done with a visual aid – slide, foil or flipchart – listing the title and headings of your main sections. You should display it, read it through aloud, and put it on one side for use as you move from point to point or in the conclusion.

The main section

The main section ('Tell them') will need a number of main headings – usually between three and six. More and the structure will be too complicated for an audience to understand or remember. You may have one or two sub-

Week Five

$\blacksquare\!\!\!\blacksquare\!\!\!\blacksquare\!\!\!\blacksquare$ M O N D A Y $\blacksquare\!\!\!\blacksquare\!\!\!\blacksquare\!\!\!\blacksquare$

headings within the main structure but, once again, there must not be too many or both you and your audience will lose your way. The main sections must follow smoothly in a meaningful order.

The conclusion

Like the end of a piece of music, you must leave your audience satisfied, and in no doubt that you have finished.

Concluding summary
If you are using a formal structure, you should conclude with a crisp, clear summary of your main points. This can be reinforced by displaying the summary with which you started.

You may follow the summary by:

Closing options

- picking up the point you started the presentation with
- a challenge or call to action
- a question for the audience to think about
- a relevant witticism or good joke

■■■■ T U E S D A Y ■■■■

Presentation aids

Having decided what you want to achieve and sorted out
the content of your presentation, the next step is to choose
your aids. The voice alone is not enough for success; there
are many aids available to help you. The room in which the
presentation will take place, its equipment and furniture,
will also affect your success. Today, therefore, we will
consider:

Presentation aids

- Why use aids?
- The dangers of aids.
- Choosing aids.
- The room.

Why use aids?

Preparing and using aids requires extra work but it is
always worthwhile. Aids offer many benefits:

Presentation aids:

- attract attention
- help understanding
- help retention
- give pleasure

Aids attract attention

The speaker's voice alone quickly loses attention, even
when skilfully used. By adding one or more other sense,
aids wake an audience up and focus their attention. In a
presentation of any length, the variety alone helps to
rekindle and hold flagging attention.

Aids help understanding

Words are often not the most efficient way to convey
messages. The nature of an unfamiliar object will be far
better understood if we see a picture; better still if we are
able to touch it. The layout of a building or a tract of
country will be best conveyed by a plan or map.
Relationships within an organisation are much clearer if
shown in the form of a chart. The meaning of statistics is far
easier to grasp from a graph. Complex theories may be
expressed by means of pictograms; the working of a
machine from a diagram.

Aids help retention
Words must be very startling or special to stick in the mind;
the other senses are much more retentive. Most people
remember things they have seen more readily than
something they have heard. If they have touched and
handled – perhaps even operated or used – something, they
are even more likely to remember it.

Aids give pleasure
Almost everyone likes pictures. Well designed and produced
aids give pleasure, especially if they make good use of colour.

The dangers of aids

We have all attended presentations which have been
wrecked by aids. Endless sequences of slides filled with
words; a video in the wrong format; a projector which broke
down; slides in the wrong order, upside down and inside
out. Above all, we have come from presentations
remembering the wonderful technology used, but without a
clue as to the message it was meant to convey.

Aids are not, therefore, automatically beneficial. To get the
benefits and avoid the dangers we must follow a few simple
guidelines.

Aids should:

- reinforce the message
- match the equipment available
- be carefully prepared
- not be too many
- not be too complicated

■■■■■■ T U E S D A Y ■■■■■■

Choosing aids

There is an ever-growing range of presentation aids.
They include:

Aids to presentation

- blank flipcharts and whiteboard
- prepared flipcharts or posters
- overhead projector
- slide projector
- videotape and film
- multimedia and other technological aids
- models and samples
- handouts

Blank flipcharts or whiteboard
Blank flipcharts are the most flexible and generally useful
aid. They can be torn off and kept on display with masking
tape or Blutac. However, they are not suitable for audiences
of more than about thirty, or for formal presentations.

Whiteboards must only be used with the special dry
markers, and cleaning can be a nuisance.

Prepared flipcharts or posters
Prepared flipcharts or posters can be produced in advance
to a high, professional standard and used to display
complicated material. However, they are only suitable for
audiences of up to forty to fifty, are clumsy to carry around
and soon get dog-eared. As the most basic of aid, they are
also unlikely to impress an especially technology-savvy
audience.

Overhead projector (ohp)

The ohp is a versatile and useful aid which is widely
available. Foils (also known as transparencies, acetates or
vu-foils) can be pre-prepared or written during the
presentation. Pre-prepared foils are easy to carry around
and store for future use. The image can be projected at
varying sizes, making them suitable for audiences of up to
several hundred. An impressive technique is to produce
foils which can be placed on top of one another – overlays –
each adding information to those beneath. In this way
a complete picture can be built up step-by-step as we
speak.

There are drawbacks. We may come to rely too much on a
set of foils and neglect the basic techniques of presentation.
Also, some older projectors have noisy fans and every so
often a bulb will blow (although many projectors are now
fitted with two).

Slide projector

The 35mm slide projector can project an image of variable
size, making it suitable (with appropriate equipment) for
very large audiences – even of thousands. Slides can be
produced to a high professional standard and are fairly
easy to store and carry around, especially if kept in a
carousel.

Here too, there are dangers. Slides can be costly to produce,
depending on the standard and the method used. As with
ohp foils, there is the danger of relying too much on a set of
slides and neglecting the other skills of presentation. Slides
may get out of order, the wrong way round or upside down.
Projection requires a darkened room, which limits contact

between speaker and audience, especially if the speaker must operate the projector from the back of the room. If remote control is not available, two people are needed with a good system of communication.

By using several electronically linked projectors and sound equipment, tape-slide presentations can be developed with superimposed images, cross-fades and other special effects. Like the multimedia aids discussed later, these are very powerful, but can also be very dangerous aids.

For both foils and slides, there are three golden rules:

The golden rules

- **Don't use too many**; 8–10 are enough; more just confuse.
- **Use plenty of graphic material**; pictures, charts, diagrams, maps, etc.
- **Don't crowd too many words on**; 20–25 on a slide or foil is plenty.

Videotape and film
Both have similar advantages and drawbacks:

Advantages of video

- can demonstrate processes and events
- is highly memorable
- adds a professional touch

▬▬▬▬▬ T U E S D A Y ▬▬▬▬▬

> *Drawbacks of video*
>
> - may take over the presentation
> - may need the room to be darkened
> - equipment may malfunction

Probably the most effective use of film and video is in the display of short clips specially produced to reinforce the presenters message.

Multimedia and other technological aids

There is an ever-growing and impressive range of electronic aids to presentation. These aids include:

> *Multimedia and other technological aids*
>
> - digital cameras
> - computers
> - digital whiteboards
> - extended desktop technology
> - full multimedia
> - interactive keypads

Digital cameras

Like the almost forgotten epidiascope, these are used to project a magnified image of either two- or three-dimensional objects onto a screen. In this way, they have a highly-specialized but extremely useful function.

■ T U E S D A Y ■

Computers

Computer-generated material (e.g. graphs, tables and spreadsheets) can be used directly during a presentation. If the computer is linked to a network, material can be provided from other computers, or from sources such as the Internet.

Computer-based presentations are the medium of choice for many in business today. A laptop is equally effective when used in a presentation to one person, or, when linked to a projector, to hundreds. In the latter case, LCD projection panels can be placed on top of an ohp and plugged into the computer, enabling the screen image to be magnified and projected for larger groups. Large-screen projectors enlarge to a much greater size, and are thus suitable for the largest audiences.

There are a number of presentation graphic programs on the market, most of which are PC and Mac-compatible. Examples include Harvard Graphics (software Publishing corporation) and Freelance Plus (Lotus development corporation). However, the most widely used in Microsoft's PowerPoint.

Graphics software allows for better use of colour and text, while features such as spell-check and templates enable consistency of logos and style throughout. It may also offer animation effects that add flair to our presentation. Other web-based software packagaes, such as Macromedia FLASH, can be used in conjunction with PowerPoint to further enhance the animated effects you may wish to incorporate.

T U E S D A Y

Digital whiteboard

A projection screen can be substituted for a whiteboard so that a PowerPoint presentation can be operated by touching the screen rather than the laptop. By using the finger as a mouse, more freedom is given to address an audience rather than continually returning to the computer to move the slide show on.

Extended desktop technology

This takes the form of a PC-card adaptor which allows laptop users to link to other monitors and retain independent control over each display area. In this way, it is possible for the presenter to view speech notes on a laptop while the audience watches a PowerPoint presentation. Internet access makes for obvious real-time benefits too as the focus of the presentation shifts in response to questions from the audience.

Full multimedia

'Multimedia' adds sound to the screen output of a computer, and may be arranged to use input from video or audiotape or CD-ROM. It thus provides an almost unlimited method for creating, blending and using textual, graphic and sound material from the widest variety of sources.

Interactive keypads

Members of an audience can be provided with keypads, enabling them to agree, disagree or react in other ways, with the results being immediately visible.

The range and power of electronic aids (especially of full multimedia) is, as we have said, growing rapidly, and offers both great advantages and serious dangers to the presenter.

Advantages of multimedia

- Highly impressive.
- Almost limitless capability; text, graphics, sound (separately and in combination), still and moving images.
- Direct input from a range of sources, including networks.
- Flexible and can accept input during the presentation.

Dangers of multimedia

- More complex software packages require training in their use.
- Comes between presenter and the audience.
- Needs darkened room.
- May appear too slick, especially for smaller audiences.
- May be very expensive.
- Complex to prepare and use.
- Subject to rapid obsolescence.

The best advice may be, therefore, to be aware of what multimedia can offer, but to use it only with the utmost care, bearing in mind the size and culture of the audience and the objectives of the presentation. You should never let machinery, however clever, stand between you, your message and personality and the audience. And if the technology you are using should let you down, you should always have a backup plan. Having paper copies of your speech in reserve ensures a presentation will go ahead – no matter how much the machinery misbehaves.

Models and samples
Models of objects which cannot be displayed, such as machinery or buildings, can be a powerful aid with smaller groups.

Samples which can be handed round will use the senses of both sight and touch. If for example, a product being discussed can be manipulated in some way to demonstrate its use, it will give instant insight and be intensely memorable.

Handouts
Handouts summarizing the main points of the presentation help understanding and retention. Unless there are special circumstances, they should always be given out at the end.

The room

The environment can make or break a presentation. There are several aspects we should consider:

The room

- size
- acoustics
- noise levels
- distractions
- ventilation
- lighting
- furniture

Size

Nothing kills a presentation more certainly than a room
which is much too small or much too big. If it is too small,
people will be cramped, uncomfortable and may not be able
to see and hear properly. If it is too big, the atmosphere will
be cold, empty and may create a feeling of failure.

People may feel embarrassed and wonder what has gone
wrong.

We (or the organisers) will have estimated how many
people we expect. If, on the day, we find we have got it
badly wrong, it is always right to consider before starting
whether we can switch to another room. If not, and the
room is too big, we can make it feel fuller by asking people
to move up to the front before we start.

Acoustics

If public address (pa) equipment is available you should check it like the other equipment. If you have the slightest doubts about the acoustics you should ask whether everyone can hear you right at the start. It is not possible to check properly in advance as a room full of people has quite different acoustics from the same room when empty.

Noise level

There is a law of nature which says that whenever a presentation is being given someone nearby is repairing the central heating boiler, hammering nails into a wall or digging up the road with a pneumatic drill. There may not be a lot you can do about such events, but bribery has occasionally been known to work(!)

Distractions

Visual distractions can ruin a presentation. If anything particularly interesting is visible through the windows, you may wish to re-arrange the seating so that it is behind the audience, or even draw the curtains.

Interruptions are a nuisance. If they are at all likely you should make use of any available aid to prevent them – a secretary or assistant outside or a notice on the door. Phones should, of course, be disconnected or diverted.

Ventilation

If the room is too hot and stuffy, your audience will get snoozy; if it is too cold, your listeners will get tense and unhappy. The choice is often between external noise or adequate ventilation; it is courteous to ask the audience to make it.

Lighting

Poor lighting creates an atmosphere of gloom. On the other hand, if the lighting is too bright, it will make ohps, slide projectors or videos harder to see. In particular, you should check that light is not falling directly on the screen. Sunlight upsets some people, especially if it is shining directly into their eyes.

Furniture

The furniture and its arrangement sets the style and feeling of the presentation. It can give a sense of formality or informality, of lecture, schoolroom or group discussion. It can enhance or spoil the use of our aids. You should never leave it to chance.

You should check that there are the right number of chairs, that they are neither too comfortable nor too spartan and that they are suitably arranged.

Desks/tables

If people will need papers, you should see that tables, desks or attachments to the chairs are available. Tables add formality to a meeting.

Final preparations

So far, you have defined exactly why you are speaking, obtained and selected your material, and chosen and prepared your aids. Before we finally take the stage, we must consider:

- speaker's notes
- rehearsal
- how to rehearse
- the rehearsal audience

Speaker's notes

Good notes give confidence and can do a great deal to minimise nerves. There are four basic approaches, and it is worth looking at the strengths and weaknesses of each:

Four approaches to speaker's notes

- no notes at all
- use of visual aids as notes
- a full, verbatim script
- prompt cards or sheets

No notes at all
A few speakers can spellbind an audience, speaking for maybe half an hour without a single note. To do this always creates a magnificent impression of competence and knowledge. People remember it for long afterwards – often far longer than they remember what was actually said.

However, this is not a sound model to follow at the start of your public speaking career. There is nothing to be ashamed of in using notes. Producing good speaker's notes is the best method of ensuring that you have structured your presentation properly; using them is the best protection against excessive nerves. If, as you gain experience, you discover a talent for noteless speaking, you can cultivate it, but this will come later – if at all – not now!

Use of visual aids as notes
Rather than preparing separate notes, some speakers use their visual aids as prompts. This can be done, for example, if you have opted for a computer-based presentation or if you are using a set of overhead projector (ohp) foils or 35mm slides.

To use this approach, you must have all the material you need on the aids. This may not always be the case, and you should never prepare aids simply to act as notes. It is possible, if you use ohp foils with card frames, to add explanatory notes on the frames, but this can be confusing. As discussed on Tuesday, aids which have too many words on them do not work well, and a presentation consisting of slide after slide, each with lengthy text or lists of words, rapidly becomes boring.

It is best not to rely on aids as speaker's notes unless you are very familiar with your material and have become practised in presenting it. Under these conditions, the method can be effective.

Full, verbatim script
Some speakers write out, word-for-word, all they intend to say in the form of a script and then read it. But this approach has many drawbacks:

The drawbacks of a verbatim script

- Few people can write a script that sounds natural when read.
- Few people can read a script so that it sounds natural.
- A verbatim script is inflexible.
- It is easy to lose one's place whilst reading.
- It is impossible to read and maintain good audience contact.

However, there are some situations in which producing a verbatim script can be justified:

When a verbatim script may be justified

- to write out and put aside
- if we are on the record
- if we are using an autocue
- if someone writes our speech for us

To write out and put aside
There can occasionally be an advantage in the discipline of writing your script in full. It may help you to organise your thoughts and material and thus give additional assistance during preparation, especially with an important and formal presentation, or if you are covering unfamiliar ground.

If you are on the record
A leading statesman, diplomat or party leader may be on the record worldwide, and every word is likely to be analysed and dissected for possible shades of meaning. For such people, a verbatim script may be inevitable, although they are also likely to have the services of a professional speech writer to prepare it. Most of us will hardly ever be in such a position, although there are a few occasions – speeches announcing a major company policy (expansion, contraction, obtaining a big contract, etc.) – when it may be justified.

If you are speaking to a conference, or presenting a paper to a learned institution, you may also need a full script for publication later in the proceedings. In this case, writing it out first will kill two birds with one stone.

If you do decide, for whatever reason, to prepare a verbatim script, you should neither read it nor try to memorise it. The next step is to condense it into good speaker's notes of the kind described on the following page ('Prompt cards or sheets'), put the script firmly aside and speak from your notes.

The autocue
There is a machine called an autocue or teleprompter which projects a rolling image of your script onto one or two transparent angled glass screens in front of your eyes. This is sometimes used at major events by speakers who are unsure of their speaking ability, or possibly need a full script for the kind of reasons mentioned above. For most speakers, the device has many drawbacks: it is expensive, needs a skilled operator and calls for much rehearsal by the speaker.

If someone writes your speech for you
If you are a prominent and busy person, you may have the services of someone to write your speech for you. However, you will still sound more convincing if you speak from good notes. You should ask the speech writer to prepare prompt cards as well as the script or, better still, prepare

your own. The reading of prepared scripts is one reason
why so many speeches by public figures are unimpressive.

Prompt cards or sheets
The commonest and best form for speaker's notes is a set of
prompt cards or sheets. The use of cards, each containing
notes for a main section or heading of a presentation, is
almost a tradition amongst some speakers, although sheets
of paper will achieve almost the same effect. Each has
advantages.

Cards
They are easier to hold and more compact. They will not
rustle and if your hands are trembling they will not amplify
the movement as much as paper. Because they are smaller,
they are less likely to be overloaded with detail.

W E D N E S D A Y

Paper
It is easier to file, and can be typed or printed neatly, possibly using a word-processor or desktop publisher.

Whichever you use, the basic layout will be the same. Each card or sheet should have:

The layout of a prompt card or sheet

(A number to show the sequence)(**1**)

- **A LARGE, VERY CLEAR MAIN HEADING**
  indicating the section of the presentation it covers
- **Not more than five or six clearly-written sub-headings**
  (If necessary) figures, or a word or two to prompt points you wish to make: stories, examples or illustrations
- Prompts on when to use your aids
- Guides to timekeeping
  (Optional – some speakers find this helps, others do not)

The format of prompt cards or sheets reflects exactly the structure you have set up during the previous step on Monday, and producing them will act as a check that the structure is good and complete.

Rehearsal

Rehearsal is not always necessary and sometimes you just do not have the opportunity. However, it offers many benefits:

Rehearsal

- reduces nerves
- improves performance
- helps judge timing
- may help to refine the content

There are circumstances in which rehearsal is particularly important.

When rehearsal is important

- for team presentations
- for particularly important presentations
- if you plan to use unfamiliar aids
- if you have unusual anxiety

Team presentations
Presentations using two or more presenters have special difficulties. Speakers may not understand how they are to work together and may leave gaps, duplicate or even contradict each other. For success, they will need to plan ahead:

Planning team presentations

Each presenter must:

- Agree who will cover which areas.
- Know what opinions each will express, especially in controversial areas.
- Plan the use of aids, and how each can help the other when using them.
- Know the handover points and the cues for each.
- Agree how questions and discussion are to be handled.

All this makes at least one proper rehearsal essential.

Particularly important presentations
In one sense, every presentation is important. However there will always be some which, for whatever reason, have special significance. They may have a key role in selling, be aimed to impress a particularly important audience, or perhaps be part of a special occasion. If you are planning a presentation in this category, one or more rehearsals will always be justified.

Unfamiliar aids
Nothing will wreck a presentation more surely than bad use of aids. If our slides are in the wrong order or upside down, we block the screen from the audience, our foils or flipcharts are too small to read, or we can't operate the controls of the video, there is little chance of success. If you are using computer software for your presentation, you should spell check and check for consistency of font type and size. It will

also help if you know the numbers of key slides so you can immediately refer back or forward should the need arise. Thorough rehearsal is the best protection against all these dangers. If it can be arranged, rehearsal in the room and with the equipment for the actual presentation will be especially helpful.

Unusual anxiety
Speakers usually feel some anxiety about a presentation, but beyond a certain level anxiety can rise to panic. Rehearsal is of the most effective methods of cutting anxiety back to size. It is particularly valuable if there is any specific problem on your mind – timing, perhaps, whether you can find the right words to express a particular point, or whether you can bring off the start or the conclusion you have planned.

How to rehearse

Take it seriously
To be worthwhile, rehearsal must be taken seriously. Surprisingly, some people feel more self-conscious rehearsing than giving the actual presentation. There is something about talking to an empty room or a video camera that can sound quite silly and this may result in skipping bits, hurrying through or giving up halfway, none of which will help.

Timing
It is natural to check the timing during rehearsal. This is helpful, but you must remember that most rehearsals are much quicker than the real thing. Whilst there is no exact rule, the real presentation will porbably take 25–30% longer than a rehearsal.

Apart from the total length of the presentation, you should check the time needed for each main section and note it on your prompt cards or sheets. In this way you can monitor how time is going and adjust before a crisis point is reached.

Location

If you have the opportunity to rehearse in the place where the presentation is to take place, you should grasp it. It will help enormously to get the feel of the place, and to learn how the table, lectern, ohp, screen and other furniture and equipment are placed. If you are unhappy with their arrangement and can move them, you should.

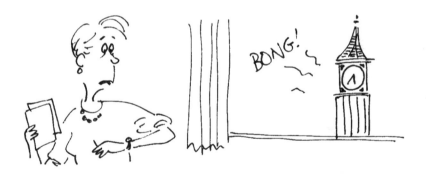

Over-rehearsal

It is possible to rehearse too much, so that you lose interest and spontaneity and become slick and unnatural. You must know when to stop.

Part-rehearsal

If you have not much time, it may be sensible to rehearse just part of a presentation; the start, conclusion or a key part or difficult section. If you have plenty of time, extra rehearsal of the difficult bits will help.

The rehearsal audience

Rehearsals are best if they give us some kind of feedback on how effective we have been and what points need attention. To achieve this, we need at least one of the following:

The rehearsal audience

- a live audience of colleagues
- a professional in presentation techniques
- family or friends
- video recording
- audio recording
- a mirror

▬▬▬ W E D N E S D A Y ▬▬▬

Colleagues
To rehearse in front of a live audience of two or three
colleagues is usually the best choice, if it is practicable.
However, to work, you must find people who are both
reasonably good judges of subject and presentation and who
are prepared to be honest and thorough in giving feedback.

A professional in presentation techniques
There are consultants who are prepared, for a suitable fee,
to give professional advice in the presentation of specific
speeches, arranging rehearsal and giving both verbal
feedback and video replay.

Family or friends
You should not despise the value of rehearsing in front of
non-experts. They can often pick out gaps on inconsistencies
in what you plan to say, and may spot assumptions which
are not justified or arguments which are not logical. Apart
from this, they are more likely to be frank and honest with
their comments than people who know us less well.

Video recording
Video recording, especially if combined with the coments of
a live audience, provides the ultimate in efficient feedback.

Audio recording
This is a poor second-best to video, but still worth doing.

The mirror
The poor old mirror is better than nothing, but only just.

Nerves

Nerves are the biggest problem for most unpractised speakers. There is no cure, but many helpful things can be said. Today we will look at these.

Getting the better of nerves

- Why bother about them?
- Facing your fears.
- Nerve-reducing tricks.
- Setting out your stall.

Why bother about them?

The great day has dawned. You feel petrified and are considering ringing up the organiser to say that you have contracted the lurgi and are on the point of death. However, this would be sad after all the work you have put in, and would disappoint the many people who have been looking forward to hearing you for so long.

Everyone feels them
To feel nerves is completely normal. All good speakers are tense before giving a presentation and the same is true of actors, instrumentalists, singers and other performers. However experienced and successful, almost all will admit to nerves before going 'on stage'.

Nerves are helpful
The sense of tension and anticipation ensures that your adrenalin is flowing and this, in turn, will key you up for maximum performance. There is a far greater risk of failing if you feel no nerves at all than if the desire to succeed gets you keyed up.

They won't notice
Since your feelings are so obvious to you, you assume that everyone else must know about them. But it is hard to guess what is going on in someone else's head at the best of times, and at a distance of twenty feet in a crowded room it is nearly impossible. Unless you tell them, or do something to give the game away such as holding a sheaf of papers in a violently trembling hand, the chances are they will never notice.

T H U R S D A Y

They want us to succeed

If a speaker or other performer gets into difficulties, the
audience usually feels more embarrassment than the person
making the speech. For this reason, the audience will
normally do whatever they can to give a speaker any help
he or she needs. They will wait patiently, suggest words,
point out the page of notes which has been dropped or the
elusive switch on the ohp. Only if you have done something
to offend the audience might help not be forthcoming.

The value of preparation

It is no accident that we have not reached actually making
the presentation until today. If you have worked carefully
from Sunday to Wednesday your task today – facing your
audience at last – will be far less stressful.

In particular, well-prepared notes will prove their worth at
this point, available as a sort of life-jacket if the waters get
stormy. If you have also rehearsed carefully this will do
much to strengthen your confidence.

Facing your fears

As with all irrational fears, it helps to face them squarely
and ask 'What exactly am I afraid of?' In the case of
speakers' nerves, there are several common answers:

What speakers fear

- not coming up to the audience's expectations
- making a fool of myself
- drying up
- not finding the right word

Not coming up to the audience's expectations
Giving an inadequate presentation is one of the commonest
fears – the worry that we are not clever enough, do not
know enough or have nothing to offer which can interest
our audience.

Audience analysis was part of the first step and if you have
carried it out carefully you shall have a sound basis for
knowing what they want and how you can satisfy them.

In fact, you will have been invited (if you have been invited) by people who were sure you had something to offer; the organisers will only have asked you if they were quite convinced you could do it and they have at least as much at stake as you do. If it was your own choice to speak, then you must have the courage of your original convictions.

Making a fool of myself
This is one of the most irrational fears, and therefore hard to quell. It is similar to the panic that grips some people when standing on the edge of a precipice. But just as hardly anyone actually jumps off, so your common sense and judgement will keep you safe in front of the audience.

If something does go wrong, it is the way you react, not what has happened, which matters. By remaining calm – adding a touch of humour if you can – an accident can be turned into a blessing. It will form a bond between you and the audience, show your common humanity and add a little light relief. It will also make your presentation much more memorable. Danger can only come if you allow yourself to show embarrassment or panic.

Drying up

If you have prepared properly and provided yourself with
good notes, there can be little danger of drying up. You
must also remember that there is nothing wrong with
occasional silence. The speaker is not bound to keep up a
continuous torrent of words; indeed, it is much better not to
do so. An occasional pause to collect your thoughts, or find
the right place in your notes, is entirely acceptable.
Controlled silence actually serves to emphasise a point and
give the audience time to reflect on the wise things you
have said. If you have a carafe or bottle of water and a glass,
you can use the legitimate ploy of pouring and sipping
some. No one will object (as long as it is not done too often).

Not finding the right word

Speakers are most likely to dry up if they search too hard
for the *mot juste*. But unlike writers, there is no need for
speakers to strive for semantic perfection; to try one or two
alternative words or phrases will often help the audience's
comprehension. Now and again in an informal presentation
the right thing may even be to invite and accept suggestions
from the audience – this can help to check understanding
and strengthen empathy.

Nerve-reducing tricks

Some speakers have their own nerve-reducing remedies. Whilst these may not work for everyone, there may be one which can help you in time of need.

Relaxation
People who have experience of relaxation techniques in other contexts may wish to try them before speaking. The easiest for general use are deep breathing or sitting in a comfortable chair reading a gripping yarn. If you know about yoga some of its techniques may help. If there is access to a hot bath that might just do the trick.

Picturing success
Some athletes, such as long or high jumpers, go to great lengths to visualise success before starting. To imagine in detail the sensations of making a brilliant presentation while waiting to start has helped some.

Sharp objects
At least one authority recommends holding some sharp object so tightly while speaking that it hurts. The idea is that the slight pain provides a focus for our anxiety and thus frees us from other more nameless fears. Suitable objects might be a bunch of keys or the sharp edge of the lectern or ohp.

Picture them in the nude
Anything which helps us to realise that our audience is made up of ordinary human beings will help to eliminate unnecessary fear. To imagine the audience unclothed helps some speakers to do this.

Dutch courage
As with driving, alcohol makes us feel better but perform worse. You should never resort to it as a cure for nerves; rather, you should make sure you avoid it, especially if you are making an after dinner speech. There is, of course, no objection to celebrating your success afterwards.

Setting out your stall

Before getting under way, and preferably before the audience has assembled, you should set out your stall properly. In large and formal presentations, such as a major conference speech, other people will help. But you should never be rushed into starting until you are satisfied everything is in order. In particular, you must always check, *before* you start, that all the equipment you need is ready.

Equipment must be

- available
- in the right place
- working properly
- understandable and controllable

Available
Organisers do not always keep their promises about
equipment. As soon as you arrive on site, you should check
that what you expect is actually there.

In the right place
It should be placed for you to use easily and without
obstructing the line of sight of the audience. You must
ensure that there is a sufficiently large surface on which you
can place the two piles of not-yet-used and used foils. If you
are using a laptop you must ensure there is no danger that
connection leads will hinder you in any way.

Working properly
To test the public address system, video, 35mm slide
projectors and ohps before you start will reassure you all is
well, or give at least warning of any problems. It is also
worth checking that the marker pens write properly, that
there is sufficient flipchart paper, or a wiper and the right
kind of pens for the whiteboard. Check too the battery in
your laptop if you are not running it off a central power
supply. Make sure there are no problems with the
functionality of the software you are planning to use.

T H U R S D A Y

Understandable and controllable
You should try out any operation (including contingencies such as focusing and switching between the bulbs of the ohp) which you may need.

If you plan to rely on someone else's help, for example to change slides, you must ensure that you understand each other clearly before starting.

Final arrangements
With the audience at last in front of you, you must pause and give yourself time to complete your final checks before you give voice:

- Rearrange things after the previous speaker.
- Put your mouse, slides, foils or notes where you want them.
- Clip on the tie mike.
- Ensure that markers, pointer and a glass of water are to hand.
- Draw breath and look up.

Presentation

You are on our feet at last and nerves, whilst still making their presence felt, are under control. Seven factors will contribute to your success during the presentation. These are:

The factors of success

- the start
- mood
- the voice
- the body
- aids
- timing
- the conclusion

The start

As with other activities, more than half the battle is getting off to a good start. There are a number of clues to success.

Don't apologise
However you feel, it is wrong to start with an apology. If you expect people to give you their time and attention (and you must) your opening statement must mean 'Listen to me. I have something of interest and importance to you!'. You must never use words which convey the feeling 'I'm not really sure whether I am worth listening to, or whether everything is as it should be, but perhaps you will be prepared to give me a chance'.

This does not mean you should sound brash or overweening, just confident.

Self-introduction

If you have one, it will be the job of the Chair to introduce you. Your responsibility will be to ensure that you talk to whoever is in the chair before the start to agree how he or she should do it and what should (and should not) be said about you.

If you do not have a Chair, you must decide whether it is necessary to introduce yourself. If you are known to all or most of your audience, there is no point in taking time and blunting the impact of your start by indulging in self-introduction.

Mood

Empathy and audience contact

As the presentation moves forward, you will need to make, and keep, contact with your audience, and to mould, understand and respond to their mood. Facial expression, glances exchanged, shuffling of feet, looking at watches, rustling of papers or frequent shifting of position all tell a tale.

F R I D A Y

Whilst the exact mood you want will depend on your objectives, some factors are important to every presentation. These include:

> ### The right mood
>
> - professionalism
> - the right degree of formality
> - controlled enthusiasm
> - pace and drive
> - good use of humour
>
> ### One factor to avoid every time is:
>
> - Arrogance

Professionalism
Whatever your other objectives, you will want to create an image of competence and professionalism. If you have prepared well, this should appear naturally, but your manner should reinforce your matter with apparent confidence and control.

The right degree of formality
Your audience analysis on Sunday suggested the degree of formality required. Now you are actually there, you will quickly learn how correct this assessment was and adjust accordingly. Most audiences today prefer a friendly and informal but not unduly familiar style. Unless there are contrary indications, this should be your aim.

Controlled enthusiasm

If you want others to be enthusiastic, you must be
enthusiastic yourself. However, it is possible to overdo it;
audiences do not like gush.

Pace and drive

As the speaker, you are the locomotive of the presentation;
you must keep it moving forward. On the other hand, you
must not gabble and rush too fast.

Humour

Natural humorists have a head start as public speakers.
Effective use of humour strengthens rapport between
speaker and audience, adds enjoyment, makes a
presentation memorable, and can disarm tension and
disagreement. The witticisms of the cleverest speakers have
gone down in history. There are few subjects which cannot
benefit from a touch of humour. If you have the gift you
should use it.

However, inexpert humour will have the opposite effect.
Old, badly-told or unfunny jokes create a barrier between
speaker and audience, cause embarrassment and tension,
and destroy confidence in the speaker. There is the danger
of offending individuals or groups within the audience,
particularly in matters of race, religion or politics by
including anything which they interpret as critical of
themselves or a group to which they belong.

You must therefore know your own ability as a humorist
and avoid stretching it too far.

Arrogance

Speakers must respect their audience and make it clear that they do so. Few things put people's back up more quickly than the feeling that the person addressing them is talking down to them. Even though they may have come to learn, the more courtesy and respect you show your audience, the more courtesy and respect they will show to you.

The voice

The voice is the speaker's main weapon (although not the only one; well-chosen and well-used aids will together have at least as much impact). You must use it with skill.

Audibility

The first aim, of course, is to be clearly audible; without this all is lost. The use of PA equipment has been mentioned; if it is available you should use it and use it correctly. If there is none, you must project your voice as clearly and loudly as necessary.

F R I D A Y

To project without shouting or strain takes practice. Hints include:

Voice projection

- keep your head up
- open your mouth wider than in normal speech
- use clear consonants
- speak more slowly

F R I D A Y

Interest and meaning

You must consciously emphasise the interest and meaning of what you are saying. You should aim to 'put a shine in your voice'. Meaning is conveyed by using variety of pace, pitch and volume.

Pace is the speed of speaking. You should speed up or slow down as the meaning requires. Fast speaking conveys enthusiasm and urgency, but becomes tiresome if overdone. Slow speaking gives emphasis, but loses attention if used too much. Occasional silence can be very effective to emphasise a point.

Pitch is the musical tone of the voice. This has much the same effect as speed, with the high notes conveying urgency and the low notes emphasis.

Volume is the loudness. You must be audible but avoid shouting. To drop the voice can add significance, if not done too often.

In all three, you must avoid any purely regular variations – over any length of time sing-song rhythms will send the audience to sleep more surely than anything else. Like an actor, you must choose which words to 'hit' – to emphasise – and which you can 'throw away'.

A good exercise is to record a short passage of a top radio announcer or broadcaster, write out what he or she has said, and speak it back into the tape recorder. This will give you a graphic demonstration of the skill with which a professional can convey interest and meaning by the inflections of his voice. The best can make a page of the telephone directory sound like a gripping tale of intrigue, murder and lust.

The body

The body can help or hinder a presentation. Inexperienced speakers feel their body is a problem and become self-conscious about it. Common difficulties include:

Using the body

- positioning
- what to do with your hands
- eye contact
- mannerisms
- gestures

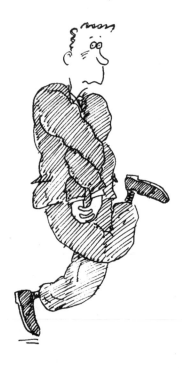

Positioning

You must bear several needs in mind, when choosing where to position yourself:

Position

You must be:

- visible to all
- convenient for your notes
- convenient for control of your aids
- well placed for the microphone (if used)

If there is a lectern, it is usually best to use it. It provides a convenient stand for our notes, and may have a light, controls for the aids and even a clock. Failing this, the natural place to stand is near the middle of the platform or speaker's area, with notes on the table. However, if a screen or flipchart is centrally placed, you must stand to one side whilst using them and may have to carry your notes. For right-handed speakers, the left side enables them to use a pointer and change foils more easily.

It is usually better to stand, even when addressing a small audience. It is easier to see and be seen and heard, and shows respect for the audience and the importance of what you are doing. Sitting is appropriate if your aim is maximum informality and audience participation; with such objectives, you might choose to sit on or in front of the speaker's table.

Pacing about by a speaker is distracting. You should have placed your aids as conveniently as possible before starting. Nervous or unnecessary moving about should always be avoided.

What to do with your hands
A lectern is a great help, as hands can be placed easily and naturally on each near corner. The same can be done with an ohp whilst it is switched off. If the table is high, it may be natural to place your hands lightly on it for some of the time. Whilst standing, the most natural place for the hands is relaxed by your sides, unless they are in use for operating visual aids, holding notes or gesturing.

You should avoid putting hands in pockets or clasping them unnaturally to front or back.

Eye contact
Eye contact with individual members of the audience is vital. It has several key functions:

The benefits of eye contact

It:

- gains and holds attention
- establishes rapport
- gives feedback

You should spend at least 50% of the time in direct eye-contact with the audience. You should take care to look around everyone, not dwelling too long on individuals unless you are, in fact, speaking to them especially.

In every group there are one or two people who are particularly responsive, indicating their attention by their facial expression and body language. You must avoid giving such people more than their share of eye contact, as you also must avoid undue attention to attractive members of the opposite sex.

Glancing out of the window or at a clock or watch, however briefly, is always noticed and has a negative effect.

Mannerisms
You should not feel that you must stand completely motionless and characterless. However, mannerisms which

■ F R I D A Y ■

are repetitive or obviously indicative of tension can be distracting. The commonest of these, which you should take special care to avoid, are:

Mannerisms to avoid

- swaying from side to side or backwards and forwards
- fiddling with markers, pointers or glasses
- placing hands in pockets
- meaningless repetitive gestures
- pacing to and fro

Gestures

Some people gesture well naturally. If you have this skill, you should use it. If you do not have it, or are unsure, it is wisest to limit your gestures until you have developed confidence and experience. Weak or repetitive gestures are a distraction.

To learn how skilful your gesturing is, you must have feedback. Video recording is ideal, and the comments of wise and honest friends or colleagues a great help. With these two aids, you can experiment with a range of gestures and practise those which seem most helpful.

Aids

Aids well used can be the making of a presentation, but the same aids badly used can wreck it. Some dos and don'ts of using aids include:

When using aids, do

- check lines of sight to the edges of the audience
- use a pointer
- write first, then read what you have written
- write from the side
- write legibly
- cover items on a list until you reach them
- remove aids when they are finished with

When using aids, don't

- block the screen or flipchart
- speak first and then write what you have spoken
- speak to the screen or board
- go overboard on special effects in an electronic presentation
- talk while something is being passed round
- show one thing and talk about something else
- give handouts until the end
- leave an ohp running for long periods

F R I D A Y

Timing

The feeling that a speaker is unconscious of the passing of time rapidly switches an audience off, especially if there are trains to catch or another speaker is waiting. On the other hand, a speaker who makes clear that he or she will keep to the allotted time inspires confidence.

Some speakers start by taking their watch off (or out), and placing it beside their notes. This allows them to consult it unnoticed, whilst also indicating to all that they intend to control their timekeeping.

The conclusion

The end of a presentation is second only to the start in importance.

Not with a whimper but a bang
It is always right to go out on a high note, and always wrong to tail off into silence or end suddenly and unexpectedly. Whatever else, you should leave no doubt that you have, in fact, come to an end.

Handling questions

Today we will look at how to deal with questions and end with a summary of the week.

No presentation (except a sermon) is complete until the speaker has handled questions from the audience. For some, this is the most frightening part of all, whilst for others it is the part they look forward to most, when they can at last relax and behave naturally. Success at question time depends on three phases:

Handling questions

- before the presentation
- at the start of the presentation
- when questions come

We will look at each in turn.

Before the presentation

The audience analysis will have helped you to anticipate
questions and identify potential sources of difficulty. Your
preparation should have provided further help. You can do
several things:

Before the presentation

- anticipate questions
- identify trouble-makers
- foresee audience tensions
- prepare reserve material

Anticipate questions

The audience analysis will help you anticipate those aspects
of your presentation which will most interest your
audience, or are most likely to raise questions. Your
understanding of the audience's interests, biasses and
existing knowledge will help you to anticipate what sort of
questions they are likely to ask, and for what reasons.

Identify trouble-makers

Most audiences do not contain trouble-makers. You should
not approach the presentation with the belief that it will.
But you may get clues as to the hobby-horses and
preoccupations of individuals who are expected to be
present. A friendly warning about Mr X, who 'always asks
questions about safety, whatever the subject', or Ms Y, who
'wants to know how single-parent families will be affected',
may save you much trouble on the day.

Foresee audience tensions

If the audience is a working group – a Board, committee or management team, for example – any clues you can get about how the members regard each other and get on together may help you to avoid traps. You may learn that Mr Z is unpopular, and others are inclined to reject his view on principle, whilst Mrs W is an unofficial leader, despite not being the top person, and her attitude commands great respect. You may find out that the board is split into two factions, and that whatever one accepts will automatically be rejected by the other – a tricky situation for the speaker, but at least it is better if you know.

Prepare reserve material
When preparing your material, it is often a good idea to prepare extra which you deliberately do not plan to use in the body of the presentation. As stated on Monday, you can use it if you find you are short, but better still, hold in anticipation of questions.

At the start of the presentation

You should guide your audience in two ways right at the start. You can take questions:

How to take questions

- after each section
- at the end

If you have one, it is the job of the Chair to tell the audience how and when questions will be taken. Before the event starts, this should have been discussed and agreed. As it goes on, the Chair should ensure that the arrangement is kept to. If you have no Chair, you must do the job yourself, having decided in advance what seems best.

As they arise
This is the best method when you are aiming at informality and participation. It can be particularly helpful if you are unsure of the level of knowledge or interests of the audience and need early feedback to help you pitch the presentation correctly.

This approach requires good skills in controlling group discussion. If not handled well, it can be distracting both to speaker and audience and can sometimes get out of hand.

After each section
To pause for questions at intervals – for example at the end of the main sections of the presentation – is the best method for a lengthy or complex presentation or lecture. It enables both speaker and audience to check that they are still in touch whilst there is the opportunity to put things right.

At the end
Holding questions until the end is the commonest method. It is essential when speaking to a large audience and on formal occasions. It allows you to develop what you are saying without interruption and is (usually) easier to control. However, it denies you direct feedback on the audience's reactions, and may allow a serious mismatch to develop between what they want and what you are giving them.

When questions come

The degree of formality and the strength of rapport you have with your audience will both affect how and when questions come and how you will be expected to deal with them. Formal presentations will generate formal questions; probably quite long set-pieces to which you will be expected to make set-piece replies. Informal presentations will generate informal questions, comments, interpolations, possibly group discussion. Your job will be to handle this as it comes, to direct it gently but firmly and guide it the way you prefer.

▬▬▬▬ S A T U R D A Y ▬▬▬▬

Panic may grip you when at last the moment arrives for questions. In fact, none may be forthcoming for what seems like an eternity. To avoid this, some speakers plant one or two easy questions amongst friends in the audience. There is nothing wrong with this – it gets the session off to a good start both for speaker and audience. The Chair may perform the same office. When the flow has started, the guidelines listed below will see you through to success:

When questions come

- listen carefully – right to the end
- if necessary, repeat or paraphrase
- decide why the question has been asked
- beware of assumptions
- separate the strands
- keep cool under fire
- never put the questioner down
- don't feel you must answer
- don't be too long or too short

Listen carefully – right to the end
If you are nervous, you may think you have picked up the questioner's drift from the first few words, but you may easily be wrong. One trap is to assume the question is hostile when it is not.

If necessary, repeat or paraphrase
Repeating or paraphrasing the question is legitimate, provided it is used sensibly and not too often. Both buy time. If the questioner is at the front of the audience, repetition may be essential for the benefit of those at the back who

have not heard. If you have the least doubt as to the drift of the question, to paraphrase it before answering is far more sensible than risking an answer which is badly off track.

Decide why the question has been asked
Inexperienced speakers always tend to assume that questioners are attacking them or trying to catch them out. Unless the subject is meant to be controversial, the audience have special reason to be hostile, you have upset them, or you have a personal enemy out there, this is unlikely. Most questions at most presentations are asked for quite legitimate reasons:

Questions are asked to

- obtain additional information
- clarify doubts
- support the speaker
- express interest and appreciation
- express another point of view
- make one's mark

S A T U R D A Y

Beware of assumptions

The assumptions on which a question is based may be different from yours in some important respect. If the subject is controversial, it will be essential not to allow yourself to be drawn onto false ground and attempt to answer from the wrong starting point. Even in less contentious situations you should always make sure you accept the questioner's presuppositions. If not, a polite statement of your own position will be essential before tackling the actual question.

Separate the strands

Questioners often ask several questions in one, either deliberately whilst they have the floor, or accidentally because they have not thought things through. In either case you must carefully and politely disentangle them before starting to answer any. Naturally, having done so, you will answer the easiest first.

Keep cool under fire

If a question is hostile or personally aimed, you must keep cool. Humour can often defuse an unpleasant situation, as long as you do not resort to sarcasm aimed at the questioner. The best plan is usually simply to ignore the unpleasantness and answer the question as if you had not noticed.

Never put the questioner down

If the question seems silly, ridiculously simple, or if you believe you have fully answered it during the presentation, there is a temptation to say something which makes the questioner look small. This must always be resisted; if it is not, the audience will always side with the questioner against you.

S A T U R D A Y

If the question does seem silly or simple, you will do well to keep your feelings to yourself and look for some hidden profundity to help the questioner out. Occasionally, there may actually be some hidden profundity which you have failed to spot. If you sense this, you may decide to explore politely by asking the questioner to explain further.

It is good practice to thank questioners, whether their questions are silly-sounding or not, either in so many words, by implication, or with a smile. In this way both the questioner and the rest of the audience are likely to remain sympathetic to you.

Don't feel you must answer
There is a natural feeling that questions must be answered, but this is not so. There are many options. Depending on circumstances, you can:

Alternatives to a direct answer

- ask for further explanation from the questioner
- throw the question to the audience
- throw the question to a colleague or acknowledged expert who may be present
- throw the question back to the questioner
- admit ignorance (and say we will find out)
- say the answer will come out later in the presentation
- answer a different (and easier) question
- give clues to help the questioner answer the question
- refuse to answer (on grounds of commercial confidentiality, national security or whatever)
- waffle meaninglessly
- turn the situation into a joke
- carry on as if you haven't heard
- walk out
- feign sickness or death

Whilst it is *not* suggested that any or all of these are suitable for general use, it *is* important to remember that there are always alternatives to a direct answer available to you.

Don't be too long or too short
Some speakers tend to use question-time as an opportunity to add large chunks of speech they forgot to deliver, spinning out answers to a great length. This may be a good idea if your aim is to take up as much time as possible and avoid having to answer many questions. Otherwise it is not

sensible, as it will frustrate members of the audience, especially those who are aching to get their question in.

It is not usually polite to answer too briefly either – single word or sentence replies sound curt, even arrogant, as if you can't be bothered to waste time with the questioner. The best length for a reply is, therefore, in between, long enough for you to show you understand and appreciate the point which has been raised, but not so long as to become another speech.

Heckling

There is the danger that members of the audience may take the law into their own hands and heckle or interrupt without invitation. In business presentations such occasions will be rare. However, if you are being consciously controversial or anticipate a hostile audience for other reasons, you must be prepared. If heckling does occur, you are inevitably thrown back on your native wit, aided by suggestions such as those given on the previous page. There are several options open to you. In approximate order of effectiveness, these are:

Reactions to heckling

- make a witty reply
- give a serious answer
- carry on as if you have not heard
- appeal for a fair hearing
- ask the stewards to throw the heckler out

Memory Techniques

JONATHAN HANCOCK
CHERYL BUGGY

WEEK SIX

Week Six

■■I N T R O D U C T I O N■■

Memory is everything. It drives every single thing you will ever think, say or do. And the way you feel about your memory is a big part of the sort of person you are and the quality of the life you lead.

At its best, memory connects you with the past, keeping alive people, places, experiences. Your memory helps you organise your work and the time in which you have to do it. It gives you access to vast amounts of information. It's stronger than the most powerful man-made computer, more versatile, more creative. It puts you in control of your world. But at its worst, memory is fallible and frustrating, inefficient and slow, prone to embarrassing lapses. It wastes you time, loses you money, puts everything into chaos.

Your memory is the most precious tool you have, but you need to know how to use it. Without proper training it will work well on some occasions and fail you totally on others. There will be things that you always remember, and things that you always forget, and you will be among the vast majority of people who feel that their memory is weak, and gradually getting weaker.

But learn how your memory works, start using it properly, and you will take your place in a privileged minority where memory is a priceless asset. However old you are, whatever job you do or stage of life you are at, you can quickly discover how to remember everything you need to know: names, faces, facts, numbers, lists, documents. You can start organising all the information that comes your way so that it is at your fingertips, whenever you need it, in a form that allows you to be efficient and creative. You can learn new skills, cope with change, improve your communication skills, your time-management, and more than anything, your confidence.

And when you understand how memory operates, you know how to make yourself memorable to others. People begin to remember the meetings you lead, the presentations you do, the instructions you give them. Your memory starts saving you time, making you money, and letting you enjoy a great feeling of control over your incredible, infinite brain.

This week includes everything you need to start putting

your memory to immediate practical effect.

Prepare to start getting the best out of your brain. There is nothing in your work, home or social life that cannot be done more successfully with a memory that is fit and active and under your confident control.

The right frame of mind

The Cray supercomputer weighs seven tonnes. Operating at 400 million calculations per second, it would have to run non-stop for a hundred years before it had achieved what your brain can do in a minute.

- You own more than ten billion brain cells.
- Your brain can make more interconnections and create more new patterns of thought than there are atoms in the universe.

The deeper we travel into external space, the more we know: but the further science takes us into the workings of the brain, the less we can say for certain. The brain's capacities are phenomenal, but its mechanisms are still largely a mystery. We race to think up new analogies for the way the brain seems to work, while struggling even to begin to comprehend its awesome potential.

S U N D A Y

> Question – How much of the average brain's capacity will be used in a lifetime?
>
> Answer – Less than five per cent.

There has never been a time when memory power was so important, and so neglected. It is undeniable that the workplace is changing at a pace never before witnessed. All of us are inundated with new information: new names, techniques, procedures, rules, facts, ideas. Stress levels are high, the need to communicate quickly and to think creatively is greater than ever – and yet few people feel mentally equipped to deal with it all.

How often do you hear or, worse, find yourself uttering the following mantras:

- 'I've got a terrible memory'
- 'I can't cope with this new spreadsheet'
- 'I can't remember where I left that lap-top'
- 'Everything's just too chaotic…'

Stop. Within your head is more than enough brain power to cope with all the new data you face, all the changes you encounter in your working life. Your brain can deal with millions of pieces of information in the blink of an eye. You just have to use it properly.

Learn how your brain works, practise making it do what you want, and you can start tapping into its enormous potential.

The first step will always be to focus on the present – the way you try to think, learn and remember *now*. It's important to consider your current approach to learning, in order to highlight the bad habits and start focusing on the things that can be changed. Here's a learning task that you're unlikely to have to do in real life, but one that can help you to see the memory strategies you naturally employ.

> How would you go about memorising the following number?
>
> 2821594434142463122635724

You have one minute to learn as much of the 25-digit sequence as you can. When the minute has passed, cover up the numbers and see how much of the order you can recall. This chapter ends with a technique for remembering the whole sequence with ease; but let's begin by considering what might currently be stopping you making the most of your brain's potential.

Negative mind-sets

You are the product of your experience. From childhood you have been on the receiving end of lessons, instructions, guidance and orders, from a number of sources. Parental influence led to that of teachers, your wider family, other adults, peer groups, and society at large. From that array of experiences, your view of yourself and the world has been formed.

The problem is, you almost certainly received far more negative messages than positive ones. Research suggests that, on average, ninety per cent of the messages a child

S U N D A Y

hears are critical or negative. It's hardly surprising then that many adults have deeply-rooted negative beliefs about themselves, and life in general. How often do you hear people say things like 'I'm not clever enough for that', 'I always failed in that in school', or 'I'm too long in the tooth to change' – and how often do you secretly agree with them?

Henry Ford said:

> 'Whether you believe you can do something, or believe you can't, you're right.'

One of the inevitable outcomes of a negative mind-set is that you're setting yourself up for failure even before you start. In many cases, you never even try something: fear of failure keeps you trapped in a familiar – but limiting – 'comfort zone'.

Yet we've all read about or spoken to people who are not limited by negative thoughts, not held back by fear of failure, not frightened to try something new. Focus on your negative ideas and challenge them.

For instance, if there's a nagging voice in the background telling you you're too old to start using your brain, you just have to look at the facts:

- ten billion brain cells
- ninety-five per cent brain capacity unused
- a memory-bank already equivalent to an encyclopedia ten billion pages long

S U N D A Y

The latest research calls into question the assumption that memory automatically deteriorates with age. If you can use it properly and keep it in trim, your brain can do things you never thought possible – and *keep* doing them.

Habit

Humans are creatures of habit in what they do, and how they think. We like routine, doing things the way we've always done them – too often not the best way, just the way we've got used to. Generally we don't even realise that we're operating in a habitual way, cutting ourselves off from options that could dramatically improve our success.

Think of a habit you've broken in the past. A habit has to be learned, so it can be unlearned. It might have been tough, it might have taken a while, but remember the satisfying feeling of success when you achieved it.

■ S U N D A Y ■

To improve your mental performance, and to start learning and remembering effectively, you need to identify the ways of *thinking* that serve no useful purpose; thinking that might be holding you back; thinking that you would like to change.

As an example, imagine you'd decided to do something about your habitual failure to remember people's names. The process of change would be built on the following key steps:

- *Accepting that your thought processes are simply habitual* – you've got into the habit of forgetting, and have no extra memory strategies to help you out.
- *Stating to yourself that this particular habit serves no useful purpose* – even when you struggle and strain to remember, you still fail to recall key names at the crucial time.
- *Acknowledge that you can change, because you want to* – a habit learned can be unlearned.
- *Knowing that you can change, however old you are* – ingrained habits are harder to shift, but never impossible: remember the longer you've failed at something, the greater and more noticeable the benefits will be when you start to succeed.
- *Seeing the advantages of change* – in this case, you would concentrate on the social and professional situations where remembering names is crucial: imagine the feeling of confidence you would have, and the sort of impact you could make on others.

S U N D A Y

- Confirming to yourself that, from this moment on, you will actively work on remembering names, using the techniques you'll learn from this book.

Congratulations: you're on your way!

The way you've been taught in the past

When it comes to taking in new information, people have different natural tendencies. Three key learning 'modalities' have been identified:

1 **Visual** – seeing
2 **Auditory** – hearing
3 **Kinesthetic** – doing

Although we all rely on a mixture of the three, we tend to dominate in one of the modalities.

Imagine you'd been given a barbecue kit to put together. How would you go about it? Would you read the instruction booklet? Would you ask someone to read the instructions to you? Or would you feel happiest simply playing around with the component pieces, exploring their construction through trial and error?

Chances are you will plump for one and that is your preferred modality. However there are those who use all three to great effect. In doing so they are practising a form of holistic learning.

It makes sense then, firstly, to know which is our preferred modality so that in any learning situation we make sure we receive information in that form.

Secondly, it's also a good idea to practise other modalities in order to flex the learning muscles and develop a more comprehensive approach to reinforce more thoroughly the information to be learnt.

By practising a multi-modality approach we can become progressive thinkers, and create a self-perpetuating circle of creative, challenging thoughts and positive feelings about ourselves.

Unfortunately, we can't always access information in the way we'd prefer. At school, it's estimated that children absorb as little of three per cent of all the material they're presented with in lessons, because of this problem. So it's often experiences at school that lead to the belief that learning is difficult: it always felt so difficult in the past.

To recap:

You have at your disposal an enormously exciting mechanism for learning and remembering – your amazing brain. You may well be limiting your brainpower because of:

- a negative mind-set
- force of habit
- trying to use it in the wrong way

You need to commit to making use of some of that ninety-five per cent of capacity that's currently standing idle.

So much for blockages to remembering and learning. What are the steps forward – the starting points for making this week work for you?

You need to be motivated

You won't succeed in anything if you can't see what's in it for you. Just as an athlete limbers up before an event, and focuses on the goal, before you begin your journey to effective memory you need to prepare yourself mentally.

What will you get out of improving your brain? Your list might include:

- dealing with information more quickly and more effectively
- saving time
- impressing others
- enjoying learning
- using new skills to boost promotion prospects
- increasing confidence

Spend a few minutes compiling your own motivating list, and make a point of looking back at it regularly.

You need a multi-faceted approach to learning

As touched on earlier, many people are turned off learning at school, and develop negative attitudes to their own abilities, because of the *way* they've been taught.

As young children, though, we don't have those problems. There was a time when we knew instinctively how to get it right. Think about the ways small children assimilate new information. They:

- engage all their senses
- give their imagination free rein
- ask lots of questions
- have little or no concept of failure
- remain enthusiastic and positive
- become totally engrossed in an activity
- try a variety of approaches

This is sometimes called 'global learning', since it involves the whole brain: the left, logical side, which deals with words and numbers, decisions and lists; and the right, random side, which attends to imagination, creativity, pictures and ideas.

As adults, we tend to limit our thinking processes, designating one thing as a problem requiring logic, and another as a challenge requiring imagination. The trick to effective memory and learning is to use both sides at once, and to benefit from all the options available.

██████ S U N D A Y ██████

You need the right learning environment

Today's workplace is often open-plan, busy, full of noise, movement and interruptions. It's fine if you can concentrate in that sort of environment – some people even prefer it – but it makes it difficult for those who need peace and quiet to think effectively. Just as we all prefer to take in information in different ways, we also have our own preferred places and conditions for learning.

Whenever possible, you need to take control of your learning environment. What sort of place would be ideal for you? Would it be:

- noisy or quiet?
- a small room or a large, open office?
- inside or out?
- heated or air-conditioned?

Experiment with the conditions, and be aware of all the tricks at your disposal for boosting focus and concentration.

- Tackle important information when you're most alert.
- Let people know when you need private time and space to think.
- Use a personal stereo, if a particular kind of music boosts your thinking power.
- Surround yourself with visual images that please you, and be aware of how colours affect your mood.
- Keep your workplace as organised and as calm as possible.

■■■■ S U N D A Y ■■■■

You need to practise

All too often we abandon something without giving it a fair
chance of working. We don't try as hard as we might to
change an old habit and replace it with a new strategy, and
reach for excuses to avoid practising it and putting in the
work. 'I'm too busy', 'It's too difficult', 'Nothing's
happening'. Suddenly the old, safe ways seem very
appealing.

There's no magic wand or instant fix. Look back at your
'motivations' list – the things you could get out of having
a powerful brain. Isn't it worth a little effort?

P.M.A. – Positive Mental Attitude

We've already highlighted the debilitating effect of the
negative drip-feed many of us have been on. The following
points will help you start to change negative into positive,
and begin building the right attitude to learning.

S U N D A Y

Remember:

- change is possible
- the techniques for tapping into your true mental potential are simple to learn
- learning can be fun
- the benefits of a trained brain are immense

Stop:

- limiting yourself
- talking yourself down
- expecting failure

Start:

- trusting in your abilities
- seeing problems as challenges
- enjoying the rewards of your efforts

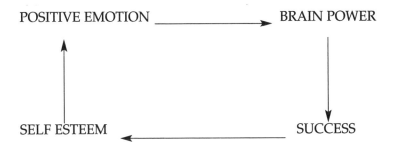

So, you need to ask yourself five key questions:

1 What's in this for me?
2 How do I learn best?

3 Where do I find learning easiest?
4 How can I start to practise?
5 How can I boost my beneficial thoughts?

Answer each of these questions in a positive way, and you take a dramatic step towards becoming a powerful and effective learner.

Learning habits may be deeply ingrained, but they can be changed – and when they are, the results are dramatic.

Near the start of this chapter you tried to learn a sequence of digits, using the approach that came naturally to you. Now, try learning it in a different way. It's possible to change information: to *make it memorable*. In this case, change the numbers into words. All you need is to remember the first two lines of a couple of very famous songs:

'I'm dreaming of a white Christmas,
Just like the ones I used to know'

and

'Should old acquaintance be forgot
And never brought to mind'.

Spend a few moments repeating the lyrics from memory, checking you can recall them accurately. If you can, then you now know the complete number sequence. Simply write down the number of letters in each word.

'I'm' has two letters, so you write down 2.

'Dreaming' has eight letters, so the next number in the sequence is 8. 'Of' has two letters, so next you write down

2 ... and so on. See how quickly you can write out the entire 25 digit number from memory.

This is clearly an artificial experiment, but it proves an important point. By adopting the right frame of mind, and showing a willingness to learn in a new way and to change information into a more memorable form, you can remember *anything*. It's even easier when you're motivated, and learning real information that's useful to you.

You've made a commitment to finding new and improved learning techniques – and now it's time to get to grips with how your memory works.

Your amazing brain

All knowledge is but remembrance.

Plato

If I had six hours to chop down a tree,

I'd spend the first four hours sharpening the axe.

Abraham Lincoln

What's *your* approach to learning? Like Lincoln sharpening his axe, how do you prepare for a memory task, to make it as easy, enjoyable and efficient as possible?

Imagine you had to learn the following shopping list of ten simple items:

chocolates, potatoes, soap, milk, paper towels, coconut, bananas, cheese, wine, bread

Spend a few moments now trying to learn this list as you would normally. As you do so, make an effort to notice what you're doing. What habits have you picked up? How do you try to remember?

By the end of today, you'll be able to learn a list like this with ease, and recall the items forwards or backwards. In fact, you'll be capable of learning a list twice as long.

To learn how to do that, you need to understand how your memory works. We'll examine the physical mechanisms of the human brain, to get a glimpse of how this amazing resource works, and how it must be fuelled and operated.

First, though, we need to ask a fundamental question: *Why* does it work? Why does the memory work sometimes – but not always?

Almost everyone claims to have a terrible memory, but they don't seem to think that it's *always* terrible. In fact, they're in no doubt that it works very well for them sometimes.

A man who forgets his wife's birthday every year may be a doctor with a mental database crammed with hundreds of thousands of medical facts. A woman who says that she can't remember telephone numbers could easily be a keen musician, and know countless pieces of music off by heart.

One of the most important steps in memory improvement is simply realising that some things are easier to remember than others. Our brains do work, and we prove our own memory power many times every day – but not every type of information sticks easily. Like Lincoln and his axe, you need to invest time preparing for the task, altering information to make it memorable.

▰▰▰ M O N D A Y ▰▰▰

We do this already. Everyone at some time will have made use of mnemonic tricks. 'Thirty days hath September . . .'; 'Every Good Boy Deserves Favour'; 'Richard Of York Gave Battle In Vain'. Perhaps you remember certain numbers by spotting patterns, noticing significant digits – your age, for example, or your house number. Unfortunately, few people ever get to know about the really powerful memory techniques – the ones that let you change *any* kind of information to make it compatible with the way your mind works.

To discover what they are, you need to test your memory. Use the following experiment to find out the characteristsics a piece of information needs to have, if it's going to be memorable. Read through this list of 25 words once or, if possible, get someone to read them out to you. As soon as the list is finished, see how many of the words you can write down from memory, in any order.

> shoe, watch, flower, Madonna, chair, lion, kettle, ball, pin, firework, pencil, tiger, phone, warm, puma, hill, time, sharpener, mugger, cheetah, hat, car, apple, book, kite

What's most interesting about this test isn't how many words you remember – but which ones. It's possible to predict with surprising accuracy which words most people recall.

book, kite – you're likely to have remembered the last two words on the list because there was very little time to forget them. No new words appeared to confuse you, so you were able to carry them in your short term memory for long enough to write them down.

shoe, watch, flower – the words from the very start of the list are also likely to have stayed with you. When the experiment began, your mind was fresh and alert. You were interested in the sort of words that might be included, and it's likely that you were making a special effort to remember.

On the other hand, the words from the middle of the list are a great deal harder to recall. Your interest wanes, your mental energy drops, your concentration wavers and the whole task just seems too difficult and confusing.

lion, tiger, puma, cheetah – most people who try this test spot the four linked words – the big cats – and remember them all as a group. Perhaps you found that this also worked for *pencil* and *sharpener* – two words that you could easily link together in your mind.

Madonna – when a word stands out from a set of information, is noticeable and unusual, it's much easier to remember.

firework – being able to picture a word is a vital part of remembering it. In this case, the word also conjures up sounds and even smells, making it particularly powerful, especially compared to the abstract words in the list like *warm* and *time*.

mugger – this word is likely to have provoked an emotional response, making it much more memorable than bland words like *pin, phone* and *hill*.

▰▰▰ M O N D A Y ▰▰▰

From this simple test, key factors about memory are revealed.

You remember:

- when your mind is alert, you're interested and motivated, especially at the start and end of any learning period
- when material is patterned or connected
- when information is unusual
- when you can picture what you have to learn
- when the information makes you feel something

You forget:

- when you lose interest and motivation, especially in the middle of a learning period
- when the material has no shape or connections
- when information is dull
- when it's difficult to picture the material
- when what you're learning doesn't provoke any emotional response

If you consider these points in terms of your day to day memory experiences, you'll see that they make sense.

The sort of information you tend to remember is:

- material you're interested in, or really motivated to learn, like statistics about your favourite sport, or material to help you make money
- songs, tunes and poems – connected into memorable patterns of sound and rhythm
- stories, also based on connections, with one event causing another, one scene linking on to the next
- faces – you know you've seen a person before

M O N D A Y

- unusual events – the days when you did something out of the ordinary
- embarrassing moments, times of happiness, fear, surprise – all occasions made memorable by strong emotions

Of course, most information we have to learn doesn't conform to these points. We waste so much time struggling to remember things that – as they're presented – simply aren't memorable:

- numbers – abstract, hard to visualise or connect
- names – you recognise the face, but what's the name? Again, the name is abstract, easily confused and forgotten
- everyday jobs – you don't feel particulaly motivated, the information is dull and uninspiring, and so you regularly forget it

M O N D A Y

So the best kept secret of memory is this: if information is difficult to learn, you need to change it, to make it memorable.

Making it memorable

It may well be a step that you've never really considered before, but it will revolutionise your learning. Learn something well enough the first time, and that's it – you don't have to re-learn it endlessly. Information is made compatible with the way your memory works, and so learning it is easy and efficient, saving you time in the long run and boosting your confidence and success. Well-learnt information is there whenever you need it, wherever you are – and in a form in which it can be explored, organised and then produced in the most effective way.

So how do you make *any* kind of information memorable?

There's a one word answer to that: **IMAGINATION**.

The Emperor Napoleon once said that 'imagination rules the world'. We all have powerful imaginations, seen in dreams and fantasies, and used when we're reading books, listening to radio plays and working through problems. It's imagination that allows us to take information and change it, to make it memorable. As long as you can return it to its original form when the time comes, it simply makes sense to explore and learn it in a form that your mind can handle.

It's time for a little imagination training. Below are four everyday words. Spend a few moments picturing each one in your imagination. In the first instance, simply try to imagine each object with as much clarity and in as much detail as possible.

- box
- tree
- car
- cake

Next, return to each item, and imagine picturing it from different angles. Can you imagine walking round it, seeing it from above, even getting inside it and looking out.

Now try adding some sense information. Imagine touching the item: what does it feel like? Is there any smell, sound or taste? Add as many details as you can to your imaginary pictures.

Next, practise making information unusual. Anything is possible in the imagination, so make each of your four images as unusual as possible. You could visualise the objects in a strange place, or doing odd things, or becoming very large or incredibly small. Exaggerate to make the images bizarre and memorable. These skills are vital when it comes to powerful learning and remembering. You take control of information in your imagination, make it visual and unusual, and give yourself a range of sense triggers.

Feelings are also important. To practise the skill of inventing emotional reactions to information, go back to the first word, *box*. You should already have a memorable image in your mind – but your task now is to imagine *destroying* it. How would you go about wrecking the box?

M O N D A Y

What would your feelings be like as you ripped it up, set fire to it or attacked it with a chain saw?

Next, imagine you're scared of the *tree*. How could you use your imagination to make this tree the most frightening thing in the world?

Turn the *car* into a source of hysterical fun. How could you picture it so that it made you roar with laughter?

Finally, invent an embarrassing moment involving the *cake*. Involve yourself in the action, and imagine the feeling of utter embarrassment.

> **Visual**
>
> **Unusual**
>
> **3-dimensional**
>
> **Stimulating to the senses**
>
> **Stimulating to the emotions**

As soon as a piece of information has been given these characteristics it can be connected with others in a memorable pattern. It's like inventing a story about your material. Each item becomes one step in the story, prompting you to remember the next.

One item can transform into another, or explode and release the next image. You can imagine joining items together, putting one thing on top of another, or seeing something come to life and do something bizarre and memorable to the next item on the list. Remember, anything is possible in imagination. The story doesn't have to have any real logic – only the connections you create.

To link these four words together in a story, you might imagine opening the box to find a tiny tree inside. You could take the tree and fix it to the rear view mirror in your car, and then drive off – straight into a giant cream cake sitting in the middle of the road.

- Think of the *box*, and you'll remember finding the *tree.*
- Think of the tree, and you'll recall fixing it in your *car.*
- Picture driving off in your car, and you'll remember how you felt when you smashed into the giant *cake.*

BOX ⟶ TREE ⟶ CAR ⟶ CAKE

However long a list is, you only need to deal with one item at a time. Make each link strong enough, and it'll take you to the end of your story.

The structure of the brain

To help you appreciate just what your brain is capable of; let's take a look at how it is structured.

Saint Augustine said 'People travel to wonder at the highest of mountains, at the huge waves of the sea, at the long courses of rivers, at the vast compass of the ocean, at the circular motion of the stars and they pass by themselves without wondering'.

Inside our heads we are wondrous indeed. In fact, the more we explore our amazing inner universe with all its range and its complexities, the more we realise there is to discover.

M O N D A Y

There are three clearly defined areas of the brain.

1 *The Reptile brain.* Also know as the stem brain, it oversees the primitive survival mechanisms such as self-protection, reproduction, nourishment and shelter. It is also responsible for understanding physical reality, collected via the senses.

2 *The Mammalian brain.* This brain area represents a quantum leap in terms of evolutionary development. It is here that feelings, emotions, memories and experiences are assimilated. It is also the part of the brain that deals with bodily needs and functions such as hunger, thirst, sexual desire, body temperature, metabolism and immunity. Having collected a vast array of information via the senses and bodily sensations, it then passes that knowledge on to the largest part of the brain, the thinking part.

3 *The Cortex.* This part makes up around eighty per cent of the total brain. Here resides the intellect, where reasoning, decision making and linguistic ability results in purposeful voluntary actions. It is here too that many believe the sixth sense of intuition can be found. This is the part of us that is able to perceive information that is not picked up by our other senses. It is the superior qualities of the cortex that stand us apart from all other living things and make us unique as a species.

As well as this tripartite brain there is another division into the left and right hemispheres. These are responsible for the different modes of thinking, and they specialise in particular skills.

The left hemisphere. This works in a logical, rational, linear and sequential manner. It takes responsibility for such things as speech, writing, details, facts and organisation.

The right hemisphere. This part of the brain works in a disorganised, random but more holistic way. It relies on intuition, and deals with feelings, emotions, visualisation and aspects of creativity. Although each part of the brain has its own particular responsibilities, all the parts communicate and interact with each other. If we delve at a more microscopic level into how the brain works, it becomes even more fascinating.

We have literally millions of neurones. These brain cells, each unique and with special responsibilities, pass messages back and forth throughout the brain to the central nervous system. They are able to do this via electrical and chemical reactions. Under the microscope a neurone could be mistaken for a minute creature from the deep. It consists of a central body with feathery tentacles known as dendrites. The dendrites have attachments called synapses, where the exchange of chemical signals takes place. Once stimulated by a chemical signal, a dendrite sends an electrical impulse to the cell body. This triggers a larger electrical pulse onto the axon, which acts like a lightening conductor. It channels the signal at great speed through its length, and out to other cells in the brain. An outer coating of the fatty protein myelin, helps enhance the speed at which the message travels. The final stage of the process occurs at the synapse, the junction between one neurone and another.

Neurones store information and act together to cause
actions and reactions. They work in assemblies, each with
specific tasks. Some deal with the outside world through
the senses and movement, while others are responsible for
internal communication between the areas of the brain to
ensure we can think, imagine, create and be aware. These
assemblies communicate with each other and with other
assemblies, simultaneously sending and receiving messages
over great distances and at phenomenal speed, while also
being aware of the whole needs of the body. Truly
formidable.

The latest research indicates we possess around ten billion
neurones in the cortex alone. Each neurone can have as
many as 20,000 synapses on its dendrites, which roughly
adds up to one million billion possible connections with
other neurones. Add to that the fact that each cell can react
or fire up around five hundred times a second, and it's
clear that the human brain is breathtaking, and its
capabilities awesome.

▉▉▉▉ M O N D A Y ▉▉▉▉

Where memory fits in

Memory itself is also complex, and most scientists now accept that memory is stored in different parts of the brain. There are also different types of memory.

Procedural memory. This is the unconscious ability to do such automatic things as run, drive a car, ride a bicycle, play a piano or juggle.

Semantic memory. This is where our knowledge of the world is stored. For example it is your semantic memory that knows that kangaroos come from Australia and that Sydney has an amazingly designed opera house.

Episodic memory. This is the memory that records and stores past events, but is not always reliable. For example your semantic memory might record facts about Australia, but you might not be able to remember all the details of a holiday you spent there.

Prospective memory. This is the system that lists the things you have to do in the future. It is one of the most unreliable of our memory systems.

In terms of our brain's development, much will have depended on our childhood experiences.

Generally speaking the raw material for full brain development is in all of us at birth. If that raw material is nurtured we will mentally blossom. For that to happen we need comprehensive physical and emotional support, and effective models that provide example and stimulus. The more meaningful your teaching and learning has been, the more effectively and thoroughly are the connections made between neurones. It is then easier to make reconnections and new connections.

The good news is that whatever your childhood experiences and whatever your age is now, you can effectively activate your brain and tap in to your remaining brain cells. That means taking advantage of the ninety-five per cent still left to use!

Storytelling

Let's return to the list of words at the start of this chapter.

> Chocolates, potatoes, soap, milk, paper, towels, coconut, bananas, cheese, wine, bread

Here's an example of how an imaginary story could be created to turn each item into a memorable picture, and then to link each one to the next.

Imagine . . .

. . . opening a box of expensive chocolates, only to discover to your horror that each one has been replaced with a potato! You investigate further by starting to peel one of the potatoes, and you discover when you bite into it that it's made out of soap. You need to get the taste out of your mouth, so you take a long drink of milk, but unfortunately the carton has a leak, and the milk pours all over you, and out across the floor. More and more milk is pouring out, and you try to mop it up with some paper towels, but it's no good. The level is rising fast. Sitting on top of the towel rail is a coconut. As you watch it grows and grows, until it's big enough for you to sit on and float on top of the milk.

A banana floats by, and you fix it on to your coconut boat as a mast – then use a large triangular piece of cheese as a sail. You find a bottle of red wine on board, and use that to paint a colourful design on your sail. Unfortunately you've been a bit rough, though, and a number of holes have been torn in the sail – which you try to patch up with pieces of bread.

Read the story through again, trying to picture it all vividly. After that, see how many of the ten shopping list items you can remember. Simply go back through the story in your mind, link by link, and write down each item as it appears.

It began with a box of chocolates. Inside that were potatoes, which turned out to be made of soap. You tried to get rid of the terrible taste with milk, but the carton leaked and you used paper towels to mop it up – in vain. As the milk levels rose, you used the huge coconut as a boat, and fitted it with a banana mast and a cheese sail. You painted the sail with

M O N D A Y

wine, tearing it in the process – and the story ended with you repairing the holes with pieces of bread.

It might help to imagine filming the strange events. Your mind's eye becomes a camera, able to zoom in on key details, move with the action, and explore everything that's going on. When you replay the mental film, you'll be able to recreate all the details of the story.

Put the technique into practice. Lay aside any other strategies or habits you might have picked up. Most important of all, be positive. Don't be tempted to think that the following list is too long to learn. You're only dealing with one item at a time, so it could be *any* length, and you'd still be able to remember it.

Bear in mind all the key points. As you go along, each item needs to be visualised, made unusual and memorable, and then connected vividly to the next. Abandon all normal logic, but make sure there's a strong reason for you to remember the next item on the list – and the stranger, more exciting, frightening, embarrassing, violent or funny the link is, the better. Exaggerate, and let your imagination run riot.

Here's the list: 20 everyday words. Take as much time as you need to transform the list into a memorable story, then play it back in your mind's eye and see how many of the words you can write down, in order. There's no reason why you can't even do the same thing in reverse. Simply follow the chain of events back to the start.

television, clown, rabbit, fire, tea, pocket, scissors, snake, bin, castle, slide, bush, money, newspaper, ant, sandwich, ring, basin, coal, cat

T U E S D A Y

Think like a genius

Global thinkers

Many of history's most famous thinkers and achievers have a single trait in common – the ability to use all of their brain.

Thumbing through a book that explores the sketches of the artist Leonardo da Vinci, one is struck by his breadth of subject matter and inventiveness. He was not only a highly gifted artist, he was also an engineer and military expert, possessing a degree of curiousity, ingenuity and universality of mind that made him outstanding. Lewis Carroll made his living teaching mathematics at Oxford University, but he also tapped into the abundant creativity of his imagination when he wrote Alice's Adventures in Wonderland and Through the Looking Glass. Albert Einstein – still one of the figureheads in the world of science – also explored the world of philosophy. He once said 'Imagination is more important than knowledge. It is a preview of life's coming attractions.'

What these exceptional men had in common was an approach to knowledge that is described as *global*. As outlined in yesterday's chapter, as well as the brain being divided into three parts, reptile, mammalian and cortex, it is also divided into two sides, left and right. The left side is responsible for logical, rational, linear and sequential thought, while the right side looks after the more intuitive, holistic, random side of our thinking.

da Vinci, Carroll and Einstein did not just tap into one side of their brain, they capitalised on both. Although specialists in their fields, they had such curiousity and vision that they made use of both the left and right sides – and thus they widened the scope of their expertise, whether it was to paint sublime pictures and design flying machines, or work on the intricacies of mathematics while writing about a young girl walking through a mirror into another reality.

Although we all do tap into both sides of our brains, we tend to prefer to use one side or the other. We shy away from pushing out of our comfort zones to explore and practise ways of thinking we consider difficult. We're leaving so much brain power untapped.

A global approach means that the brain is being utilised fully. Learning becomes easier, more can be achieved, thresholds and limitations challenged. The saying, 'None of us is as good as all of us', could well be applied to how we approach using our brain's capabilities. What we need to do is to develop our right-brained modes of thinking, such as feelings, emotions, music, creativity and visualisation, as

well as the left-brained modes of verbal and written
communication, organisational and rational abilities – and,
crucially, start putting the two sides to work *together*.

Global learning is further enhanced by using the senses and
by immersing oneself in a subject. By diving in and
becoming engrossed and asking the who? what? why?
when? how? questions, understanding is enhanced and
learning becomes even more effective.

The added advantage of adopting the global approach is
that it also produces positive emotions via increased brain
power, and encourages us to be even more adventurous in
our thinking.

More memory practice

Don't worry that you'll get confused between the different
mental pictures you create and stories that you invent. Your
memory is unbelievably powerful, and able to keep all the
different batches of information separate.

Put this principle to the test by learning another list of
words, and then checking that you can still remember the
20 words you learned at the end of the last chapter.

Here's the new list of words:

> grass, elephant, computer, matchbox, mirror, football,
> rocket, biscuit, caravan, fence, spade, cow, tent,
> cloud, lamp, shorts, basket, train, sun, glass

Remember the key characteristics of memorable
information. These words need to be visualised in as much

colour and detail as possible, exaggerated and given sense
and emotion triggers, then linked together into an unusual,
connected story. Give yourself a maximum of ten minutes
to commit this list to memory – to *make it memorable*. As
soon as you've completed your story and checked that you
can remember all 20 words, return to the first list, and read
out *those* twenty words – beginning with *television*.

You now have 40 items committed to memory, in two
distinct mental 'files'. As long as each story is built on
strong links, they won't overlap or become confused. In
each case, the first word is all you should need to start off
the chain of images – and you'll find that you can recall the
list backwards as well as forwards.

> Memory techniques like these may seem disordered
> and fanciful, but in fact they create a real sense of
> organisation and precision.

Picture clues

So far we've worked with lists of objects, each of which
provided a definite image. This means that you can
memorise lists of shopping or presents, or all the items to
be taken on holiday, but what about information that's
harder to visualise? What happens when you need to
remember words that suggest no obvious pictures?

The trick is to use *picture clues*. You think up a picture to
remind you of your original information. It may well be
very different from the actual word you're trying to learn,
but it'll be enough to jog your memory. Picture clues can be

T U E S D A Y

based on how a word sounds, what it looks like, or on an image that it suggests. You can use any picture that works for you.

As an example, imagine you had to learn the following list:

> *First ten U.S. Presidents since the Second World War*
>
> Truman, Eisenhower, Kennedy, Johnson, Nixon, Ford, Carter, Reagan, Bush, Clinton

Here are some suggestions for picture clues but the best ones are always those that you think up yourself.

- *Truman*: perhaps a cricketer, like *Freddie* Truman, or someone taking a lie-detector test to prove that they're a 'true man'.
- *Eisenhower*: maybe you simply think of 'ice' – or it could be an 'ice shower'.
- *Kennedy*: you could picture Barbie's boyfriend Ken, or maybe a rocket being launched from the Kennedy Space Centre.
- *Johnson*: the image here could be of Johnson's baby powder, or the actor *Don* Johnson.
- *Nixon*: perhaps a Nikon camera, or a thief 'nicking' something.
- *Ford*: a river-crossing or a Ford car.
- *Carter*: a man pulling a cart.
- *Reagan*: a ray gun.
- *Bush*: a bush.
- *Clinton*: Clint Eastwood perhaps.

T U E S D A Y

Spend a few moments coming up with an image clue that works for you, for each of the ten presidents' names. Once you have your images, learning them is as easy as learning the items on a shopping list. Simply take each one in turn, connect it with the next, and build up a memorable story.

You might imagine . . .

. . . Freddie TRUMAN, still wearing his cricket gear, climbing into an icecold shower – EISENHOWER – only to find Barbie's plastic boyfriend Ken – KENNEDY – in there already. Ken is covering himself with Johnson's baby-powder – JOHNSON – before he poses for photographs taken using a top-of-the-range Nikon camera – NIXON. The photographer races off to get the pictures developed in his FORD car, but he's driving so fast that he crashes into a CARTER. Enraged, the carter pulls out a ray gun – REAGAN – and the poor photographer tries to hide in a nearby BUSH but Clint Eastwood – CLINTON – is already using it to hide from the Indians . . .

Whatever kind of story you create, run though it a few times in your mind, checking that you can remember all ten picture clues and that each one links clearly to the next. When you're confident with your imaginary tale, use it to write down the names of the ten presidents from memory.

Check that you can still remember the two lists of twenty words – one began with *television*, the other with the word *grass* – and the ten item shopping list. All the pieces of information should be there in their individual files: already that's 60 pieces of data memorised with ease.

T U E S D A Y

Image illustrations

With practice, you'll get used to thinking of a picture to represent any kind of information. Often you don't need to worry about every last bit of the original material – just think of a picture that's going to jog your memory. After all, without these techniques you'd probably remember the information *eventually*. It's in there *somewhere* – you just need a prompt to retrieve it when you really need it.

Say you wanted to learn the following list of jobs to do in a day at work:

1 Set a date for the office party
2 Order new calendars
3 Buy a present for Paul
4 Arrange a game of squash
5 Pay cheques in to the bank
6 Book your holiday

You might come up with the following image 'illustrations' for each job:

1 The party itself, full of sounds, tastes and feelings
2 A large, colourful calendar
3 Paul, holding his present
4 A squash racket
5 Large cheques
6 A sun-baked beach

You could then connect the images into a story like this:

The office party is in full swing, and the noise is so great that all the calendars fall off the walls. One hits Paul as he's opening his present and he collapses, unconscious. You prod him with your squash racket to check he's OK, then write him a cheque for compensation, which he uses to pay for a holiday in the Caribbean.

If you ran through that chain of images a few times on your journey to work, you'd have a powerful memory story to help you organise your day. You could consult this mental checklist wherever you were, and make sure that all the key tasks were completed by the end of the day.

Numbers

So far we've concentrated on remembering words and phrases, but it's also possible to use the same basic techniques to memorise numbers.

These days, most of us don't need to remember large amounts of numerical information. What we need to get to grips with are PIN codes, burglar-alarm settings, addresses, extension numbers, birthdays, times – all mostly made up of just a few digits. Having a strategy for learning these small groups of numbers saves a great deal of time and trouble.

As with the lists you've learned so far, the trick is to think in pictures. You need to invest a little time deciding on a picture to represent each of the ten digits, 0–9, so that you always have an image-clue to use.

On a blank piece of paper, jot down the ten digits, with enough space alongside each one to write a brief description – or make a quick sketch – of the image you give it.

You could base your images on what a digit looks like. In that case, you might draw a ball next to 0, or write 'sun' or 'orange'. Next to the number one you could write 'pen' or 'pencil', or draw a needle or pin. You just need to think of one key image for each digit.

You might base some of your images on what a digit sounds like, choosing something that rhymes with it. Two could be 'shoe', three might become 'bee', four 'door' and so on.

Another possibility would be to make use of the significance a digit might already have. If you were born on the sixth day of the month, for example, you might illustrate six as a birthday present, or write 'birthday cake' on your piece of paper. Seven could become one of the Magnificent Seven, eight an After Eight mint.

When you've come up with an image for each of the digits, check that no two are so alike that you'll get confused. You can also fine-tune your system as you use it, so don't be afraid to develop and improve your set of ten images.

Using this number system is simple. To learn a group of numbers, you just transform each digit into the image you've assigned it, then connect the images together into a scene or story. The one crucial extra step is to make the scene appropriate to your reason for learning the numbers in the first place.

For example, if the code to disarm your burglar alarm was 3264, then your number system might give you these four images:

T U E S D A Y

BEE SHOE BIRTHDAY PRESENT DOOR

You could imagine a huge honey-bee landing on your shoe. You try to squash it with a birthday present, but the bee flies off and out of the house through the open front door.

BEE on SHOE, threatened with BIRTHDAY PRESENT flying through DOOR – this simple scene gives you the four important numbers: 3264.

The final step would be to connect this scene with your reason for learning the four numbers. You might imagine sounding the alarm as the bee escapes – to remind you that these images give you the code for the alarm.

Perhaps you want to remember that the PIN code on your bank card is 7205.

For seven you might have an image of HEAVEN (rhyme).

Two might be represented by a SWAN (shape).

Zero could be a FOOTBALL (shape).

Five might turn into a HOOK (shape).

You might picture yourself standing in heaven, when you see a majestic swan. You climb onto its back, and enjoy flying – until you realise that people on the ground below are pelting you with footballs. To get your own back, you burst every one you can catch, using a large metal hook.

To connect this strange tale with the original numbers, you might imagine seeing an animated version of it on the screen of a familiar cash machine. Every time you use a machine for real, you'll remember the cartoon – and see yourself in HEAVEN, climbing onto the SWAN, being pelted with FOOTBALLS and bursting lots of them on a HOOK: your bank card PIN must be 7205.

Practise using your own number system by memoriing the following historical dates.

> *Remember*
> - Step One: Turn each digit into the appropriate image.
> - Step Two: Connect the images into a short story.
> - Step Three: Connect the story with your *reason* for remembering.

Dates:
Gunpowder Plot: 1605
Death of Ovid: 17
Battle of Waterloo: 1815
Henry the Eighth born: 1491
Ruin of Pompeii: 79

Below are five UK dialling codes. See how quickly you can use your system to commit them to memory – and remember you don't need to worry about the first two digits each time, because all STD codes begin with 01.

Dialling-Codes:
Newcastle: 0191; Liverpool: 0151; Oxford: 01865
Peterborugh: 01753; Birmingham: 0121

Any kind of information can be given a picture clue, and those pictures linked into memorable stories. The information is simply being made compatible with the way human memory works.

■■■■ W E D N E S D A Y ■■■■

How to remember anything

One of the best things about the sort of learning described in this week is that it cuts out wasted repetition. Once you've created pictures and stories to remind you of a set of information, you never have to start again from scratch. You can quickly recap the material even if you haven't used it for months, simply by reminding yourself of the key images – and every time you do so you're strengthening the memories, rather than just learning the same material again.

Spend a few minutes now recapping some of the information you've learned so far, the images and stories that allow you to recall:

- the ten item shopping list, beginning with CHOCOLATE
- the list of twenty words beginning with TELEVISION
- the list of twenty words beginning with GRASS
- the first ten U.S. Presidents since World War Two
- the dates of
  - the Gunpowder Plot
  - the death of Ovid
  - the Battle of Waterloo
  - the ruin of Pompeii
  - the birth of Henry the Eighth
- the dialling code for:
  - Newcastle
  - Liverpool
  - Oxford
  - Peterborough
  - Birmingham

W E D N E S D A Y

You're able to remember any kind of information by *making* it memorable, and so far you've learned more than seventy distinct pieces of information.

Practice makes perfect – so try memorising the first ten numbers in Japanese. Don't be tempted to think that this is too difficult. The technique is one you're well used to by now. You simply invent an image-reminder for the way each number sounds, then link all ten together.

1 ichi	6 roku
2 nee	7 nana
3 san	8 hachi
4 she	9 q
5 go	10 ju

Image ideas:

1 and 2 – itchy knee
3 – sand
4 – sheep
5 – 'go' sign
6 – rock
7 – bananas
8 – a sneeze (it sounds like 'hatchoo!')
9 – a queue
10 – juice

Perhaps you imagine yourself . . .

. . . rubbing your itchy knee in the sand, when a flock of sheep rush at you, knocking you flying across the beach. You try to get rid of the sheep by holding up a large sign saying 'Go', but it's no good: they're all settling down for the day on rocks by the shore, and opening up their picnic boxes – which are all full of bananas. Unfortunately, sheep must be allergic to bananas because they all start sneezing – 'hachi!' – and form a long queue at a stall selling juice, which they hope will wash away the offending taste.

> itchy knee... san(d)... shee(p)... go... rock(u)...
> (ba)nana... hachi... q(ueue)... ju(ice)

Ten images, each jogging your memory about a Japanese number.

The best images and stories are always the ones that you think up yourself, so spend a few minutes putting your imagination to work on this list. Check it through a few times, reinforce or change difficult or confusing parts – then test yourself by covering up the list and reading all the numbers back from memory. If you were to recap your story a few times every day, within a week you'd know this list by heart.

The best kept secret

Stories are powerful tools for giving otherwise abstract and unconnected pieces of information a memorable structure. But there is another strategy – one that has been called 'the best kept secret' about your memory. It makes learning faster and easier, it works in the way your brain likes to work, and it has been used with incredible success for centuries.

Ancient Greek legend has it that super-rich Scopas threw a huge banquet, during which disaster struck. His banqueting hall collapsed on his hundreds of guests – among them Simonides, the poet, one of a handful of survivors. Identifying the bodies would have been impossible, had it not been for Simonides' trained memory. By closing his eyes and mentally rebuilding the banqueting hall, he was able to connect every guest with their location in the room, and provide a perfect guest list and seating plan from memory.

Simonides lived at a time when memory systems were taught and celebrated. How else could one teach, speak, argue cases of law or compose epic poetry without a practised ability to do it from memory? By Roman times, using mnemonic strategies came as second nature to great orators such as Cicero, who is known to have addressed the senate for days on end from memory. Before they were taught what to remember, students were taught how to remember it – and the central element of every memory system was what has come to be known as the 'Roman Room' concept, or the 'Memory Palace'. Simonides used the framework of a banqueting hall to contain the information he needed to remember the guests, and you too can use the frameworks – buildings, golf courses, towns, walks – of your everyday life to store vast amounts of information in an incredibly useable way.

It is a natural tendancy of the human brain to think spatially, and to connect abstract information with concrete places. Have you ever got to the top of the stairs and forgotten what you were coming up for? If you return to the spot where you were standing when you had the urge to go up, your memory may well kick back into action. Detectives often take eye witnesses back to the scene of a crime to help them remember exactly what they saw. If you listen to music as you drive around, it is likely you can recall where you were the last time a particular song or piece of music came on. The Roman Room technique capitalises on this strong link between memory and location. It makes use of the fact that you already know from memory many hundreds of mental frameworks into which information can be slotted and stored.

The route system

Step 1. Pick a building you know well. This technique also works well when you use walks, car journeys – even golf courses – but it's easiest to start with a simple building: your home, where you work or perhaps a hotel you visit regularly.

Step 2. Divide this building into ten separate areas. It often helps to sketch out a quick plan on a piece of paper. The areas could be rooms, particular features or whole floors – just however you think the building can best be divided into ten zones.

Step 3. Decide on a route, from area one to area ten. It's important that you're sure of the route, because you'll always take the same mental walk around this building. What would be the most logical way of getting from the first area to the last?

Step 4. Close your eyes and imagine moving along the route. Start by picturing yourself standing in area one. What can you see? What does this place smell like and sound like, and what details set it apart?

From there, visualise yourself moving to area two. Again,

bring this zone to life in your mind's eye. Keep doing this, going from place to place and spending a few moments in each one, until you arrive at the end of your route.

Step 5. As a final check, see if you can imagine making the journey in reverse. This shouldn't be a problem: in real life you have no difficulty remembering the way out of your house or back home from work. It's just a good way of making sure that you're fully confident with this memory route.

When you've completed these five steps, you're ready to put your route to use. It's been time well spent: you'll be able to use this mental structure many times, to help you remember many different types of information.

To use a route, you simply locate a different piece of imagery in each of the ten areas. These are exactly the same sort of image clues used to remember words, names, ideas or numbers. The route system just removes the need for a story to link them together: instead, the connecting structure is already decided upon. All you have to do is slot in the images.

Use your imagination to fix each image in place as powerfully as possible. As you make the mental journey around this building, think of unusual, funny, violent, memorable ways of placing an image into each room.

As an example, here's a sample route around a typical house:

1 front porch
2 hallway
3 living-room

▬▬▬ W E D N E S D A Y ▬▬▬

4   dining-room
5   kitchen
6   sun room
7   staircase
8   bathroom
9   bedroom
10 study

If you were using this route to memorise a shopping list –
apples, coffee, cakes, butter, sugar, oranges, mineral water,
salt, treacle, cereal – you could imagine . . .

. . . stepping into the front porch, and finding a huge
APPLE filling the room. You have to squeeze around it to
get into the hallway, which is flooded with hot COFFEE.
Imagine the smell, and the feeling of the hot liquid as you
paddle out into the living-room. Here, all the furniture is
made out of CAKE: a cake sofa, cake dresser – even a cake
TV. You walk into the dining-room, where a meal has been
set out on the table – but the only thing on every single
plate is a block of BUTTER – hardly a balanced meal! In the
kitchen, every cupboard, tin and pan is full of SUGAR.
Imagine opening up a high cupboard, and being showered
with an avalanche of sugar.

The next area on this route is the sun room. Here, ORANGE-
trees are flourishing in the warm sunshine – and the whole
room is painted bright orange. The staircase has been turned
into a cascading waterfall – but a very expensive one, using
gallons of MINERAL WATER. There are three rooms
upstairs. In the bathroom, the bath is full to the brim with
salt. Imagine what it would feel like to take a bath here – and
how it would taste if you accidentally got a mouthful! Lying

down in the bedroom is just as uncomfortable, because someone has spilled sticky TREACLE all over the bed clothes. Your journey ends in the study, where the books on the huge bookcase have been removed – and replaced with packets of CEREAL. There's cereal all over the carpet, and the desk – it's even got into the expensive computer.

In practice, filling up a route like this is extremely fast. Once you've done it a few times, you'll be able to imagine moving from room to room with ease, and take just a few seconds to visualise fixing each image in place. Try it, and you'll find that retrieving the imagery is almost unbelievably easy.

In the example route, you'd instantly remember:

- the apple blocking up the porch
- the coffee flooding the hallway
- the cake furniture decorating the living-room

- the butter served up in the dining-room
- the sugar filling the kitchen
- the oranges growing in the sun room
- the mineral water cascading down the staircase
- the salt filling the bath
- the treacle spilled in the bedroom
- the cereal all around the study

Design a route of your own. Follow steps 1 to 5, then put your framework to use straight away to learn the following list of items to pack for an imaginary holiday.

sunglasses, suncream, swimming costume, passport, travellers' cheques, camera, sandals, maps, tennis racket, toothbrush

It's useful to have several routes organised in your mind, so that you can use them in rotation. Once used, you'll find that the imagery has disappeared from each route by the time you come to use it again. On the other hand, you can fill a route with information of lasting value to you, recap it every so often, and retain it as a permanent resource.

Take time now to design a second route. Make it memorable, different from the first, but follow the same five steps. When you're confident of this second mental structure, practise using it by committing the following information to memory:

Bodies of the Solar System, in order from the sun

1 Sun
2 Mercury
3 Venus

4 Earth

5 Mars

6 Jupiter

7 Saturn

8 Uranus

9 Neptune

10 Pluto

As with the list of U.S. Presidents and the Japanese numbers, you first need to come up with an image-clue for each of these heavenly bodies. Here are some suggestions, but feel free to think up your own:

1 Sun – your son, or the Sun newspaper

2 Mercury – a thermometer

3 Venus – goddess of love

4 Earth – a pile of muddy earth

5 Mars – a Mars bar

6 Jupiter – perhaps a duplicator, or a 'dew pit'

7 Saturn – Satan

8 Uranus – uranium

9 Neptune – sea god

10 Pluto – Mickey Mouse's dog

Once you've got your ten image clues, you simply fix them into place around your route. Always be on the lookout for appropriate ways of slotting them into place, and try to make use of things already present in your mental structure – items of furniture, for example, as 'hooks' to hang them on.

If your second route was based on your workplace, for example, you might imagine pages from the Sun newspaper pasted across the window of your office; a thermometer fixed to the control panel in the lift; a pile of earth in the middle of the boardroom table etc.

▰▰▰ W E D N E S D A Y ▰▰▰

Give yourself enough time to fix each of the ten images in place, then see how quickly you can write them all down, in order, from memory. If you have trouble recalling any of them, simply leave a space and go on to the next area. It may take a little time to recall a few stubborn images, but all the clues are there somewhere.

When you're confident with this new data, spend a few minutes recapping the other information you've learned:

- the ten-item shopping-list, beginning with *chocolates*
- the list of twenty words, beginning with *television*
- the list of twenty words, beginning with *grass*
- the first ten U.S. Presidents since World War Two
- the dates of:
  - the Gunpowder Plot
  - the death of Ovid
  - the Battle of Waterloo
  - the ruin of Pompeii
  - the birth of Henry the Eighth
- the dialling codes for:
  - Newcastle
  - Liverpool
  - Oxford
  - Peterborough
  - Birmingham
- the first ten numbers in Japanese
- the ten items to take on holiday
- the ten items on the shopping list beginning with *apples*

Along with the Solar System list, that's 110 separate pieces of information, neatly arranged in mental files. Every time you recall them like this, you fix them even more firmly in your mind.

One of the most powerful benefits of the routes system is that whole sets of information can be fixed into each mental space. This means that you could easily create a single route to hold details of all the projects you were working on, or all the jobs you wanted to get done in a given week, month or year. The route system gives you the power to be highly organised – but, within that framework, to be creative too, adding and removing images whenever necessary.

Memorising sets of information

Using the 'house' route described earlier, here's an example of how *sets* of information can be included and memorised.

You might decide to make the front porch your 'staff training' room, if that was a key part of your work. You could decorate it with picture clues to remind you of:

- the outdoor activity course you need to book (rope swings and balance beams fitted around the porch)
- the names Judy and Roy, staff members you need to see about their appraisals (Judy might be performing a Punch and Judy show in a cupboard, and Roy could be sitting on the window-sill dressed as Rob Roy)
- the date 1st July, an important deadline (the digits to remember are 1 and 7, and this might give you the images PAINTBRUSH and HEAVEN – so you could imagine using the paintbrush to create a dramatic illustration of heaven on the front door)

Whenever you return to the front porch in your mind, you'll find it filled with image clues for all the key details to remember about staff training. You can add new pictures when necessary, and remove those that are no longer required. To do that, either visualise the old images being removed or rubbed out, or simply stop highlighting them in your mind, and let them slip away naturally from your memory.

You might decide to make the bathroom your area for remembering details about the key tasks you need to accomplish before the end of the month. You could imagine:

- finding the bath full of old door signs (since you need to order new ones)
- flushing computer disks down the toilet (to remind you to replace a key software product)
- discovering Ben Hur using the shower to wash his golf clubs (to make sure you remember to organise a game of golf with your colleague Ben)
- seeing Ben Hur use his shoe to kick oranges around the bathroom (giving you the digits 2 (SHOE) and 0 (ORANGE), and thus a reminder to arrange the match for the 20th)

The mental routes you create can also help you read, digest and remember texts and documents. As you read, get used to breaking the information down into key points. You're going to be illustrating each point with an image clue – so what *are* the key points? How much detailed information do you need to retain, and what images would jog your memory about each main point?

As you're reading, jot down key words or phrases that would act as a sufficient 'crib sheet'. Reading a memo about a change of premises, for example, you might jot down:

- moving
- 5th December
- Derby
- 3 new jobs
- Paul in charge of project

When you'd finished, you would give each point an image clue. Perhaps you imagine choosing slides to illustrate this information in a visual presentation. What picture would be appropriate for each idea?

You might choose:

- a removal van
- someone using a hook (5) to pull a nail (1) out of a shoe (2) – 5/12
- a Demolition *Derby*
- worker *bees* (3)
- the dome of St. *Paul's* Cathedral

Fixing the images into one of your memory routes, you might imagine:

- a removal van crashing into the porch
- a cobbler at work in the hallway, using his hook to prise a nail from a shoe
- a Demolition Derby taking place in the living-room
- three worker bees eating at the dining-room table
- the kitchen transformed into St. Paul's Cathedral

As always, the process written down looks more complicated than it is in practice. You could easily slot images into your route as you read through the text, and the habit of thinking in pictures is an easy one to pick up. Soon you'll be condensing all the material you read automatically, and coming up with memorable illustrations with ease.

Reading like this is almost certainly slower than you're used to but how often have you 'read' a whole page without taking in a single piece of information? *Active* reading is much more focused, so it feels more tiring to begin with, but you do it in shorter bursts – and get out exactly what you put in. Give it a try, and soon you'll be reading not just for the sake of reading, but to understand and learn.

A recent newspaper article analysed a report about the things people liked least about their working life – and how they would go about making changes if they could. It broke the 'moans' and 'wishes' into two lists of ten key points – just as you could have done if you were presented with the entire research document.

To practise illustrating ideas picked out of larger texts, and fixing the images into a route, try coming up with a picture to represent each of the ten 'wishes' printed below, then arranging them around one of your mental frameworks.

Top Ten Wishes
  1 to work shorter hours
  2 to change 'company culture'
  3 to work flexible hours
  4 to avoid commuting
  5 to work from home
  6 to change job
  7 to have more staff
  8 to earn more
  9 to retire
 10 to have less stress

Learning to learn

You have a test approaching, your emotions are in a turmoil as you realise you have just so much to remember. Your mind appears blank as you spin into panic. There is an important presentation looming, you feel stressed and anxious, convinced you will forget everything and make a fool of yourself. The radio interview which will give you the opportunity to talk about your company and its work is tomorrow, but how will you remember your name, let alone get your message across? Such responses are typical: we've all felt that sinking feeling. Somehow it seems that whatever it was we did know has been lost in the recesses of our brain.

However it doesn't have to be that way. If you begin to put the following advice into practice and do the necessary preparation, you are putting yourself in the best possible setting to meet with success. It's good to know that by regularly using these tips and techniques you can enhance your ability to learn, remember with ease, get those answers right, interview with high impact and make a memorable presentation without reading from copious notes.

Step one: put yourself in the best learning environment for you.
There is little point struggling to learn effectively if where you are working is too noisy, too quiet, too hot or too cold, too untidy or too bare and unwelcoming. Whatever is best for you, try to create it before you start to tackle whatever it is you have to learn and remember. It is worth mentioning that current research concludes that the colour of the room you are in, the music you might be playing, the smells you are inhaling, the pictures on the walls, even how you are sitting, can all have a profound impact on your emotions and therefore your attitude to your work.

Step two: ensure you are in a positive frame of mind.
Feeling good about yourself and your abilities and anticipating a good outcome to your endeavours is very important. Just as no athlete worth his salt would dream of approaching the starting blocks of a race with a negative mind set, so you should see a successful outcome to your work. Recognise negative self talk and replace it with something more constructive and positive.

You might find using creative visualisation techniques could help you here. This is a method of relaxing and mentally creating a positive outcome to whatever it is you are about to embark on. It is a way of setting yourself up for success not failure.

Other techniques include using affirmations. This is a method of repeating positive statements about yourself and your abilities. There is also the reframing technique. Here you choose to banish negative self talk and select the positive way of viewing something.

Remember everything has a positive aspect to it if you really look hard enough. Choose to view your abilities and your approach to learning in a new way.

Step three: see what's in it for you.
Now that may be easier said than done especially if you have to deal with information that does not exactly excite you. But whatever you're tackling, you're much more likely to remember it if you can see what use it will be to you and how it will help you. In this way you become an *active*, not a *passive*, learner. Remember, there is a positive gain in everything, if you are prepared to look for it.

T H U R S D A Y

Step four: be prepared to re-learn.

We are creatures of habit in the way we think, and consequently we can limit ourselves by the mental boundaries we have set ourselves as a result of past experiences. Reframing, thinking outside the box, accepting there might be other ways of approaching a subject, and seeing the big picture, all help to encourage a more proactive stance to learning and retaining information. Remember too the importance of the global approach to learning that we covered in the previous chapter.

Step five: be courageous and don't be defeated by past mistakes or learning problems that seem insurmountable.

It could be the case that the way you were taught in the past did not suit you, but you can do something about that now by knowing and using the learning style that is right for you, be it visual, auditory, kinesthetic, or a mixture of all three. It's all too easy to stay in one's comfort zone rather than going out and trying new ways of learning and new areas of knowledge. Don't limit yourself or subscribe to the 'Better the devil you know' mentality.

Step six: be clear about what you want to achieve from what you are about to learn.

At the same time realise how much you already do know in order to boost your confidence. Be willing to look back at past successes and victories to see how far you have come already. Why not make a list of what you have achieved so far? Keep a note book that celebrates your successes, on the walls stick up pictures, photographs, certificates, anything that is a constant reminder of good positive experiences. Do not subscribe to the negative statement that self-praise is not good for you.

▬▬▬▬ T H U R S D A Y ▬▬▬▬

Step seven: reward yourself regularly for what you are achieving.
If you have been working hard and meeting the targets you
have set yourself, what's wrong with taking a day off to do
something you really enjoy, or treating yourself in the
shops? It's also important to nurture yourself if the going
gets tough. Be kind to yourself. A day at a health spa, a
relaxing aromatherapy bath, laying in a hammock with a
glass of wine and a good book might be ideas you would
like to consider.

*Step eight: keep yourself in tip-top condition by eating well,
sleeping well and taking regular exercise.*
A balanced healthy eating programme not only helps
prevent unnecessary wear and tear on your body, it also
energises you and helps you keep mentally fit. Getting
enough good quality sleep should also figure in helping
you operate at your optimum level. If you are not sleeping
well consider how you can relax and let go before going to
bed.

▰▰▰▰▰▰▰T H U R S D A Y▰▰▰▰▰

Do you need to invest in a new mattress? Would using essential oils on your pillow help? or playing relaxing music? or using ear plugs? Also try to ensure you are taking regular exercise, at least twice a week. Sometimes just getting up a little earlier for a brisk walk can help set you up for a more energetic positive day, and certainly after a day full of pressure, exercise helps burn off excess stress.

Step nine: crucially, practise by going over the knowledge you are acquiring and have acquired.
Ensure you put the information you need into your brain in a meaningful way, then revisit it regularly to further reinforce it.

By using these tips and techniques you will find that you are building a strong and healthy mental attitude to learning and remembering. Your outlook will be positive as you approach new information. Also your ability to absorb facts more comprehensively and with greater ease, means you will have far more confidence when it comes to recalling information for any tests, or approaching interviews, presentations or communications of any kind.

So how can you begin to take action to ensure you incorporate this advice into your everyday life so that you are in the best possible frame of mind to learn and remember?

Action

1 Are you in the best learning environment?
  What changes can you make?

2 Do you have a positive mental attitude?
  What improvements can you make?

T H U R S D A Y

Action

3 How can you get the most out of any learning experience?
What's in it for you?

4 What mental barriers have you set up? Name a limitation around learning or memory that you have imposed on yourself?
Where has it come from?
How can you change it?

5 What is your preferred learning style? How could you improve your abilities in the other modalities?
Mentally revisit a mistake or failure. How can you now regard it in a more positive way?

6 List five recent successes in order to appreciate your abilities.
List five more you want to achieve.

7 How can you reward yourself when you do well?
How can you pamper yourself?
How can you nurture yourself when the going gets tough?

8 How can you improve your diet?
How can you improve your exercise regime?
Are you getting good quality sleep?
Are you taking time for relaxation?

T H U R S D A Y

Action

9 How can you practise what you are currently absorbing about memory and learning?

To conclude today, let's see how well you have remembered the lists from the previous days.

What are:

- the ten item shopping-list, beginning with *chocolates*
- the list of twenty words, beginning with *television*
- the list of twenty words, beginning with *grass*
- the first ten U.S. Presidents since World War Two
- the dates of:
  - the Gunpowder Plot
  - the death of Ovid
  - the Battle of Waterloo
  - the ruin of Pompeii
  - the birth of Henry the Eighth
- the dialling codes for:
  - Newcastle
  - Liverpool
  - Oxford
  - Peterborough
  - Birmingham
- the first ten numbers in Japanese
- the ten items to take on holiday
- the ten items on the shopping list, beginning with *apples*
- the top ten 'wishes'

People skills

One of the traditional party-pieces of the stage memory performer is remembering the names of every member of the audience. American magician and mnemonist Harry Lorayne made it his trademark, reciting theatrefuls of names night after night. One estimate put the number of names he had successfully recalled at eight million.

Many great military leaders, politicians and businesspeople have demonstrated equally breathtaking abilities to remember names. And yet for most people, remembering even one new name at a time is too much.

Perhaps you know what this feels like: you are at a conference, talking to a colleague, when a recent acquaintance comes over to join them and it's up to you to introduce them to each other – and suddenly you cannot remember either of their names. But imagine the opposite effect. Think how powerful it would be to be able to put names to faces at meetings and parties; how effective to remember key facts about the people you do business with; and how useful to know enough about memory to make everyone you meet remember you.

Step One is to listen, to hear people's names when you are introduced to them. Slow the process down: practise asking people to repeat their name if you missed it. Give yourself time to take it in.

Step Two is to be interested in every new name you hear. Ask where it comes from, what it means, how it's spelled.

Step Three is to switch on your mind's eye and visualise the name. Spend a couple of seconds imagining what the name would look like written down, or how it might come out as a signature.

Step Four is to think of picture clues. What images come into your head when you think of the name? You're only looking for image triggers, so you might pick just part of the name to turn into a picture – an object, place or animal. Perhaps you think of a well-known person who shares the name, or a friend or relative of yours. You are making a vital memory move – moving away from abstract names to images that are real, unusual, interesting, colourful and memorable.

As the pictures start to emerge, Step Five is to try to make some connection with the real person in front of you. Imagine them holding whatever image has occurred to you, standing in the place that came to mind, or turning into the famous person you thought of. Think of their name as *illustrating* them in some way, and use your imagination to connect them with the image clues their name suggests.

For example, if you meet John Butcher, his name might well suggest meat, knives, chopping boards, roast dinners. As you talk to him, picture him taking out a huge meat cleaver and chopping great hunks of meat. As always you can involve your senses, switching on every facet of your memory, fixing your new friend in your mind with some powerful memory joggers.

With practice you can carry out these five steps quickly, without them getting in the way of conversation, and learn to give yourself enough memory clues to negotiate a

F R I D A Y

meeting or party. Afterwards, it is up to you how many of the new names you choose to remember permanently. You can invest time in rehearsing the most important names and adding extra details so that you remember them long into the future.

Here are some more examples of image clues:

Surnames

- Anderson: perhaps someone hiding in an Anderson air-raid shelter, wearing a gas-mask
- Shelley: covered in sea-shells
- Rowling: constantly performing forward rolls
- Jones: singing in the style of Tom Jones
- Cathcart: pulling a cart piled with cats

First names

- Leo: lion
- Kate: kite
- Mark: covered in dirty marks
- Mike: holding a microphone
- Donna: prima donna ballerina

Leo Shelley could be visualised roaring like a lion *and* covered with shells. Mike Rowling could be trying to talk into his microphone *and* do hundreds of forward rolls. The trick is to build up a set of images, using all the time at your disposal to add extra reminders.

Every new piece of information can also be given an image

and added to the mental scene. You might picture Kate Jones flying a kite while singing Tom Jones songs – at the same time as working out on an exercise bike and reading a book – representing the two hobbies she's told you about. If you recalled an image of Donna Anderson dancing around her air-raid shelter – and talking to a man in a fig-leaf – you'd remember that her husband was called Adam.

Remember people's names a few times by using these techniques, and you'll soon find that you know them off by heart. The strange imagery fades away, and you'll have forgotten *why* you know them – you just *do*.

Don't worry about getting names wrong. There are plenty of jokes about people confusing mental images and making embarrassing gaffes, but in reality this rarely happens. Mnemonic techniques just give you extra chances for learning more names – and when you get in the habit of remembering, that feeling of confidence is often enough in itself to make you remember.

Printed below are ten names, along with an extra fact about each one. Learn them all by using one of your mental routes. Think up images to jog your memory about each first name, surname and personal fact, then fix them in the spaces around the route.

Tom Bird: enjoys fishing
Sheila Walker: comes from India
Richard Welsh: works with computers
Arnold Donald: has a wife called Jean
Tracey Cole: keen tennis player
Jane Webster: American

F R I D A Y

Ronald Smith: enjoys cooking
Tara Singh: accountant
Shaun MacDuff: keen horse-rider
Juan Domingo: married to Maria

To recover the information, simply retrace your steps, moving from room to room in your mind. Each area on the route should contain clues to three key pieces of information: first name, surname, and personal detail.

When you're confident with the imagery you've created, see how much of this information you can write down from memory. You may not remember every single person you meet, but these techniques will certainly help you feel more confident about keeping track of the important ones.

Thinking creatively like this is also a good basis for creative conversations. If you get used to thinking in pictures from the first moment you meet someone, then you're in the perfect frame of mind to discuss ideas and possibilities, and to solve problems. You'll also be aware of what it takes for other people to remember *you*. Give them time to hear your name and take it in. When you're talking about yourself, try to speak in pictures and stories, suggesting images and emotional responses for them to latch on to.

It can only benefit you if people remember you, and even simple strategies like these can be more effective than the most expensive business card.

F R I D A Y

Communicating effectively from memory

Talks, interviews and presentations

What you have already learned about how the brain functions, and how we learn and remember best, can stand you in good stead when it comes to performing in the public arena. You can tailor-make your message to appeal to all of your audience by considering the following nine points.

1 Ensure you paint pictures with the words you use. Remember how the brain likes unusual, dramatic exciting images. Make use of similes and metaphors.

2 Tap into the three modalities by giving your audience something to see, hear and do.

3 Include such information, and present it in such a way, that it will appeal to both left- and right-brained thinkers. Make use of the power of tapping into the senses of your listeners. Is it possible or appropriate to appeal to their sense of sight, feel, taste, smell and touch?

4 Put yourself in the shoes of your audience. Carry out some research. How do they think? Create empathy by understanding that people are mentally moved first by the way they habitually think, then by their feelings and emotions. Help them to make connections with things they already know in order to lead them into new territories, and if possible personalise the messages you are sending them. Tap into what will move or influence them emotionally.

5 Know that the way you open and close your presentation is important in terms of the powerful images you create. People pay most attention at the beginning and end of an interview or presentation, so it is also crucial to ensure your audience don't lose interest in the middle of what you are saying. Pay special attention to how you structure that part. Again make use of images, paint pictures, tell a story, give your listeners something to see, hear and do. Make links and connections with what has already been said and signpost where you are taking them next.

6 Before you begin any presentation or interview, anticipate success by visualising how it will be. See yourself being well prepared, dynamic and interesting and being well received by your audience. See and feel how receptive and appreciative your audience is. Experience how great you'll feel as you pat yourself on the back! Now practise and rehearse to perfect your performance. Imagining is powerful but certainly not enough on its own.

7 Using the learning and memory techniques you have been introduced to in this book, you can now create your whole presentation mentally by organising the key information in one of your chosen routes. Take memory joggers by all means, but just think how impressive it will be to give your performance without once losing eye contact with your audience or fiddling with pages of notes. We are always impressed with those who show they know their subject so thoroughly that they speak without a script.

8 If you are going to use visual aids, remember to make them colourful and meaningful to give them impact. Use images and few words. Don't forget, 'a picture paints a thousand words'!

F R I D A Y

9 Remember the importance of positive self talk. Cultivating a positive mental attitude not only transforms the way you feel about yourself, it also gives a new and powerful dimension to the way you appear to others. You find you are full of energy and conviction, qualities that make your audience sit up and listen. Don't forget you are your best visual image!

So what action can you now take to improve the impact you will have when you next give a talk, interview or presentation?

Checklist

1 How can you improve the language you use?
2 How can you tap into the three modalities?
3 How can you appeal to left- and right-brained thinkers?
4 How can you engage the senses of your listeners?
5 How can you empathise with their points of view, their needs and their emotions?
6 How can you open and close powerfully?
7 How can you keep them interested in the middle?
8 Can you visualise success?
9 Can you select the key points of your presentation interview or talk and place those points in one of your mental routes or settings?
10 How can you improve your visual aids?
11 Finally what positive messages can you send yourself about your abilities and skills as a presenter or interviewee?

Lifelong learning: your personal memory improvement plan

Becoming a lifelong learner

The term 'lifelong learning' seems to be on everybody's lips these days. However, it is something that has always been practised by high achievers and those who have become great and inspiring role models over the centuries. Such people have naturally high curiosity and great enthusiasm for knowledge. They automatically keep their minds stimulated, challenged and exercised, as we saw earlier with the likes of da Vinci, Carroll and Einstein.

You may not feel that you wish to emulate those who have reached such dizzy heights of achievement, but by reading and taking part in the exercises over the past week, perhaps you now realise just how much potential you have inside

S A T U R D A Y

your head. Your brain is waiting, willing and very able to help you learn and remember. As it is bursting with potential, why not choose to tap into it and stimulate some of the spare millions of brain cells!

The good news is, the very fact that you have bought and read this book puts you in the category of lifelong learning already. To continue the process, here are some suggestions.

See the advantages
As a result of committing to lifelong learning you are likely to:

- Continue to build and maintain high self esteem
- Stretch your mental muscles
- Push out of your comfort zone and explore exciting new realms of knowledge
- Develop new skills
- Keep fresh, stimulated and motivated
- Create and sustain a positive learning energy cycle
- Improve your knowledge
- Improve your earning potential
- Become more creative
- Use more of your brain
- Feel more excited by life and all it has to offer

How to do it
How can you ensure that lifelong learning becomes part of your everyday existence?

- Create the space to learn. Make use of travelling or waiting time and use books or audio tapes to gain new knowledge. Get up a little earlier than usual and combine jogging with a walkman or an exercise bike with a book!

Read in the bath and in bed. Turn the television off more often.

- Sign up for some classes, or another professional qualification. There is so much on offer these days. Such courses offer structure, aid purpose and direction, and sharing learning aids stimulus.

- Identify the need. What could you learn that will give added benefit to the work you do or the quality of your life?

- Is your learning environment as beneficial as it could be? Could you create a space where you know you will be in the best possible atmosphere to learn? Don't forget, even on a crowded train you can make use of a walkman. Remember too that you will have a preferred time of day for learning, and that the short intense burst approach might be better for you than taking huge chunks of time for studying.

- Try to immerse yourself in your chosen subject or subjects. Be wide and deep in your approach. Be aware of how much you already do know.

- Check out your health. Do you need to make changes in your diet? Are you fit? Do you need a routine medical check? Are you sleeping well?

- Are you using your preferred learning style? Make sure you are absorbing new information in the way that is most beneficial to you. At the same time, try to build your strengths in the other modalities to enhance the global approach. Consider your brain as an exercise gym. The more you use the different apparatus on offer in a gym, the fitter your whole body becomes.

- Also try to use both sides of your brain to capitalise on left- and right-brained learning. Challenge yourself. If, for example, you consider yourself to be poor at mathematics, challenge that assumption. Realise that it is a negative thinking habit holding you in that frame of mind, and start some maths classes, or buy some books to help you improve. Think what that will do to your confidence, as well as developing more of the left side of your brain.

- Keep hold of a positive mental attitude and don't put yourself down when you make mistakes. Be enthusiastic and excited by knowledge. An outlook like this will simply grow and blossom.

Tips for retrieving stubborn memories

Work has been done to highlight strategies for improving the recall of eyewitnesses to crimes – and it reveals tips for retrieving stubborn memories. There are four key points.

■■■■ S A T U R D A Y ■■■■

1   Recreate the initial conditions

Witnesses to crimes or accidents are often asked to try to remember exactly what the weather was like. How warm did the air feel? Was it windy? They also try to bring back their own feelings. Were they hungry or thirsty, sad or happy, excited or bored, on the day the incident occurred?

This is also useful when you're trying to recall imagery from a memory story or route. Try to tap into general memories, and to recall feelings, and you may well recover the precise images you're looking for.

2   Concentrate on details, no matter how unimportant they seem

We've seen that the brain works on a pattern of interconnections, and that information needs to be patterned and connected to suit it. It follows then that any details you remember can be used as a starting point, to begin a chain of associations back to the detail you're trying to recall.

If, for example, you return to an area on one of your mental routes and remember a detail that seems unimportant to the main image you're looking for, it's still worth concentrating on it and seeing what it yields. It could suggest something else; that might link to another thought – and suddenly the key image appears.

3   Visualise a remembered scene from another point-of-view

Witnesses to bank robberies might be asked to imagine what the *robbers* must have seen – and you can use the same principle to boost your recall. Get used to visualising a mental route, story or scene from different angles, and letting your mind's eye search out the detail you're missing.

■■■■■■ S A T U R D A Y ■■■■■■

4   Replay a memory in reverse
After road accidents, eye-witnesses are sometimes asked to
replay the events backwards: visualise the crashed cars ...
then describe what happened just before the crash ... and
what led to *that* ...

It's a particularly useful strategy when you're trying to
remember by using a story or route. If it doesn't work
perfectly one way, try recalling it in reverse.

Your personal action plan

No matter how much you read about a subject, or how
inspired you become, the only way to make any knowledge
work for you in a purposeful way is to actually put it into
practice.

You have already discovered that by using some of the
exercises in this book you have been able to remember
nearly 200 things so far. There is nothing like doing
something for it to have impact. All too often though, after
finishing a course or a book, we put the written material
away on a shelf and carry on as before.

That is why preparing a personal action plan is such a good
idea. Giving yourself written goals and timelines, putting it
somewhere where it will be a constant reminder of what
you want to achieve, means you are far more likely to take
and sustain action.

Select from the following as guidelines, adding more if you
need to, then lay out the information to suit you. For
example, when considering 'Continue lifelong learning',
you might have several topics or areas that you want to

tackle under the **How?** heading, with a number of timelines under **When?**

What?	How?	When?
• Become a more positive thinker		
• Adopt a global approach		
• Continue lifelong learning		
• Move out of comfort zones		
• Acknowledge recent successes		
• Obtain optimum health		
• Find time		
• See the advantages		
• Knock down mental barriers		
• Reward yourself		
• Pamper yourself		
• Practise and review		
• Develop your imagination		
• Memorise useful facts		
• Memorise useful numbers		
• Develop new routes for remembering		

▬▬ S A T U R D A Y ▬▬

Tests

You should now feel confident about your memory, and aware of what you have to do to make it work. The basic principles are simple, and the applications are endless.

Give the information you have to learn

- imagery
- emotional triggers
- exaggeration
- pattern

Anything can be made compatible with the way your memory works, and represented as a set of linked pictures: jobs, names, times, dates, facts, presentations, interview answers, memos, reports. In the right form, your brain can hold unlimited amounts of data.

To confirm the progress you've made since starting this book, take part in this final set of tests. Use any of the techniques you like, individually or in combination. You can make up similar tests yourself in the future to help keep your memory in trim.

Test 1: word list

Memorise the following list of words. Try to do it in less than five minutes, then check your success.

sword, handbag, curtain, custard, rake, bomb, trombone, shark, mountain, dragon, leaf, cafe, biscuit, CD, boot, comb, gate, ice, oven, camera

Test 2: job list

Learn this list of jobs. Again, give yourself a maximum of five minutes.

1 order new letterheads
2 take laptop to be repaired
3 arrange meeting with Kelly
4 cancel trip to India
5 go to bank
6 submit invoices
7 play squash
8 call Chris (ext 263)
9 lunch with Andy
10 book holiday, starting August 25th

Test 3: numbers

Use your number system to memorise the following imaginary extension-numbers. You have ten minutes.

Scott: 8305
Rita: 1876
James: 2236
Pam: 4907
Daniel: 9301

Test 4: names

Below is a list of ten people you'll be looking after at a conference. You have ten minutes to learn all their names, so that you can write out the entire list from memory.

▬▬▬ S A T U R D A Y ▬▬▬

Jack Braine, Holly Harper, Christian Attley, Ashley
Verne, Debbie Green, Frank Shepherd, Ray Oates,
Helmut Schreiber, Dougal MacMillan, Hattie Chandler

To finish the test, see how much of the information you've
learned throughout the week is still fresh in your mind.

- the ten items on the shopping list, beginning with
  chocolates
- twenty words on the list, beginning with *television*
- twenty words on the list, beginning with *grass*
- the first ten US Presidents since the Second World War
- the dates of
  - the Gunpowder Plot
  - the death of Ovid
  - the Battle of Waterloo
  - the ruin of Pompeii
  - the birth of Henry VIII
- the dialling-codes for Newcastle, Liverpool, Oxford,
  Peterborough and Birmingham
- the first ten numbers in Japanese
- the ten items to take on holiday
- the ten items on the shopping-list, beginning with *apples*
- the top ten wishes of workers in the research document

Along with the four tests in this chapter, that's 175 distinct
pieces of information – and still just a glimpse of your
memory's infinite power.

Conclusion

Remember:

1 It's important to understand how you learn best.
   What is your preferred learning style? Are you a left- or
   right-brained thinker?
   Do what you do well, but try to harness the full range
   of your learning possibilities.

2 You need to organise your learning.
   Look for the easiest ways to arrange the information
   you have to learn.
   Organise your approach to learning to make the process
   smooth, quick and fun.

3 You should tap into your imagination.
   Children have a naturally fertile imagination and so can
   you.

4 Adopt the best mental attitude.
   Be positive. Break bad thinking habits, motivate
   yourself, reward and encourage yourself.

5 Find the right learning environment.
   What surroundings will encourage you to be at your
   most receptive?

6 Match your healthy mind with a healthy body.
   Eat well, exercise regularly and get a good night's sleep.

7 You are never too old to learn.
   Don't be tempted to use age as an excuse for not
   continuing to learn and remember. You have more brain
   cells than you need, however old you are.

8 Practise.
   Do it! Start using the techniques you have learned in
   this book, and they will soon become second nature.

9 Be a lifelong learner.
    Keep your brain stimulated and use it to go further in
    everything you do.
10 Your brain is amazing.
    Never underestimate your learning power. Its potential
    for storage and creativity is immeasurable.

The average brain has the capacity of an encyclopedia ten
billion pages long: start making entries and fill it up.